Building High-Performance
People and Organizations

Building High-Performance People and Organizations

Volume 2
The Engaged Workplace: Organizational Strategies

*Edited by
Martha I. Finney*

PRAEGER PERSPECTIVES

Westport, Connecticut
London

Library of Congress Cataloging-in-Publication Data

Building high-performance people and organizations / edited by Martha I. Finney.
    p. cm. — (Praeger perspectives)
    Includes bibliographical references and index.
    Contents: v. 1. The new employer-employee relationship — v. 2. The engaged workplace: organizational strategies — v. 3. Case studies and conversations.
    ISBN: 978-0-275-99271-2 ((set) : alk. paper)
    ISBN: 978-0-275-99272-9 ((vol. 1) : alk. paper)
    ISBN: 978-0-275-99273-6 ((vol. 2) : alk. paper)
    ISBN: 978-0-275-99274-3 ((vol. 3) : alk. paper)
    1. Employee motivation. 2. Employee motivation—Case studies. 3. Organizational effectiveness. 4. Organizational effectiveness—Case studies. 5. Personnel management. 6. Personnel management—Case studies. I. Finney, Martha I.
HF5549.5.M63.B85   2008
658.3'14—dc22   2007048780

British Library Cataloguing in Publication Data is available.

Copyright © 2008 by Martha I. Finney

All rights reserved. No portion of this book may be reproduced, by any process or technique, without the express written consent of the publisher.

Library of Congress Catalog Card Number: 2007048780
ISBN: 978-0-275-99271-2 (set)
      978-0-275-99272-9 (vol. 1)
      978-0-275-99273-6 (vol. 2)
      978-0-275-99274-3 (vol. 3)

First published in 2008

Praeger Publishers, 88 Post Road West, Westport, CT 06881
An imprint of Greenwood Publishing Group, Inc.
www.praeger.com

Printed in the United States of America

The paper used in this book complies with the Permanent Paper Standard issued by the National Information Standards Organization (Z39.48-1984).

10 9 8 7 6 5 4 3 2 1

Contents

Acknowledgments	vii
Preface *Martha I. Finney*	ix
1. The Six Degrees of Preparation *Bruce Ferguson*	1
2. Being Connected: The Effects of Technology on Employee Engagement *Thomas O. Davenport*	11
3. Driving Long-Term Engagement through a High-Performance Culture *Christopher Rice*	30
4. The Lost 20 Percent: Engaging the Almost Great *Craig Mindrum*	48
5. Essential Building Blocks to Successful Engagement Survey Programs *Nancy DeLay*	64
6. Spirit: A Vital Key to Engagement at Work *Pat McHenry Sullivan*	79
7. No "Best Practices" *Tamara J. Erickson*	95
8. Managers: The Key to an Engaged Workplace *Derrick R. Barton*	110
9. Work-Life Means Business *Kathleen M. Lingle*	124

10. Coaching for High Potentials to Become High-Performing Leaders
    Duncan Mathison — 141
11. The Five Points of Peak Performance
    Louis S. Csoka — 158
12. Rebuilding Trust within Organizations
    Dennis S. Reina and Michelle L. Reina — 168
13. Fun: Essential to Creating the Culture of Engagement
    Leslie Yerkes — 182
14. Ten Things You Should Know about Executive Search Now
    Gordon Thomas — 192
15. Compensation Strategy: A Guide for Senior Managers
    Sibson Consulting — 208
16. Engagement Journey: Caterpillar
    Brian Gareau, Kate Parker, Sarah Zigler, and Tom Doolittle — 220

Index — 245

About the Editor and Contributors — 251

Acknowledgments

This multivolume book set represents thousands of hours of volunteer effort from some of the world's leading experts on all aspects of the people side of business. Every single one of the contributors in these volumes said "yes" to my request for their best and latest thinking, and then produced masterfully written chapters, adding their voices to this community of engagement. I can't thank each one of these contributors enough.

There are two other people, though, who deserve my deepest gratitude. Colleen Cayes, my friend and founder of Healthy Buildings, kept telling me month after month to keep my eyes on the finish line (when multiple bags of Hershey's Kisses seemed like the better, more immediately gratifying option).

And then there's Jeff Olson, my editor and long-distance taskmaster. For me to fully express my appreciation for his steadfast, enduring patience (and ever-so-consistently applied pressure) would appear to be unseemly pandering. He knows how I feel, so I won't embarrass him in public. Suffice it to say, I'll miss those predawn exchanges of emails.

Preface

What is the secret to success? Some would say, "Why, design a better mousetrap, of course." They would be only partly right. But then we would have to ask ourselves, who would keep building those mousetraps after they've been designed by the entrepreneur? Who would keep an eye out for the quality of these mousetraps? Who would get the word out about those mousetraps? Who would source the raw materials? Who would build the distribution channels? Who would keep the proverbial path to your door well groomed and inviting? Who would make sure your designs aren't stolen by a competitor? Who would continuously improve on those designs? And who, for that matter, would be hiring all those people to do all those things?

A company's journey to great success may start with a great idea that arrives like a bell in the middle of the night. But it would be a very short and sad journey indeed if that idea wasn't backed up by a cadre of high-performing, dedicated, inspired people who not only invested their best in the service of your company's dream but also told their friends about what a great employer you are. *People* are your secret to success.

High-performing organizations depend on high-performing people, perhaps now more than ever. Never before has the chase for innovative advantage been so high-speed, so global. And in the face of massive shifts in the populations around the world, never before has the chase for the people advantage had such high stakes. This chase for the people advantage is being called *employee engagement* these days.

And the argument for engagement is quite compelling. As you will read in Volume 1's engagement journey chapter by Intuit, the Corporate Leadership Council estimates that engaged employees perform 20 percent better than their nonengaged counterparts. ISR statistics show that companies that score high in engagement outperform their industry average by 6 percent, while low scorers perform under industry average by 9 percent. Hewitt Associates research has shown that the stock market performance of the companies that appear on its own "best employer" list shows an average shareholder return of 20.2 percent, while companies that have fewer than 40 percent engaged employees show a shareholder return of negative 9.6 percent.

It's one thing to talk employee engagement, but it's quite another thing to *do* engagement. Where do you begin to create an engaged culture? How do you begin? Do the answers to either of those questions really matter just as long as you do begin? Understanding what employee engagement is all about, especially in the context of running a high-performance organization, would be a good place to start.

To that end, I have organized *Building High-Performing People and Organizations* into three volumes, each addressing a specific level of understanding about what it means to fully engage the hearts, hands, and minds of an impassioned workforce that is committed to the same organizational objectives its leadership is. Volume 1, *The New Employer-Employee Relationship,* focuses on the theory underlying all approaches to employee engagement—and, in a broader sense, organizational development. Chapters include multiple points of view on employee surveys; the importance of aligning people strategy with the organization's business strategy; building a culture of trust; a look at the changing demographics; linking customer branding with internal branding; how nonprofit organizations can uniquely benefit from the extra passion that engaged employees bring to their work; and the role that engaged employees play in helping an organization move toward a desired change state.

Each volume concludes with what I am calling an *engagement journey chapter*: an in-depth look at a single corporation and what it has done to develop its own engagement initiative. Accordingly, Volume 1 concludes with a look into the work that software giant Intuit has done to understand the dynamics of what it means to be engaged from an individual's perspective and how it has leveraged that knowledge into truly effective engagement programs. The Intuit engagement journey chapter is ideal for this volume because it also presents an assembled body of research into the business case for employee engagement, drawing from the latest data of many of the independent researchers and statisticians in the field. It's an excellent primer into the world of engagement.

Volume 2, *The Engaged Workplace: Organizational Strategies,* moves beyond theory and dives directly into the application of many approaches to creating engaged cultures inside an organization. This volume opens with a challenge to all leaders to candidly assess their own preparedness for taking on engagement in their organizations. Assuming that the readers have passed their own *am-I-really-ready-for-this?* test, this volume invites them to look at the many facets of people-centric organizations, specifically as they're played out inside cultures that are committed to engagement: the uses of technology; how to plan for engagement survey programs; how work/life balance benefits the engaged culture; the role that managers play in keeping employees engaged (or disengaged); the essential ingredients for peak performance; the role of spirituality in the workplace; rebuilding trust; how fun enlivens innovation; the essential elements of executive searches; and how to capture the "lost 20 percent," those valuable, talented employees who might have slipped through the cracks for one reason or another.

The engagement journey chapter in Volume 2 looks at the celebrated engagement initiatives at Caterpillar, a global heavy manufacturing company. This chapter looks at how its engagement program was launched by the essential commitment of its chairman, and how that commitment has been realized on factory floors around the world, including China, Brazil, and France.

As with every aspect of the human story, there is no shortage of diverse opinions coming from deeply passionate, highly regarded experts. So Volume 3, *Case Studies and Conversations,* invites a wide variety of thought leaders to weigh in with their opinions and insights into such core aspects of running a high-performance organization as leadership; high-performing teams; diversity; learning cultures; employee branding; organizational values; appreciative inquiry; collaborative problem solving; and the organizational advantages of formal employee communications programs. These interviews conclude with a forecast into the future.

Volume 3 also features a selection of case studies, mostly of small- to medium-sized businesses and how they took the high-level concepts around engagement and made them real in their own workplaces.

The engagement journey chapter for Volume 3 features Starwood Hotels and Resorts Worldwide and tells the story of how this company determined that uniquely engaged employees were their most essential value proposition, especially in pushing forward their brands to their guests. This chapter demonstrates the service value chain to readers, showing how inextricably linked the internal brand message is with customer experience.

Everyone who contributed their time and talents to this book set was already supremely busy before I called them with the invitation to participate. Each expert has either written books of their own or certainly has plenty of material with which to write their own books. So I am especially grateful that they were willing to add their voice to the choir and collectively paint the large picture of what it means to create a high-performing organization full of passionate people. As I write these words, I realize that this book set is precisely that—the representation of a high-performing organization full of passionate people.

VOLUME 1: THE NEW EMPLOYER-EMPLOYEE RELATIONSHIP

Employee engagement is a topic that has assumed a whole new vogue in recent years. What company doesn't want to have an organization completely staffed with over-the-top, over-the-moon employees who completely love their work, their company, and their jobs? The business case for this is indisputable: profits go up; workplace injuries go down; innovation is cutting edge; all that leadership effort that might have gone into micro-managing indifferent employees can now be invested in building the company's future. All that sounds like excellent return on investment by anyone's standards.

But underneath all these shining benefits lie the questions: What exactly is an engaged culture? And what are you prepared to give up to get there? In Volume 1 I asked experts in the areas of organizational development to explore these questions and answer the essential questions to help readers understand why this is a critical topic today—and perhaps for the next several generations. As a group, we collected chapters on

- What is employee engagement really?
- How to look at organizational talent as people equity as a way to develop a company's long-term objectives.
- How to align people strategy with business strategy.
- How to design a global employee engagement survey process that really serves your company.
- The essential ingredients for trust in the workplace.
- The changing demographics and how they will impact hiring and retention in the immediate future.
- The power of linking external brands with internal brands.

VOLUME 2: THE ENGAGED WORKPLACE: ORGANIZATIONAL STRATEGIES

Volume 2 provides the essential tools to support any leader who resolves to transform the organization into a high-performing company that attracts, keeps, and inspires employees who want to function at their optimum potential. These chapters speak directly to leaders, both challenging and inviting them to regard their organizations in new ways:

- Six ways to tell whether you are really ready to take on the challenge of transforming your culture into one that attracts and keeps engaged employees.
- How to use technology to truly leverage engagement in your culture.
- How to use a high-performance culture to promote long-term engagement.
- How to take the initial steps necessary for creating an employee engagement survey that's relevant to *your* organization.
- How work/life balance programs and built-in flexibility promote high performance among your employees.
- How to help high-performing leaders sustain their levels of achievement through coaching.
- How to make the best use of executive search firms.

VOLUME 3: CASE STUDIES AND CONVERSATIONS

Employee engagement is nothing if it's not a conversation with the people essential to helping you achieve your mission-critical objectives. So Volume 3 offers a collection of critical conversations with thought leaders on all the aspects of employee engagement and high-performing organizations. I have collected the insights and advice from some of the most dynamic experts in their field:

- People-centric cultures: Ann Rhoades of Southwest Airlines and JetBlue.
- Leadership: Dan Walker, formerly of Apple, and David Russo, formerly of SAS Institute.
- Employee branding: Scott Bedbury, formerly of Starbucks and Nike.
- Corporate universities: Susan Todd of Corporate University Xchange.
- Talent management: Susan Gebelein of Personnel Decisions International.
- Diversity: Tiane Mitchell-Gordon of AOL.
- Employer regard: Beverly Kaye, coauthor of *Love 'Em or Lose 'Em*.
- The ROI of employee communications: Kathryn Yates of Watson Wyatt.

In addition to featuring Starwood Hotels and Resorts Worldwide as the anchor chapter, this volume also offers smaller case studies of companies that have found ways to speak to their employees in the fundamental language of mutual commitment, skills, passion, and dedication to a cause that's larger than any one person inside the organization—including the senior-most leaders themselves.

At the conclusion of each interview—be it a case study or a conversation—I ask the same question: "From your perspective, what's the single-most essential ingredient to running a high-performance organization with engaged employees?" Each answer, taken as an individual response, may not surprise you. But my hope is that all the answers banded together will give you the vision and hope you need to make it happen for your own organization. And yourself, for that matter.

Chapter 1

The Six Degrees of Preparation*

Bruce Ferguson

Thanks largely to the efforts of Stephen Covey, over recent years leaders in their pursuit of effectiveness have developed the practice of discerning *nice to do* from *must do*. The ambition of developing a high-performing culture of engaged employees certainly embraces both categories, as we'll see in a moment. This chapter looks at yet a third point of effective discerning that is especially important when it comes to employee engagement: *Are you absolutely, positively prepared to assume the personal challenges that come with the pursuit of effectiveness through employee engagement?*

It is commonly said that employee engagement must be sponsored from the absolute top of the organization. If you are at the top of your organization—perhaps the CEO of the entire enterprise or simply the manager of your department—employee engagement must start with you. For it to really take hold, you personally must be ready to take on the commitment, no matter how rough the ride might be as your engaged culture begins to take hold in your organization. And it will get rough at times. You can count on that.

This chapter briefly reviews the *nice-to-do* and *must-do* aspects of employee engagement but only to set the stage for the hard personal work that is in store for you. Then it will cover the Six Degrees of Preparation—six areas of *your* personality and philosophy that must be in place if you expect to be able to lead your organization to high-performance greatness.

---

*Copyright © 2007 by Bruce Ferguson.

NICE TO DO AND MUST DO

At this point in history—in a global society of employers—it hardly seems necessary to lay out the nice-to-do and must-do facts of running high-performance organizations through the passions of engaged employees. Other chapters go into greater detail on these topics. They are quickly addressed here as a review of the benefits leaders stand to enjoy when they take on the rewarding challenge of improving their internal cultures.

Nice to Do

Engaged employees are generally more productive and pleasant to be around. They lend their companies their best innovation and discretionary energies. They're more likely to stay on the job, and they are more likely to spread the good word about you in the community as a great employer. As a result, you may not have to compete so hard for quality candidates in an ever-tightening labor market.

Companies with a reputation of being great places to work also have good relationships among their customers. Southwest Airlines, the Container Store, Whole Foods, and Google are four commonly referred to examples of this principle. As anyone who has been on a Southwest flight or bought a bundle of free-range, hormone-free chicken breasts can attest to, when employees and customers interact with each other in a common expectation of cheerful, high standards, they share the mutual obligation to meet those standards of interaction. The result: Happy employees serving happy customers. A good, high-quality experience is in store all around.

This results in a good reputation in the community. Good press and good word of mouth are very nice to have for a company that wants to prosper through the efforts of its employees and the collaborative loyalty of its clients and customers. There is hardly ever a shortage of well-qualified candidates willing to stand in line—not to mention turn down other job offers—to work for you. Your customers wouldn't mind standing in line to do business with you; they're even willing to pay a premium for the pleasure of working with you. (As this chapter was being written, the iPhone first hit the market. Its ultimate prospects are still yet to be known, but the first-day lines are indisputable.) When your good reputation precedes you, your work life is just that much easier. You have—as they say at Apple—"insanely great" people creating "insanely great" products for "insanely loyal" customers.

Companies can do well without these advantages, of course, and they do. But why make things unnecessarily difficult or unpleasant for yourself and your organization—especially when the employer down the street is building a reputation for itself as a great place to work?

Must Do

Over recent years consulting and research firms, such as Gallup, International Survey Research (ISR), Towers Perrin, and so on, have studied the hard business returns associated with employee engagement. Many compelling, irrefutable observations have emerged that directly tie engagement with business performance.

In 2005, Melcrum Publishing released a report offering a compilation of many of the statistics reported by these firms. Some of them are listed briefly here.

- A Gallup study of stores showed that stores scoring in the top 25 percent on its survey on engagement performed on average 4.56 percent over their sales budget for the year. In contrast, those scoring in the bottom 24 percent of the same survey performed at 0.84 percent below budget. This represented a difference of $104 million of sales per year between the two groups.
- Another Gallup study quoted in the Melcrum report said that disengaged workers are 10 times more likely to say that they will leave their organization within a year.
- A Towers Perrin study reported that engaged employees were more likely to focus on customer service—building customer retention and loyalty.

The cost of disengagement is also essential to keep in mind. According to Gallup data quoted in the Melcrum report, actively disengaged employees cost U.S. businesses between $270 billion and $343 billion every year due to low productivity. Decreasing the number of actively disengaged workers by only 5 percent would lead to $94 billion increase in productivity.

Among disengaged workers, only 13 percent would recommend their company's products and services, as opposed to 78 percent of engaged employees recommending their company's products and services.

Are You Absolutely, Positively Prepared?

With all these arguments and data in favor of running high-performance, high-engagement workplaces, it is easy to forget that there's a very good reason engagement must start at the top. It can be very confusing, and some of the pro-engagement choices you will have to make could fly in the face of what might be considered good business practices in other circles (for instance, say, layoffs for a fast spike in the stock market or the termination of a high-performing star who also happens to be brutal to his own support staff).

Perhaps the most challenging aspect of creating high-performance organizations through the passions of your people is more about the self-awareness you must achieve before you're ready to go public with your intentions of creating a workplace where great people will want to come to work. Employee engagement isn't about surveys, balanced scorecards, free coffee, or the most beautiful office building in town. It's not about flex-time or tuition reimbursement. It's not about fully paid health benefits and four weeks' vacation in the first year. It's not even about your business's make-the-world-a-better-place mission. All those things are meaningless without a senior leader who not only espouses the value of engagement but also takes a good long look in the mirror and asks, "Just how far am I willing to go with this engagement thing?"—and then committed to the answer, whatever it may be.

YOU ARE YOUR FIRST DIRECT REPORT

There really is no right or wrong answer to that question, only true and untrue. You can say, "I'm going to go whole hog with engagement," or you can say, "Engagement is just the latest flavor of the month" (however, given the must-do data outlined above, you might want to reconsider that extreme notion). You can position your strategy anywhere on the scale between those two points. When it's your business, it's really your choice. The important thing to know is that whatever you announce, you're stuck with it. Or you can move forward. It's like exiting the rental car parking lot. If you even think about backing up from your position, serious damage will be done.

If engagement is about anything, it's about a change in behaviors and beliefs driving from your office—specified and sanctioned by you with the promise that these changes represent values that your employees can count on, come what may. The key words here are, "come what may." Trouble comes when leaders want to be known as pro-engagement visionaries, but really haven't thought through what that will mean to them on a daily basis, especially when the heat is turned up.

This is why self-awareness is so essential. Do you really want to be a pro-engagement leader—with all the hard work that goes along with that set of values? Or do you just want to be *known* as someone who believes in engagement?

Before you call in your management team and your corporate communications staff to brainstorm nifty slogans, you may want to undertake this exercise of Six Degrees of Preparation. These are six essential characteristics of a pro-engagement leader. Measure yourself against these characteristics to see whether you personally have what it takes; whether you really want do the hard work to acquire what it takes; or whether you'd prefer to just give the whole thing a pass—for now.

DEGREE 1: PRO-ENGAGEMENT LEADERS MUST BE AUTHENTIC

Running a high-performance organization is challenging for anyone (that's why you get the big paycheck), but it is a lot easier when you believe in what you're doing. Authentic leadership begins when you believe in four things.

Yourself—Are you doing the work that speaks to your own set of dreams, principles, and values? Do you actually enjoy leading people? Does running an organization—with all its creative challenges—ignite your own personal passion? Or would you prefer to be sailing toward the Southern Cross or letting the horses out at dawn in Montana? Biking through Moab before the sun gets too high? When the alarm goes off in the morning, are you glad? Or do you feel dead inside?

Your company's mission and values—Are you actually proud to be associated with your company? Do you respect your customers? Would you be a customer if you weren't its leader? When you see it mentioned in the paper, do you smile? Or do you cringe? When you consider the company's values, can you actually tell stories about how you've personally witnessed those values in action? Or, given half the chance, would you rewrite the mission and values statement to more accurately reflect your own principles—or more cynically, what's really going on in your organization?

Your company—Do you support the business model? Do you respect its board? Does the board respect you? Are you still dragging the ghost of your predecessor around with you? What are you trying to live up to? What are you trying to live down? Do you feel that your stakeholders are giving you a chance to succeed? Or are you constantly defensive and in reaction mode?

Your people—Here's where we really get down to it: What do you really believe about people in general and your employees specifically? Do you believe that people are basically lazy and need to be prodded, punished, or bribed before you can expect to see any results? Or do you believe that people basically want to do a good job and that when you treat them with respect, they'll treat the business with respect?

Remember, there is no one right set of answers to these questions, just true and untrue as a measure of what *you* believe in and what passions, attitudes, and expectations *you* take to work every morning. When you know who you are, you can authentically lead from that self-awareness. If you choose to, you can authentically strive to improve aspects of yourself that you've identified as being counterproductive in your efforts to build and run a thriving, engaging workplace.

This kind of continuous improvement is essential not only for your organization but also for your own personal growth. We're all flawed, and nothing is going to show those shortcomings faster than the exposure you get as you go public with your vision of how your ideal organization will be run. Authenticity also requires personal humility. Are you willing to show those flaws and foibles? Are you willing to let your people know that you are committed to strengthening your weaknesses and improving your own behaviors?

As the authentic leader, your obligation is to model the behaviors you expect to see in your organization throughout the ranks. If you want to see wisdom throughout your company, in which people make decisions for the long view instead of short-term benefits, then you have to choose the long view in your decisions. If you want to see tight teamwork in which your people share the credit, then you have to be a team player and share the credit. If you want your people to be constantly challenging themselves and each other to be better, know more, do more, and build their skills, then you have to take on a personal philosophy in which you challenge yourself every day to be better than you were the day before.

To be an authentic leader, you must demonstrate what you believe through the way you behave. Your people deserve to count on believing that you are who you say you are—today, tomorrow, next year. This principle, conveniently, leads us to the second Degree of Preparation.

DEGREE 2: PRO-ENGAGEMENT LEADERS MUST BE CONSISTENT

When you're truly authentic in the way you approach your leadership role—for both the organization and for the people themselves—it is easier to be consistent in your behaviors and the way you make your decisions and choices. In a leadership culture that's based on authenticity, there will be fewer challenging moments of truth, because your culture will be saturated with the automatic expectations of how you will behave and how you will expect your employees to behave.

The more publicly you are committed to the engaged workplace, the more rigorous you must be with your standards—and the courage of your convictions will be put to the test. That is something you can count on.

How rigorous do you have the courage to be? Say your company has a stated value that everyone treats each other with respect. What specifically does that mean? Must everyone address each other as Mr. or Ms.? Probably not, but that's what "respect" might mean to some people. Must subordinates always defer to their superiors? Maybe, if that's what "respect" means to your senior leaders. But does "respect" mean the same thing to the individual contributors? Probably not. How can they feel respected by their bosses?

You have to be rigorous in your definitions by being specific. So "respect" means specifically that your organization is a zero-tolerance zone for rudeness and unfair management practices. That seems straightforward enough. But what happens when your preferred supplier—or, heaven forbid, a key customer—is discovered to have those very unfair management practices that are specifically banned in your own internal culture? Your relationships with these external business associates are crucial to your company's business prospects. What would happen if your employees got wise to the fact that you were doing business with people who violated the internal standards that you hold sacred? Do you really have the courage of your convictions? Could you really terminate an essential business relationship in the service of your standards?

Could you make a case for the argument that their internal practices are none of your business? Whether you can rationalize drawing the line between what's your business and what's your suppliers' business, your employees and customers probably won't be able to. Not for long, at any rate.

In the past 40 years, consumers have become increasingly aware of their power to exert their values over their favorite brands—even brands they're loyal to. The grape growers of the 1960s and 1970s certainly felt the heat during consumer boycotts on behalf of farm workers. Less than two decades later, apparel companies that were using child labor in other countries felt the immediate anger of U.S. customers once the word got out. Business in South Africa during apartheid pulled out of the country. Today, companies are discovering that customers will pay extra for "fair trade" coffee and chocolate. And consumers are also discovering that many products made in China are very poor bargains indeed when safety is concerned.

As the labor market continues to swing in the direction of favoring individual employees, they are also going to feel their economic power and, just as customers have been, make their career choices according to their values as well as their ambition. As a result, they'll be watching you very carefully to make sure that your espoused values are just as consistently applied with external relationships as they are internally.

Your employees are going to expect you to behave consistently in line with your values, with them, with your market, and with your engagement philosophy.

DEGREE 3: PRO-ENGAGEMENT LEADERS MUST BE IMAGINATIVE

This can be one of the most challenging degrees of preparation, because not everyone thinks of him- or herself as being naturally imaginative. There are different degrees of imagination, creativity, and originality. You don't have to be a creative genius to be a visionary leader. But you do have to capture your employees' imaginations and help them see how their dedication is essential to the future of the organization—and by extension, their own prospects. When people believe that they have a future with a company that is committed to helping them grow, that they can be proud of, and that will allow them to stay on top of their field, they are more likely to stay and invest their own visionary efforts.

Even for the CEOs with the least imaginative powers, it is still essential that they understand how important it is to drive the company toward a specific future—a future that their employees can envision as clearly as the CEO can.

A key component of being imaginative is being curious. That is an attribute that every leader has control over. It's not a talent so much as a habitual way of thinking. And it's essential to leading in an environment that is so changeable, as every market is today. Every engaging, mission- and values-driven leader must be constantly processing a regular menu of questions when considering new prospects, new markets, new futures, new candidates. What does this mean to my company? What will this mean to my people? How can we leverage this new idea into an even better return on our efforts? Is this something we should avoid? Is this something we should embrace? How can we make the most of this situation and drive its outcome from the very beginning?

Imaginative leaders must process these questions on both global and local levels. Any leaders who think that they're not running global operations are kidding themselves. No matter what you do, it has ramifications on some level throughout the world. If you choose to off-shore some of your talent, you're definitely global. If you choose not to but some of your products or services go off shore, you're global anyway. Citizens of countries that represent your big markets are going to wonder why you don't extend your opportunities in their direction as well. If you have no presence at all beyond domestically, but your competitors are all over the world, you're global. At the very least, your global question will be, "If not, why not?"

You had better have some well-thought-out answers to that question—answers that show you continue to invest a great deal of imagination to all the questions regarding who you are as an employer.

DEGREE 4: PRO-ENGAGEMENT LEADERS MUST BE FLEXIBLE

The need to be flexible does not negate the absolute expectation that you are also consistent. As the leader, you must be both. Flexibility gives you the skills to stay open and receptive to new ideas from unexpected sources, as well as remain easily adaptable to unforeseen changes—not only to respond to shifts in the marketplace but also to take advantage of them.

Two words come to mind when we consider flexibility: *inclusive* and *responsive*. Let's look at *inclusive* first.

Inclusive is commonly a word that's linked with diversity—which then takes leaders into the conversation of providing equal opportunities to all qualified candidates, regardless of race, gender, religion, sexual preference, or national origin. However, just as the conversation of diversity has evolved over the years to include the fact that businesses benefit from having an internal representation of their external community and customer base, the concept of inclusivity has also evolved toward the discussion about what it takes to create a corporate culture where everyone is confident that their voice will be heard and respected. Truly inclusive cultures lower all barriers for employees—barriers to employment and promotion, certainly, but also barriers to achievement and expression.

Being inclusive is using the collective genius of your entire organization. It used to be that leaders would tell their employees, "I'm the boss, I have the answers. So just keep your heads down and do your jobs." The truth is that no one does well with his or her head down. No one can see the future that way. No one can see what's coming at him full-speed—whether it is a problem to duck or an advantage to seize. You need to have employees who look up and speak out. Include everyone in the conversation of how the business can thrive; commit yourself to respecting all opinions. It could be that unique point of view that will see things differently—so differently that even your competitors will miss it.

When you're flexible, you're *responsive*, ready to make a fast move in response to new insight from unexpected corners of your workforce. How quickly can you change direction? How much faith do your people have that you will make the critical moves in a timely way so that all their efforts and dedication continue to be well invested? What does your track record say about you so far? Can they trust you to make the wise decisions in time to seize the opportunity?

DEGREE 5: PRO-ENGAGEMENT LEADERS MUST BE SERVICE-ORIENTED

For generations, the automatic assumption was that employees worked for their bosses, and collectively everyone worked for the CEO. In the mid-1990s a new expression started making the rounds of conferences and leadership conversations: *servant leadership*. This idea flipped the traditional relationship of who is working for whom on its head—which provided a refreshing point of view and invited everyone to reconsider what it means to be the boss. It wasn't long, though, before the idea of the leaders working for their employees began to get tedious, not to mention disingenuous. Front-line managers still had the hire/fire prerogative. In fact, the senior leadership continued to be working for the CEO, but the CEO certainly wasn't working for them. He was reporting to the board and stockholders. No one was kidding anyone with this servant leadership notion (not for very long, at least).

The truly engaged workplace offers up a third model of the leadership food chain: *collaborative* leadership. Yes, there is still the hierarchy. When push has to come to shove, the power of the hierarchy is invoked. You can bet your last paycheck on that.

But in a high-engagement workplace environment that attracts top talent, leaders aren't really the managers of subordinates anymore. They're the coordinators of experts. Individual contributors want to, well, *contribute*. Engaged, high-performing contributors don't need to be bossed around or managed on a short leash. They need to be given the tools, direction, and training to stay on top of their game. They need to be given the opportunity to stay on top of their profession and field of expertise. And they need to be given the chance to do what they do well. They need their managers to collaborate with them by behaving more as team members bringing to the table their own specific roles, which might include determining how best to use all the other team members. Extract any given moment of the day of a high-performing organization and analyze it for its essential components, and you'll have a hard time determining who is actually the boss.

Service-oriented leaders committed to leading a high-performing, engaged organization are also patient. They know that change doesn't happen just because they mandate it to, especially when they're trying to create change in a community of committed experts. They know the burden is on themselves to influence change, not enforce it. They influence it by taking the time to communicate with their people that a particular change is a good idea. This is, of course, assuming that they have already been inclusive in seeking out the expert opinion, advice, and observations of their people.

DEGREE 6: PRO-ENGAGEMENT LEADERS MUST BE COMMUNICATIVE

You can't overestimate the essential power of engaged leaders who are communicative. Almost every day you read headlines of yet another leader who is forced to step down—deservedly or not—because he lost the confidence of his people.

The more engaged your staff is, the more empowered they are, and therefore the more demanding they will be in being completely informed and current on the business that is most essential to them.

When business culture threw away the so-called employment contract but still wanted employees to remain dedicated to their work and be dependable to show up every day, smart employees had to transform themselves into educated consumers of their career opportunities. In the process the really high-value talent evolved into business partners of sorts. They want to—and deserve to—know what's going on in the company in order to determine for themselves whether their continued partnership is a good investment for them. They may not be stockholders, but they are giving you their prime productive years, their energies, their innovation, their dedication, and their excellence. Your transparency will help them discern whether they are getting a good return on their investment.

Leaders can't hide themselves behind the power of their position anymore. You have to be out there with complete and timely information on the essential data that are affecting your business. Every employee should have access to the business news of the day, even factory floor employees halfway around the globe. It is possible, as you will see in the chapter on Caterpillar in this volume. It is also essential. No excuses.

Your employees also want to see you. Even the graveyard shift deserves your attention. At least once a quarter, if not more often, plan on being there in the early morning hours. Show up on the weekends, if your company has weekend shifts. Show your people that your passion for the work they do extends around the clock, all week long.

When you think about organizational leaders who are highly visible, it's easy to immediately picture leaders like Herb Kelleher or Richard Branson—exuberantly extroverted leaders who are famous for the infectiousness of their joy for their work. This doesn't have to be you. In fact, it probably shouldn't be. Kelleher and Branson already have the jobs of being themselves. Your job is to authentically be you. If you're not especially extroverted, that's fine. That will make you a strong listener instead. If wacky toys and training gimmicks leave you cold, so much the better. You'll be known as someone who doesn't waste your employees' precious time with party tricks. Leave those kinds of antics to the people who can authentically make those behaviors work for them. *Authentically* . . . there's that word again. It looks like we've come full circle.

One of the key hallmarks of an organization that is dedicated to high-performing engagement is that employees know that this is where they can be themselves, being their best and doing their best work. That's you, too.

As a leader, it's your responsibility to build a company that is growing toward a specific, intentional future that serves all its stakeholders—including your employees and yourself. Many leaders today are finding that seeking an internal culture that thrives on the engaged passions of employees who love their work is a really good business model. You may choose a different approach instead. It is entirely up to you.

Either way you decide to go, no matter where you decide to position yourself on the continuum of high-performing engagement, just be sure you put yourself there intentionally. And definitely make sure that you're prepared.

REFERENCE

Employee Engagement (London: Melcrum Publishing, 2005).

Chapter 2

Being Connected: The Effects of Technology on Employee Engagement*

Thomas O. Davenport

One of the biggest technology stories of 2006 wasn't really about technology at all. The biggest story—or at least the one with the most far-reaching implications for technology users—came from the Danish Cancer Society. Researchers in Copenhagen tracked 420,000 Danish cell phone users, including some 52,000 who had used cell phones for 10 years or more. The scientists concluded (with high confidence, if not absolute certainty) that cell phone use will *not* cause cancer of the brain, eye, neck, or salivary gland. There's also no such thing as cell phone–induced leukemia.[1] So slap that Bluetooth headset to the side of your face and chat away. Your physical health is not in danger—at least according to the findings of this study.

On one level, the Danish study presents an important and reassuring finding. We can now be confident that our most common technological companion probably won't kill us (unless it distracts us in traffic and creates another highway statistic). On a deeper level, the study also underscores the ambiguous relationship with ever-more ubiquitous technological connections. Underlying the study is a simple, yet significant implication: Technology has become so widespread that we worry about its effects on our health. These concerns lie at the root of urban legends about cancer caused by cell phones, the very legends that prompted the Danish doctors to assess the health effects of cell phone use in the first place.

Technology is everywhere. It affects just about every dimension of our daily lives. Technology helps us get cash, make friends, send overnight packages, pay bills, and order T-shirts. Moreover, almost every technology application that touches our

---

*Copyright © 2007 by Thomas O. Davenport.

everyday lives also affects the way we work. Without a cell phone, BlackBerry, email, wireless computer, Internet connection, and even social networking software, work would be a different place. Beyond influencing the way we perform work tasks, what effects does technology have on what it feels like to work—how we spend our time on the job, how much we accomplish, how we connect with our peers, how we feel about our jobs and our organizations? In other words, what effect does technology have on employee engagement?

ENGAGEMENT IN A TECHNOLOGICAL WORLD

As a concept, employee engagement goes directly to the heart of the relationships people have with their work and their organizations. Engagement doesn't mean satisfaction, happiness, or even high morale. It gets at something deeper—the inspiration people feel about their work and the energy they invest in doing a good job for a specific enterprise. At its simplest, engagement manifests itself as an individual's willingness invest more than the minimum effort required to keep his or her job.[2] Mounting evidence suggests that higher levels of job engagement lead to outcomes that organizations value. For example, Towers Perrin's research shows that highly engaged employees are more likely than other employees to say that they can have a direct impact on the

- Quality of service provided to customers
- Quality of the organization's work product
- Revenue growth and profitability of the company
- Operating costs of their work units.[3]

Highly engaged workers also say they plan to stay with their organizations longer than less engaged employees. This commitment reduces the considerable costs and disruption associated with turnover.

Engagement comprises two major components, a yin and yang of employee attitude. *Emotional engagement* refers to the bonds people form with their organizations, work teams, and fellow workers. This form of engagement addresses the will people have to do their work conscientiously and maintain a commitment to their teams and companies. *Rational engagement* encompasses the understanding people have of how their individual and departmental contributions benefit the larger enterprise. Workers with high rational engagement are more likely than others to invest discretionary effort in their jobs (i.e., to contribute beyond the minimum requirements to stay employed). Figure 2.1 illustrates this two-part concept and shows the elements of each form of engagement.

Going down another level, one can identify the main elements that influence each type of engagement. Towers Perrin's analysis reveals five key factors that taken as a whole, drive both emotional and rational engagement:

- **Work itself.** The sense of accomplishment that work provides, with special emphasis on autonomy and decision-making power and a clear understanding of how one's work contributes to department and enterprise success.

Figure 2.1
The Two Sides of Employee Engagement. (*Source*: Adapted from Towers Perrin, *Winning Strategies for a Global Workforce: Attracting, Retaining and Engaging Employees for Competitive Advantage* [2005], p. 14.)

Emotional Engagement
- I would recommend my company to a friend as a good place to work
- My company inspires me to do my best work
- I am proud to tell others I work for my company
- My job provides me with a sense of personal accomplishment
- I really care about the future of my company

Rational Engagement
- I understand how my unit contributes to the success of my company
- I understand how my role is related to my company's overall goals, objectives, and direction
- I am willing to put in a great deal of effort beyond what is normally expected to help my company succeed
- I am personally motivated to help my company be successful

- **Collaboration with others.** The effectiveness with which the content of the job and the structure of the organization encourage and facilitate cooperation both within work teams and across teams and functions.
- **Development opportunities.** The means, both formal and informal, by which employees can build their skills and abilities and realize the benefits of their ability-building efforts through increased performance, enhanced confidence, and fair recognition for success (through financial and other means).
- **Senior management behavior.** The degree to which employees believe senior management possesses and expresses a genuine interest in employee well-being and acts to ensure the long-term success of the organization.
- **Connection to the organization.** The belief that the organization has a clear and effective focus on its customers, has products and services that engender pride in employees, and through these maintains an appealing corporate culture.[4]

Some of these factors have greater effect on the emotional side of engagement (skill development and connection to the company, for example). Others work their influence more directly through the rational side (such as the effect of work itself, especially autonomy and participation in decision making). This text looks for patterns and likely connections, stopping short of striving to find hard-wired causal relationships.

This chapter examines those patterns in several categories, from technologies that directly influence how work is accomplished to those that affect how workers interact with each other and manage their working lives. Granted, these categories are arbitrary, and they certainly overlap. Nevertheless, dividing them into these groups helps in showing that just as technology itself takes many forms, so its affect on engagement varies across applications and contexts.

TECHNOLOGY THAT AFFECTS HOW WORK GETS DONE

The use of technology for accomplishing work has manifested itself in just about every kind of job that exists, from computer-aided design and manufacturing to data capture for retail transactions. As one researcher noted, "This infusion of technology has had a tremendous effect on employee morale, changing the nature of jobs, and impacting interactions with coworkers."[5]

One study looked at the reaction of health care workers to the introduction of record-keeping technology, specifically how nurses and other workers responded to the transition from using laptop computers for patient care documentation to using hand-held devices. Nurses also had to move from printed patient care plans to automated clinical planning software. These changes focused on making nurses more efficient, improving the continuity of patient care, and reducing the expense associated with copying and pushing paper.[6] The researchers found that greater involvement in the planning and roll-out of these changes correlated with more positive reactions to the new technologies. Likewise, people who had greater clarity about job content and contribution (that is, lower uncertainty about how their work affected the health care process and patient outcomes) also reported more positive feelings about the new devices.[7]

This study reinforced that the engagement effect of introducing work-altering technology depends on three things.

1. **The effect of technology on actual work tasks.** Do computers and other devices make the job easier or harder? Are workers more or less productive? Does the introduction of technology bring out what is essential and important about the job? Or does technology distract workers from what seems most interesting and involving about their work? Do technological factors make mastery of the job more feasible and attractive or less so? When a job becomes more interesting and its mastery more fulfilling, individual performance should improve. Engagement should also increase. In this research example, technology may have enhanced engagement by helping people build what psychologists call *self-efficacy*, a feeling of mastery and competence on the job. But technology's effect on self-efficacy can be a double-edged sword. If technology reduces job complexity and challenge to the point where work becomes simplistic, laden with minutia, or devoid of challenge, the aspects of engagement driven by involvement in work may actually decrease.

2. **The degree of involvement exercised by the affected workers during the introduction of new technologies.** Did the affected populations have some say on when and how technology would be introduced? Did management seek their advice on how employees (and customers) might respond to new ways of doing things? Involvement enhances control over the circumstances of change. Control, in turn,

increases the likelihood that workers will accept technology-driven modifications in how they do their work. Also, involving workers who have direct influence over production and service delivery will likely increase their confidence that new technology will *enhance* (and not degrade) their ability to produce high-quality products and serve customers effectively. For broad changes, a cross-section of employees from various departments can organize into planning task forces to guide the implementation process. If technological changes extend across a large geographic area, participation and involvement can be supported by discussion boards, teleconferences, and even occasional meetings in central locations. Regardless of the mechanisms chosen, the goal is to give people some measure of influence over their own technological destinies. Doing so produces the feelings of autonomy and self-determination that increase engagement through elements of the individual job.

Following a circular path, self-efficacy also promotes the adoption of technological innovation. According to Albert Bandura, a well-known psychologist,

> Early adopters of beneficial technologies not only increase their productivity but can gain influence in ways that change the structural patterns of organizations. Burkhardt and Brass (1990) report a longitudinal study showing that efficacy beliefs promote adoption of new technologies, which, in turn, alter the organizational network structure. They traced the diffusion within an agency of a computerized system that performed a variety of functions in data management and dissemination that were previously contracted out. Beliefs of personal efficacy to master computers were predictive of early adoption of the computerized system. Early adopters gained more influence and centrality within the organization over time than did later adopters.[8]

The engagement path progresses like this: involvement boosts control and engagement, which increase self-efficacy, which fosters rapid adoption of job-enhancing technology, which increases engagement-driving connections with the organization. A virtuous circle, if there ever was one.

3. The clarity of individual roles within the affected organizations before new technology came on the scene. Did people understand their jobs and their means of organizational contribution before they had to deal with new ways of working? Role clarity goes to the heart of rational engagement; it is the sine qua non of connection between individual work and organizational success. Ambiguity about the roles and lack of clarity about contribution to department and enterprise success will engender negative reactions to technological changes.[9] Conversely, workers who have a better line of sight between their jobs and the success of the organization show more inclination to embrace changes of all kinds. Their comfort with change becomes all that much stronger when they can foresee a positive effect on product and service outcomes.

Whatever direct effect technology may have on an individual's work, its implications for engagement will flow chiefly through three channels: the individual's sense of effectiveness at work, the degree of influence over how the job is executed before and after technology introduction, and the ability to understand and concentrate on what matters most about serving customers and producing a high-quality output.

TECHNOLOGY THAT ENABLES COMMUNICATION

The impact of technology at work is perhaps most dramatic—or at least most recognizable—in its effect on how we communicate with our peers. Take email, for example. A minor factor in everyday work life 10 years ago, handling email now takes precious work time for everyone who sits at a desk facing a computer. Email messages of all types are expected to reach nearly 3 trillion in 2007. That's 10,000 messages for every man, woman, and child in the United States. By one count, people at work receive upward of 130 messages a day.[10] Of the total time workers spend using the Internet for communication, the highest percentage—but only 39 percent, not even close to a majority—constitutes communication with business associates and co-workers.[11] Much of the rest is personal, and a significant proportion is spam. According to a study by Fortiva and Harris Interactive, 28 percent of employed U.S. adults acknowledge that the volume of email they receive causes them to fall behind in their work.[12]

For all the irritation it brings, email could not have ascended to a dominant position in the communications food chain without some clear advantages. Sitting at the top of the advantage list are five key features we have all come to appreciate about email and other electronic communication modes.

- **Network breadth.** The ability of users to send and receive messages from a wide array of contacts—presuming the definition of *network* encompasses almost anyone whose email address you have (or who has yours).

- **Speed.** The time that elapses between when messages go out from senders and are delivered to the recipients. This can range from a few seconds (or shorter) to days (or longer). Email and instant messaging (IM) rate high on this criterion. They don't make communicators wait for planes, trains, and automobiles to carry words on paper from a writer to a reader.

- **Parallelism.** The ability of participants to carry on multiple, almost simultaneous conversations with members of the broad network.

- **Rehearsability.** The rehearsability of such modes as email and blogs comes from being *asynchronous*, a reference to the time lag between when a receiver gets a message and when he or she must respond to it. Face-to-face conversation is synchronous—people talking (usually) respond immediately to the comments of their conversation partners. With email, you can wait as long as you want to reply. Because the sender controls the timing of an email transmission, he can review and rewrite each message, drafting the content and editing it before sending it. Judging by the amount of flame mail burning its way through networks, this feature remains underused.

- **Reprocessability.** This feature of electronic communication allows users to retain an archive with the historical threads of conversations that might otherwise be difficult to place in context. Email and blog users rely on reprocessability to keep track of content that would soon overload their organic storage capacity (i.e., their brains). Reprocessability also has a disadvantage, one known to many IT staffs in U.S. companies: Users can amass virtual mounds of messages in archives that clog servers across the corporate landscape. Of course, there is the added disadvantage that deleting doesn't entirely eliminate email, an inconvenient aspect that plays a part in grand jury hearings now and then.

These shortcomings remind us that for all their advantages, electronic conversation modes like email, IM, and podcasting have features that can hinder communication. The disadvantages include the following.

- **Lack of immediacy.** The advantage of asynchronicity—a potentially useful time lag between message and response—is also its disadvantage. Face-to-face and telephone communications take place *now*. Exchanges are all but seamless and are sometimes just about simultaneous. We don't need to wait to see how our conversation partners have responded to our message. In contrast, the immediacy of electronic communication varies. It can be high for IM and much lower for a podcast.
- **Low symbol variety.** With face-face communication, much of the information transferred comes from facial expression, body language and tone of voice. These symbols can come into play simultaneously, conveying converging or contradictory meaning, but nevertheless adding variety and nuance to communication. Electronic communication like blogs and email carry verbal information, but lack vocal and visual cues. Podcasts and conference calls add vocal information but still lack the visual element. The verbal content carries information, but vocal and visual nuances often convey richer symbolic content. Emoticons (symbols like this ☺) make a poor substitute for a winning smile or a devastating frown.

Think of email and face-to-face communication as points on a communication mode continuum. Other points on this continuum appear in Figure 2.2. Their performance on the evaluation criteria appears in Figure 2.2.

Understanding the advantages and limitations of various modes enables users to match communication methods with requirements. This, in turn, makes it possible to use them in ways that enhance rather than reduce employee engagement. For example, the speed, rehearsability, and reprocessability of email make it ideal for task clarification and providing objective information for immediate (or subsequent) review and assessment. Indeed, email is sometimes the fastest way to get simple directive messages to teammates. These features foster collaboration and expedite work, two pillars of engagement with both emotional and rational components. Virtual meetings via the Web have many of the same advantages, but with the added upside of immediacy. Team sessions via the Internet can work well for bringing a whole group up to speed on a new idea or on the results of an analysis. Videoconferences can be almost as good as face-to-face team meetings (except that audio transmission delays and poor visual resolution can limit the richness of communication cues). For teams that are geographically dispersed, the occasional videoconference can facilitate information exchange that is almost as good as being together in person. Intra- and interteam collaboration can thrive, and work can get done more effectively.

Figure 2.2
Evaluation of Communication Modes. (*Source:* Based on analysis by L. M. Maruping and R. Ararwal, "Managing Team and Interpersonal Processes through Technology: A Task-Technology Fit Perspective," *Journal of Applied Psychology* 89, no. 6 [December 2004]: 975.)

Communication Mode	Evaluation Criteria							
	Network Breadth	Speed	Parallelism	Rehearsability	Reprocessability	Immediacy	Symbol variety
Face-to-face conversation	Can be broad, but most conversations have few participants	High	Low	Low	Low	High	High
Telephone	Can be broad, but most conversations have few participants	High	Low	Low	Low	High	Moderate – allows vocal but not visual cues
Videoconferencing	Moderate	High	High	Moderate	Moderate	High	Moderate/High – technology limitations may limit vocal and visual clarity
Web Meetings	High	High	High	High	High	High	Moderate
Instant Messaging	High	High	Low	High	High	Moderate/High	Low
Email	High	High	High	High	High	Moderate/Low	Low
Blogs	High	Moderate	Low	High	High	Low/Moderate	Low
Podcasts	High	Moderate/High	Low	High	High	Low	Moderate

Workplace blogs represent a special form of communication technology, one that crosses organizational boundaries and brings particular advantages and disadvantages. A blog is defined as one individual's Web-enabled communication, unmediated by any editor, about any issues he or she considers worthy of comment. Blog publishing allows others to post their own comments and make them available for anyone who cares to read the whole continuum of musings. As Figure 2.2 indicates, blogs offer great network breadth, moderate speed, and off-the-charts rehearsability and reprocessability. People blog to document their lives, comment on topics that interest them (including their companies and their work), achieve emotional catharsis, and bond with a community. Employees have been known to use blogs to complain about company practices and rally support for anti-organization causes. Indeed, by one count, letting off steam about work issues is the number one reason why people generate work-related blogs.[13]

Can blogs function as useful communication tools in a work setting? Consider how allowing (and even encouraging) employees to blog about their work during working hours could open up a channel through which organizations can harness and promulgate the tacit knowledge of workers. Blogs can act as "spaces for intelligence gathering, construction and dissemination," in the words of one observer.[14] Businesses can also use blogs to communicate with employees (and customers, potential candidates, and indeed, the whole world). Blogs provide a forum that feels more organic, more genuine, and less formal than more conventional communication modes like advertising, promotion, and company newsletters.

What about the engagement effect of blogging? On one hand, it's easy to see how connecting with a blog-enabled community would enhance an individual's bonds with that community. On the other hand, the community will almost certainly stretch beyond organizational boundaries. This means that some (if not most) of the derived engagement will inevitably be directed toward a group outside the enterprise. Similarly, knowledge-sharing via blog might help build individual competence and self-efficacy; remember that the opportunity to develop skills and abilities tends to increase engagement. But at least some of the knowledge sources (and recipients) are bound to be extra-organizational. Is the organization willing to tolerate some misdirected energy or potentially subversive blog messages if the payoff includes potential enhancements to engagement through group connection and job-related knowledge enhancement? As of this writing, only a few organizations have had to address this question, but many will in the near future.

Here again, while remaining mindful of the many advantages of electronic communication, we can't forget their shortcomings. For all their attractions, no form of electronic communication can match conversation (even over the phone) for immediacy and symbol variety. The emotional aspects of engagement require that employees have a personal connection with their peers and supervisors. We've all heard the horror stories about the misuse of electronic communication. One of the most dramatic took place in 2006, when RadioShack used email to tell 400 employees they were being laid off from their jobs. The email message itself came straight from the corporate-speak lexicon: "The work force reduction notification is currently in progress.

Unfortunately your position is one that has been eliminated."[15] The unwritten message was even more disheartening: "We don't care enough about you to invest the money and manager time to tell you in person that you're losing your job."

Conveying sensitive information that demands immediate dialog and explanation doesn't lend itself to IM and email (or any other electronic communication approach). When the speed and simplicity of email trump the immediacy and symbol variety of direct face-to-face contact, something may literally get lost in translation. Even if the message isn't about a layoff, it's easy to imagine that substituting electronic communication for face-to-face contact in sensitive situations can only reduce an employee's feeling of connection with the organization.

An additional element enters the engagement calculus when we consider how intrateam relationships evolve over time. Relationships among the members of task-oriented work teams develop as the team defines and clarifies its task, decides how to approach it, makes work assignments, and meets (face to face or virtually) to pursue its goals. At each point in the team's progress, questions and conflicts may arise. Team dynamics in the early stages of a project are particularly sensitive. Resolving differences of understanding and opinion requires nuanced understanding and use of communication modes. Some straightforward questions and differences lend themselves to quick resolution over an electronic channel. Other conflicts may require the inclusive, immediate, and symbolically rich connections that only a face-to-face meeting can afford. The smart project manager must know when to hit the keyboard and when to hit the hallway. At stake is the success of the team as a collaborative unit—and consequently, the engagement of its members.

TECHNOLOGY FOR MANAGING WORK LIFE

Technology has become a major factor in how companies and their employees manage what one might call the *context of work*. In many cases, cost reduction has been the driving motive. For example, as health care costs have risen, companies have taken steps to stem expense increases. One strategy has called for shifting responsibility for both the management and the funding of health care to employees. Technology has come to dominate the process by which employees choose and use the benefit programs their organizations provide. Part of the cost-reduction strategy has called for substituting employee self-service for the direct personal service the human resources function used to provide. Employers now require employees to use electronic tools for:

- **Acquiring information.** Gathering data on the various health care benefit programs the company offers.
- **Performing analysis and making decisions.** Using computerized analytical tools to compare and choose among benefit programs.
- **Performing transactions.** Making benefit selections or recording status changes in the human resource information system.
- **Checking results and status.** Confirming benefits coverage and account balances (e.g., determining the current balance in a flexible spending or 401(k) account).

How effectively have technology tools performed in these roles? To a large extent the answer depends on the person. In a report on implementing employee self-service technology, an IBM research team points out some of the potential advantages to employees.

- Using self-service technology, employees can often get answers to questions faster than working through a human intermediary.
- Self-service lets people obtain information at times when it is convenient for them and in the language with which they are most comfortable.
- Self-service technology can give people access to a wider range of information than is available through human sources.
- By providing such services as retirement calculators and health benefit comparisons, companies can give employees the ability to take control over their personal finances and health care choices.[16]

As the authors of the study acknowledge, technology-enabled self-service can also have a dark side.

- In many organizations, important employee populations (sales representatives, retail store clerks, line manufacturing workers, for example) do not have access to Web-enabled computers throughout the day.
- For some workers, noise, lack of privacy, and limited physical space make personal computer use difficult.
- Limited computer literacy may make self-service too difficult for some employees.[17]

The authors conclude, "Not only are workers who are unable to access self-service more likely to revert to previous sources of HR information (such as managers or local HR staff), they can be easily demoralized by what they perceive as the organization's inability to address the needs of the entire workforce, not only those working with personal computers."[18]

What does all this mean for employee engagement? Towers Perrin research shows clear linkages between employees' connections with the organization and their attitudes toward the tools employers provide for benefits management. When workers agree that their organizations provide useful information and tools to help them make health care decisions and handle retirement planning, they record higher scores for commitment, motivation, and trust in senior management.[19] In other words, their attachments to the organization and their faith that senior management cares about them increase to the extent that benefits management tools help them make sound decisions quickly and easily. Of course, the opposite is also true: Clumsy tools that waste time and produce confusing results can only reduce these key engagement drivers.

Benefit programs are not the only context in which technology plays the role that live, caring HR professionals once played. Under pressure to cut employee acquisition costs and improve new workers' productivity, companies are looking for ways to use technology to introduce newly hired employees into the organization. Historically, orientation and organizational socialization occurred through a combination of classroom instruction and informal, on-the-job learning. To some extent, of course, the information required to navigate an organization still gets conveyed informally, through peer contacts and mentor relationships. How else can one learn that the cafeteria is down the hall, the restroom is around the corner, and the boss always uses the teddy bear coffee cup? Increasingly, organizations have turned to technology to expedite the orientation process and reduce the cost associated with conducting formal classroom sessions. They have achieved mixed results.

This use of technology for employee orientation brings into sharp relief two distinct goals of the process. One goal, of course, is informational. New employees need to know a few important things about the organization and work environment. Objective information about such topics as organizational history, competitive positioning, product offerings, and organizational argot (the acronyms, slang, and jargon used in the company) is critical to functioning effectively within the organization's culture. Another, more subtle goal is socialization. Newcomers require more than just objective information to adapt to new organizational surroundings and perform their jobs well. They also need to establish relationships with their co-workers and understand the formal and informal power structures of the enterprise (i.e., its politics). New employees must also learn the organization's goals and values and come to an understanding of how they are expected to contribute to the company's success. Effective orientation represents a key aspect of individual development, a critical first example of the organization's willingness to invest in building the skills and competencies of employees. The goal of all this is proficient performance—getting the individual quickly to a reasonable level of productivity, partly by creating a foundation on which to establish employee engagement.

For one organization, researchers compared the effects on new employees of two orientation approaches. Program A consisted of a one-week session with plenty of social contact. Newcomers were flown to a central location where they spent a week secluded with fellow new hires, orientation instructors, and guest speakers from various parts of the organization. The program consisted of presentations, videos, reading assignments, team-building activities, and Q&A sessions. Program B used a self-guided computerized approached designed to reduce travel and other costs associated with the orientation sessions. The self-guided orientation package covered the same material as the more socially focused approach. It incorporated a multimedia program containing written, audio, and video-based sections. Program B was designed to be completed in two to three days.

When the researchers compared the results of the two approaches, they found similarities in some outcomes and dramatic differences in others. As Figure 2.3 indicates, the socially intensive and computer-based approaches produced comparable levels of newcomer understanding of organizational language and history. In contrast, the traditional socially focused orientation yielded significantly better outcomes in the less information-intensive, more personal areas: understanding organizational

Figure 2.3
Comparison of Orientation Programs. (*Source*: Adapted from W. J. Wesson, and C. I. Gogus, "Shaking Hands with a Computer: An Examination of Two Methods of Organizational Newcomer Orientation," *Journal of Applied Psychology* 90, no. 5 [2005]: 1023.)

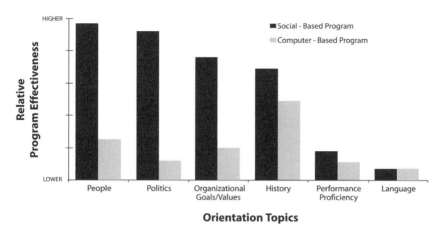

goals and values, establishment of relationships with other employees, and understanding organizational politics.

Here we have a clear illustration of the kinds of situations in which substituting technology for social contact can reduce engagement. On one hand, relying on technology at the expense of personal contact may meet individuals' needs for objective information about organization terminology and history. These can help new employees become quickly and effectively engaged in their work. On the other hand, this approach falls short when it comes to building bonds among people (who may later on want to call on their orientation classmates for advice and guidance), between new employees and their bosses, and between people and the organization. Thus, on two key engagement dimensions—collaboration with peers and affinity with the organization's mission and goals—the socially heavy, technologically light orientation effort produced better engagement-related outcomes. Overall, the research findings support the conclusion that orientation programs built on extensive personal interaction have better engagement effects than those relying more heavily on technology. In this research case, participants in the social orientation program also expressed higher organizational commitment and job satisfaction.[20]

TECHNOLOGY THAT ENABLES WORKPLACE FLEXIBILITY

Remote work—telework, if you will—has gone from phenomenon to accepted practice in not much more than a decade. Remote work takes several forms. An employee can work at home or from many other distant locations: the library, the coffee house, the beach. Telework flexibility extends to time as well: morning, noon and night, to name three. Some estimates place the number of teleworkers in North America as high as 50,000.[21] Other estimates come in substantially lower, partly because, while the definition of telework may be reasonably precise, the definition of *teleworker* is not. Does one qualify as a teleworker if he or she works at home once a month? Or is the minimum requirement for inclusion at least one day a week of remote work? Whatever the definition, the number of teleworkers has multiplied as their mode of working has gained favor among employees and organizations alike.

Technology-supported telework has made real the notion that work is not a place you go, but a set of activities you perform. Telework assumes (indeed, could not happen without) the support of technology. Absent email, fax machines, IM, telephones, and of course, computers themselves, we would all remain anchored to our desks. Technology frees us from the fetters of the workplace and makes the physical location irrelevant. How does working away from the workplace, supported by technology but personally unconnected from other workers, affect an individual's emotional connection with enterprise and co-workers? How does working remotely affect the depth of involvement someone has with the job itself? These effects of teleworking are considered on two engagement drivers: the content of work and the productivity required to produce a feeling of success; and the degree of collaboration that occurs within work teams.

Much as the census of teleworkers remains open to debate, so does the question of the productivity effects of teleworking. Some organizations make extravagant claims for the productivity gains associated with telework, suggesting that output can increase by as much as 15 to 40 percent.[22] After all, teleworkers can move through their daily tasks relatively unhindered by the incidental interruptions that often plague the work process. They can avoid everything from unexpected visitors and unproductive meetings to fire drills (figurative and literal) and tedious birthday celebrations. Fundamental to the telework concept is giving teleworkers productivity-enhancing advantages that incidentally go directly to the heart to of the relationship between work and engagement. Those precious advantages are autonomy and control over the work process. When these are present, one can reasonably conclude, teleworkers may experience a productivity advantage (and potentially an engagement boost) over their workplace-bound colleagues.

Productivity, of course, is notoriously elusive to measure for knowledge workers in general and teleworkers in particular. What metric best reflects output for a teleworker? Words typed? Lines of code written? Customers served? Problems solved? What about the *quality* of output produced by the teleworker? Is it as high as the yield from those who have the benefit of direct contact with others on the team? Companies encourage (or in some cases, compel) people to work at home to save the cost of office space and related overhead. But does a teleworking arrangement also require an incremental investment in equipment and connectivity? And what might such an investment mean for the net productivity return to the organization on its work-support investment?

Other sticky questions focus on the collaboration effects of telework. What if the productivity of the teleworker declines because lack of personal access to team members makes information harder to acquire or interpret? What if the productivity of the rest of the team drops because critical interpersonal interaction declines? What if, as one observer commented, "Some teleworkers add to their colleagues' workload through email requests sent from home while making themselves unavailable for the requests of others?" [23] In other words, what if frustration rises (and engagement falls) for those back at the ranch when teleworkers are out on the range? Net engagement for the team as a whole may take a hit as collaboration becomes more difficult.

Ultimately, the engagement effects of telework on both teleworkers and their teams will depend on four factors.

- **The individual employee.** Such traits as low need for socialization; comfort with technology tools; effectiveness at independent, minimum-supervision work; and skill at time and space management enhance the teleworker's prospects for success in a remote setting. When a teleworker has these qualities, a teleworking arrangement will afford sufficient opportunities for satisfaction with work and connection with the organization and its goals.
- **The work itself.** Factors such as high individual control over work content; little need for face-to-face support; modular management of tasks (as opposed to fast-changing, organic flows that require interpersonal negotiation and immediate response); readily observable (and, if possible, measurable) quality and quantity of output; and effective support from technology tools increase the likelihood for telework success. Work that has these elements, when matched with individual worker qualities, can be productive and afford sufficient (if not extensive) collaboration opportunity.
- **The organization's culture.** When values are placed on output rather than just effort, when there is overall acceptance of different work modes, when the organization encourages only *essential* meetings, when there are enough in-person events to maintain social networks, when status and power derive from performance rather than just managerial titles, teleworking has a chance to succeed. These cultural features mean that people can experience their connections to the organization without being present at the work site.
- **The behavior of the manager.** When managers know how much to stay in contact, trust employees, manage by results rather than effort (or rather, appearance of effort), plan and organize work to integrate both on-site and remote contributions effectively, understand the value of recognition and use it to support the whole team's engagement, then a good foundation exists for a successful manager/teleworker relationship. Managers who approach the oversight of teleworkers this way are likely increase employee engagement by providing meaningful work, fostering suitable collaboration, and reinforcing the connections between individuals and the organization.

Just as with the optimistic claims of higher productivity, questions still exist about whether telework provides an attitude boost among those who work outside the workplace. One source says that 28 percent of people who work from home describe themselves as engaged, compared with 25 percent who work primarily in an office setting.[24] Others disagree. Researchers who have studied the attempts to measure the attitudes of teleworkers reached this conclusion: "There is little clear evidence of increased job satisfaction among teleworkers in the studies we examined."[25] Job satisfaction isn't the same as engagement, but comes from work experiences and is an outcome of high engagement.

Ultimately, teleworker engagement will almost certainly rest on the alignment of the four factors. When a person's low need for socialization coincides with work that requires mostly individual rather than team effort, when the organization's culture focuses on and rewards production rather than on-site face time, and when managers recognize the efforts of remote workers and reward those workers as frequently and as richly as they do their on-site team members, then teleworkers are likely to express high engagement and produce effectively. But both productivity and engagement will likely suffer when even one of these factors falls out of alignment.

WHAT IT ALL MEANS FOR MANAGERS AND COMPANIES

Technology has multiple, sometimes contradictory, and often unpredictable effects on work and workers. How then should managers and executives handle the introduction and use of technology in the workplace? Can we define useful guidelines for the deployment of computer and communication technology, rules of thumb to help organizations take the actions that foster employee engagement and avoid those that reduce engagement?

We might begin by reviewing the discussion of the last section. The discussion noted when and how technology-supported telework reinforces employee engagement, in spite of some obvious challenges of disconnection and isolation. Four factors define when telework is appropriate: consistency with employee characteristics and needs, suitability for specific work tasks, cultural support from the organization, and astute manager judgment. When these four factors come together, teleworkers tend to express high engagement and produce effectively.

These may look like the criteria for effective management in any high-engagement workplace. To a large extent, they are. Indeed, it falls largely to the manager to ensure that the work experience and the organizational environment (whatever influence technology may have) address the five drivers of rational and emotional engagement. Technology will reinforce a competent manager's efforts to the extent that it

- Makes jobs richer and more interesting and makes people more effective at doing their work.
- Increases and makes more gratifying the interpersonal contact people have with their teammates.
- Facilitates the development of skills that improve self-efficacy and fulfill people's basic desire to learn.
- Reinforces that senior management understands employees' needs, cares about those needs, and takes steps to increase employee well-being.
- Helps people understand and connect directly with an organizational mission that makes employees proud to say they work for the enterprise.

Beyond the manager's role, however, the power of technology, especially for communication, introduces other challenges for companies and individuals alike. For example, what happens to employee engagement when organizations deploy so much technology that people can't escape the electronic tentacles of the company? One blogger, writing about the advantages of podcasting messages to the sales force, sounded gleeful about the prospect of giving iPods to every busy salesperson. He mused about how wonderful it would be if busy salespeople could listen to company messages while working out in the hotel gym.[26] Heaven forefend a salesperson should have enough downtime to catch a quick workout without having to be plugged in. Requiring people to connect to the company around the clock via an electronic umbilical cord can't be a formula for enhancing their emotional linkages with the organization.

Some organizations worry that employees may be too plugged in, or at least that they may be using workplace technology for purposes other than doing work. They have instituted processes for policing employee's use of the Internet, email, blogging, and social networking capabilities in the (real or virtual) workplace. About three-quarters of companies monitor employees' Web site connections, and about two-thirds block access to specific sites.[27] As with all complex issues, however, policing of technology use can have unintended consequences. Consider two scenarios.

Company A worries about misuse by employees of communication technology and institutes a program of monitoring. This action demonstrates that the organization values compliance and rule-following more than the collaboration and work-enhancing aspects of technology. Employee trust of the organization falls, they question the motives of senior management, and consequently, engagement drops. As one observer comments, "Colleagues who trust one another have synergy and work better as a unit. Eavesdropping, electronic or otherwise, is always going to tear that fabric of trust."[28]

Company B wants to build an environment of trust and therefore minimizes monitoring of employee's technology use. Indeed, the organization encourages people to make suitable use of technology to enhance collaboration. Some abuse the privilege, but most do not. Job effectiveness goes up, as do teamwork and trust in senior management's understanding of what employees need to perform effectively. Employee engagement increases as people connect with the organization. Their pride in the organization helps motive them to self-monitor communication technology use. Engagement goes up as most people focus on their jobs and use technology appropriately.

Granted, these scenarios seem simple, even stylized. Nevertheless, they demonstrate a key point: The effect of technology on employee engagement follows a circular path. Technology affects engagement, but engagement also affects how (and how effectively) employees use technology. Highly engaged workforces do many things well: They are better at serving customers, working productively, generating high-quality work products, increasing revenue growth, and pushing up organizational profitability than their less-engaged counterparts. They are also more adaptive and accepting of technology introduction, and more likely to use technology judiciously.

Ultimately, we should see technology as a lens through which engagement drivers are focused. High-engagement organizations provide interesting jobs, collaboration opportunities, development pathways, means for senior management to demonstrate concern for employees, and line of sight to organizational mission. They also willingly involve employees in developing and introducing technology solutions into the work environment. These companies are likely to find that technology, introduced into a high-engagement context, will act to preserve and even enhance employee engagement levels. Without this foundation, however, the slickest technology on the planet will only engender frustration and disconnection. In other words, employee engagement lies at the beginning of the technology change path, as well as at the end.

NOTES

1. "Cellphones Don't Trigger Cancer, Big Danish Study Says," http://breitbart.com/news (December 5, 2006). Original study published in the *Journal of the National Cancer Institute* 98, no. 23 (December 6, 2006): 1717–1713.

2. D. R. Roberts and T. O. Davenport, "Job Engagement: Why It's Important and How To Improve It," *Employment Relations Today* (Autumn 2002): 21.

3. *Winning Strategies for a Global Workforce: Attracting, Retaining and Engaging Employees for Competitive Advantage*, Towers Perrin (2005), p. 10.

4. Ibid.

5. R. Morrison, "Employee Involvement, Attitudes and Reactions to Technology Changes," *Journal of Leadership & Organizational Studies* (Spring 2006): 1, http://www.allbusiness.com.

6. Ibid., p. 3.

7. Ibid., pp. 6, 7.

8. A. Bandura, *Self-Efficacy: The Exercise of Control* (New York: W. H. Freeman, 1997), pp. 459, 460.

9. Morrison, "Employee Involvement," pp. 6, 7.

10. D. Hallerman, "E-mail: Turning up the Volume," *eMarketer Report* (April 29, 2005): 2.

11. N. H. Nie, "Ten Years after the Birth of the Internet: How Do Americans Use the Internet in Their Daily Lives?," Stanford Institute for the Quantitative Study of Society, 2005 Report, p. 6.

12. "27% of U.S. Corporate Employees Reached the Amount of Storage Space for Their Corporate E-mail Inbox," http://www.itfacts.biz.

13. J. Richards, "Unmediated Workplace Images from the Internet: An Investigation of Work Blogging," Paper presented to the 25th International Labour Process Conference, Universitiet van Amsterdam, April 2–4, 2007, p. 22.

14. Ibid., p. 17.

15. "You've Got Mail: You're Fired," http://laptoplogic.com (August 30, 2006).

16. "Taking Information into Your Own Hands," IBM Business Consulting Services (2004), p. 5.

17. Ibid., p. 7.

18. Ibid.

19. "From Responsibility to Action—Making Benefit Change Work," Towers Perrin (2006), pp. 15–16.

20. J. Wesson and C. I. Gogus, "Shaking Hands with a Computer: An Examination of Two Methods of Organizational Newcomer Orientation," *Journal of Applied Psychology* 90, no. 5 (2005): 1024.

21. M. Turek, "The Number of Teleworkers Is on the Rise," http://www.collaborationloop.com (November 27, 2006), p. 2.

22. D. Westfall, "Does Telecommuting *Really* Increase Productivity?" *Communications of the ACM* 47, no. 8 (August 2004): 93.

23. E. Bailey and N. B. Kurland, "A Review of Telework Research: Findings, New Directions, and Lessons for the Study of Modern Work," *Journal of Organizational Behavior* 23 (2002): 393.

24. J. Robison, "Getting the Most out of Remote Workers," *Gallup Management Journal* (June 8, 2006): 2.

25. Bailey and Kurland, "A Review of Telework Research," p. 389.

26. http://blogs.businessweek.com, posted June 9, 2005.

27. S. Armour, "Employers Look Closely at What Workers Do on the Job," *USA TODAY* (November 8, 2006): 2B.

28. Ibid., p. 1B.

Chapter 3

Driving Long-Term Engagement through a High-Performance Culture*

Christopher Rice

Culture may take top honors as the most mysterious and difficult-to-get-your-arms-around lever of employee engagement. Other commonly recognized engagement levers appear easy to move in comparison. Got bad managers? Fire the worst, then train—and compensate—the remaining managers for behaviors that engage. Experiencing a disconnect on the branding front? Enlist the marketing department to lead an inside-out brand campaign to rally the workforce.

But culture? It's amorphous and intangible. Not long ago, biologists were the only ones creating it—in petri dishes. Organizational development experts studied it, and there were a few maverick businesspeople, like Herb Kelleher of Southwest Airlines, who credited culture as the secret to their firm's success. Most businesspeople dismissed it as soft HR stuff—until leaders like Kelleher started getting attention for the successes they enjoyed, especially in adverse economic times.

Organizational culture is far from fluff. It's potentially the most powerful engagement tool at your disposal. If you get culture right, it provides a foundation for high engagement that can sustain a workforce through good times and bad. That's because culture, like the air you breathe, touches all employees. Culture is not an engagement program portioned out to a select group of managers or a workplace perk that drives high employee survey scores but can succumb to budget cuts when times get tough. Culture is there whether you have deliberately shaped it or not. It makes good business sense to make sure your culture is working for you—to drive high performance and engagement.

---

*Copyright © 2007 by Blessing White, Inc.

This chapter explores the links between culture and engagement, what a high-performance culture looks like, the steps for creating one, and the pitfalls into which even the most well-intentioned leaders can fall.

WHAT DOES A HIGH-PERFORMANCE CULTURE LOOK LIKE?

Corporate culture at its most basic level is the *sum of an organization's behaviors and practices*. It reveals itself in big and small decisions as well as daily practices ("how we do things around here") that tend to perpetuate themselves. Culture often goes unnoticed by employees (like the air you breathe), yet a healthy culture (like clean air) is essential to a healthy organization.

A firm's founder naturally places his or her stamp on the organization—shaping the culture through early hiring decisions and policies as well as his or her own values, communications, and behavior. But most often, as the organization grows organically or through mergers and acquisitions (M&As), its culture naturally changes and is allowed to evolve.

However, culture—and then subsequently employee engagement—is too critical to leave to the evolutionary forces. You must *deliberately* mold and cultivate a high-performance culture to drive engagement. And you can.

High-performance cultures are shaped around the following three components:

- **A clear, compelling corporate mission.** A mission, or *purpose* as some firms call it, is a statement that answers the question of why the company exists: "What's your reason for being?" It needs to inspire, inform business decisions, generate customer loyalty, ignite employee passion, and motivate discretionary effort. "Making money" doesn't qualify as a mission, although profitability is essential to a firm's survival. Although a mission does not have to reflect a "save the world" tone, it does need to be aspirational and clear enough to engage employees. Its mere existence serves as the organization's North Star, providing a fixed point to which the workforce can connect.
- **Shared organizational values.** Core values guide employee behavior and influence business practices as your organization delivers on its promises to customers, employees, and other stakeholders. Core values answer the question: "What are your guiding principles, your authentic, enduring 'rules of the road?'" Your business strategies shift to meet market demands. Your core values don't.
- **Shared accountability.** High-performance cultures require an environment that encourages employee ownership of both the organization's bottom-line results and its cultural foundation. Culture affects everyone and is everyone's business. It's essential, then, that the entire workforce understands the core drivers of your culture and share responsibility for sustaining them.

CULTURE'S IMPACT ON ENGAGEMENT

Numerous studies connect the dots between organizational culture and employee engagement. The Corporate Leadership Council, for example, labels culture a "public good" engagement lever—meaning it is not subtractable, nor is it excludable. Unlike "private good" levers (e.g., coaching or career development programs), culture does not require direct investment in individual employees, it is "scalable" (by touching all levels of employees), and it requires minimal resources to maintain (providing benefits indefinitely). If you're serious about employee engagement, it's worth taking the time to shape your culture because your efforts can provide wide-reaching, long-lasting value.

A high-performance culture can positively impact employee engagement in the following ways.

1. **Provides meaning and emotional connection** to a workforce searching for employment that offers more than just a paycheck. That connection translates into increased commitment and pride, which in turn results in higher retention and discretionary effort.
2. **Prevents bad business practices and behavior** that may not necessarily land your leaders in jail but can certainly alienate customers and employees who come to work each day with good intentions and high achievement needs. High-performance cultures weed out leaders who don't live the core values before those leaders' behaviors damage morale and drive top talent out the door.
3. **Guides and inspires employee decisions** in a flatter, fast-paced workplace so that employees do all the right things when you need them to—whether or not their manager is watching.
4. **Encourages innovation, risk taking, and trust** — all qualities characteristic of an environment that encourages employee use of talents and discretionary effort. Plenty of studies make the link between high engagement and the ability of employees to do what they do best when they show up for work each day.
5. **Supports "fit."** A strong culture helps ensure that those who don't fit leave or aren't hired in the first place. That's important to sustained employee engagement, because disgruntled, out-of-place employees bring everyone down. When an organization focuses on values, not just results, hiring and firing decisions are easier to make. Better yet, bad hires often self-select out.
6. **Attracts and retains star performers** who not only have the skills required to achieve ambitious business goals but are also so invigorated by the company's core beliefs that they give 110 percent. "Meaningful work" has appeared as one of the top three career drivers in the last four career development studies conducted by BlessingWhite. Although each employee has a unique definition of "meaningful," when an organization has a well-established culture based on a clear mission and shared values, it's easier for employees to determine whether their job will provide the meaning they seek.
7. **Provides fixed points of reference and stability** during periods of great change or crisis. Think of a lighthouse with its beacon during fog and rough seas. In the same way, a high-performance culture can keep employees motivated and aligned when business strategies are constantly shifting or marketplace pressures mount. It also helps ensure that if a crisis hits, leaders at all levels act in a way employees can be proud of.
8. **Aligns employees with diverse interests around shared goals.** A high-performance culture creates a sense of community and encourages teamwork, creating a common bond among individuals with different experiences and expertise. The result: A feeling of belonging to something bigger than one's self.

There's no doubt that managing your culture requires constant attention, and if it's not something you have addressed before, it's likely to be a lot of hard work. Kotter and Heskett, in the landmark study that led to their classic book *Corporate Culture and Performance,* estimate it can take 5 to 15 years to actually change a culture, depending on its size.[1]

It seems daunting, but if you're committed to employee engagement, the ultimate, long-range benefits of taking action outweigh the organization that you might get by default:

- A culture that may be supportive of engagement now (by luck or market forces) but is not necessarily sustainable.
- A neutral culture that forces your organization to work harder and invest more in private good engagement efforts.
- An organization that continuously incurs preventable expenses in image repair and turnover costs.
- A toxic culture that undermines all your other employee engagement strategies.

BEST PRACTICES FOR BUILDING AND SUSTAINING A HIGH-PERFORMANCE CULTURE

Since every organization's culture is unique, the following recommendations do not constitute a process of lock-step actions. What is critical to remember, however, is that culture creation is a *continuous effort.* You can never check these steps completely off your list and say, "our culture is done." Organizations with high-performance cultures continuously monitor results and regularly return to these strategies to sustain their success:

- Clarify your mission and values
- Assess your starting point
- Communicate and translate your mission and values
- Model your values
- Inspire employees
- Align employees
- Align business practices

Clarify Your Mission and Values

If you don't have a published mission or set of organizational values, you need to identify and define them. You won't actually start with a blank slate. Having no *espoused* values, for example, is not the same as having *no* values. Your organization has rules of the road, even if they are unspoken. (Which means, of course, that you may have to undertake an abrupt, painful, and expensive reverse course if you discover that the mission and values that are in place are detrimental to your company's long-term interests. The change won't be fun, but it's better than continuing down the wrong road.)

One executive of a global high-tech firm explains it this way:

Defining our mission and core values was a natural step in our evolution. When we were small, everyone knew what we were about. But as we've grown to over 16,000 employees, we felt it was important to step back and formally write down the core principles that guide our behavior. They aren't foreign to anyone. We just want to be crystal clear how these values contribute to future success and ensure they remain on everyone's radar screen.

This has to be an inclusive process. Senior leaders may be tempted to hole up in a small clubby group to define mission and values, in order to shortcut a values clarification process of seemingly endless drafts and word-smithing (see the sidebar for sample mission and values statements) with all stakeholders to get to a concise statement of purpose and five to eight core values. What they get, if they do it this way, is a document that will reflect their own hubris and delusion rather than a real-world picture that the entire company can endorse.

EXAMPLES OF MISSION STATEMENTS
Why does your organization exist?

- The Walt Disney Company: To make people happy.
- Merck: To preserve and improve human life.
- Charles Schwab: To provide customers with the most useful and ethical financial services in the world.
- BlessingWhite: Reinventing leadership and the meaning of work.

Authenticity

Clarifying your mission and values requires looking inward, not outward. You can't benchmark other companies to determine what you stand for. You can't contract a set of desirable core values from a consulting firm (although consultants can facilitate your clarification process). You need more than a passionate senior leader to distill and give definition to the guiding principles that will be authentic for your organization. You need to bring yourself to the table and stay there until the job is done.

Some firms establish cross-functional teams to identify their values from the rank-and-file up. Others may start at the top but then actively solicit input from managers and employees through focus groups and online surveys. Either way, the process needs to delve into the following questions.

- What are the organization's unwritten rules?
- How does work get done?
- What do new employees think that the organization values?

- What do veteran employees believe?
- How do those perceptions compare?
- Which values are most critical for success moving forward?
- How is each value defined?

The process can be time-consuming, yet it ensures that the mission and values reflect the essence of your organization. There's nothing more demotivating than executives espousing values that are totally foreign to the workforce.

EXAMPLES OF CORE ORGANIZATIONAL VALUES
What are your organization's rules of the road?

Xilinx

- **C**ustomer Focused: We exist only because our customers are satisfied and want to do business with us . . . and we never forget it.
- **R**espect: We value all people, treating them with dignity at all times.
- **E**xcellence: We strive for "best in class" in everything we do.
- **A**ccountability: We do what we say we will do and expect the same from others.
- **T**eamwork: We believe that cooperative action produces superior results.
- **I**ntegrity: We are honest with ourselves, each other, our customers, our partners, and our shareholders.
- **V**ery Open Communication: We share information, ask for feedback, acknowledge good work, and encourage diverse ideas.
- **E**njoying Our Work: We work hard, are rewarded for it, and maintain a good sense of perspective, humor, and enthusiasm.

Starbucks

- Provide a great work environment and treat each other with respect and dignity.
- Embrace diversity as an essential component in the way we do business.
- Apply the highest standards of excellence to the purchasing, roasting, and fresh delivery of our coffee.
- Develop enthusiastically satisfied customers all of the time.
- Contribute positively to our communities and our environment.
- Recognize that profitability is essential to our future success.

General Electric

- Passionate
- Curious

- Resourceful
- Accountable
- Teamwork
- Committed
- Open
- Energizing

U.S. Army

- **Loyalty.** Bear true faith and allegiance to the U.S. Constitution, the Army, and other soldiers. Be loyal to the nation and its heritage.
- **Duty.** Fulfill your obligations. Accept responsibility for your own actions and those entrusted to your care. Find opportunities to improve oneself for the good of the group.
- **Respect.** Rely upon the golden rule. How we consider others reflects upon each of us, both personally and as a professional organization.
- **Selfless Service.** Put the welfare of the nation, the Army, and your subordinates before your own. Selfless service leads to organizational teamwork and encompasses discipline, self-control, and faith in the system.
- **Honor.** Live up to all the Army values.
- **Integrity.** Do what is right, legally and morally. Be willing to do what is right even when no one is looking. It is our "moral compass," an inner voice.
- **Personal Courage.** Our ability to face fear, danger, or adversity, both physical and moral courage.

Buy-In

This clarification process also builds commitment and jump-starts the communications required to familiarize the workforce with the power of core values. One financial services firm with a founder and chairman who had a very clear vision of the organization's values took 10 months and the input of 80 executives to revisit its purpose and formally document its values. The CEO's rationale: "The challenge was not document creation, it was commitment generation. To achieve that objective, a process of much broader inclusion was essential."

The process can work at a department level as well. An IT department that weathered a tumultuous acquisition typical in the pharmaceutical industry found that defining what the larger organization's values meant at the *department level* helped everyone get on board—on the same page—for the way the reshaped department needed to behave in order to succeed under the new ownership.

Assess Your Starting Point

If you already have a published mission and core values, you need to know where your organization stands. Take the posters down from the wall, revisit the words, and most important, assess whether these tenets actually guide the practices and behaviors of your organization.

Look at your mission.

- Does everyone know it?
- Does everyone agree on what it looks like when it's in action, especially in moments of tough choices?
- Do leaders use the mission to guide business decisions about product and service offerings, alliances, and expansion opportunities?

Look at your core values. Are they

- *Posted?* On the walls? On your Web site for investors and potential new hires to view? In your annual report?
- *Known?* How many senior team members can rattle off the list? How many middle managers and employees can do the same?
- *Embraced?* Do leaders refer to them regularly? Do your employees reference them in meetings when facing a decision about an action? Are there opportunities to convene discussion groups that focus on one or more of the values at any given time?
- *Lived?* Do leaders model desired behaviors?
- *Embedded in daily decisions and practices?* From organizational mechanics, to processes and functions that touch the employee, the customer, and other stakeholders, where are business practices on the culture spectrum? Are they reinforcing its core values or flying in its face? Can your employees tell stories of incidents when they have seen the values in action?

When sizing up the situation, take extra care to look at differences that may exist across your organization. Field offices are often less aligned with the organization's mission and values than headquarters. Leaders of divisions or departments tend to set the tone—good or bad—for interpreting your culture's core drivers. This reality check will bring to light gaps between espoused values and day-to-day operations in addition to well-aligned behavior and business practices. Run internal focus groups to gather stories of values in action or behaviors in conflict, conduct random employee conversations and check-ins, or use a more formal employee survey. This "scan" of your culture can help you prioritize the areas of greatest need and the actions that will provide the greatest leverage.

One manufacturer in the computer industry, for example, had clarified its core values in 1996 through a worldwide initiative in which every employee had the chance to provide input. When its senior team assessed the culture after four years of rapid growth, it realized that the values were known but were not always influencing practices and behaviors to the extent the leaders wanted. As a result, they implemented several initiatives, including the addition of culture-building tools and content in their manager boot camp. Their goal was to renew a focus on values and ensure that managers could fulfill their role as custodians of the strong culture of shared values that historically had set the firm apart from its competitors.

Communicate and Translate Your Mission and Values

Communication is a critical step for organizations with a newly clarified mission and values, but it remains a key success factor for those trying to build and sustain a high-performance culture. We're not talking about a check-off-the-box communication strategy orchestrated by your marketing staff (although that can certainly help in the beginning).

A high-performance culture requires continuous communication to provide meaning. Meaning—not abstract terms, catchy phrases, or executive missives—drives employee engagement.

Starting at the Top

If senior leaders aren't crystal clear—and in complete agreement—about the organization's mission and values, attempts to cascade their message will act like a crack in a foundation, with the fissure growing larger and larger as communications work their way down through the organization. Many senior leaders admit to us that they haven't memorized the organization's values. Most usually get only 50 percent of the values correct. Some leaders actually try to bluff their way through interviews, recounting values that sound lofty but don't actually belong in their organization. Research by the Hay Group confirms these observations, suggesting that senior team members in large and small organizations can suffer from a disconnect on the organization's mission, vision, values, and short-term strategies.

Staying on Message

Leaders need to talk about the organization's culture and core mission and values at every opportunity. When they think they're done, they need to keep going. In addition to the "what," leaders need to include the "why" to add commitment to clarity. Why do they personally care? What will the organization (or the market or the world) look like when every person and practice is aligned with the firm's mission and values? A managing director of a financial services firm based in Ireland explains, "I try to be proactive. When I communicate about strategy and decisions, I always refer to our values too. We need people to see and hear the priority we give the values."

Making Abstract Concepts Real

For employees to align their behavior and decisions with core values, they need to be able to do more than recite pithy statements. They need to understand, see, and feel the meaning implicit in the words. Meaningful communication requires two-way dialogue to make it real. Employees need to know, "What does this mean to me? How can I make a difference?"

Storytelling is an excellent way to translate a mission and values into tangible actions. It also provides an emotional element that inspires individuals to *care enough* to act. To be most effective, stories need to be first-person accounts that

- Contain specific, sensory-rich details so that the listeners can actually feel a part of the scene.
- Cover feelings *and* facts.

Firms with high-performance cultures routinely begin meetings or business dinners with storytelling about the mission and core values in action. They make sure to post stories of "culture keepers" on their intranets not only to celebrate successes but also to offer concrete examples of what living the organization's values actually looks like.

Model Your Values

Defining values in the abstract and providing vivid examples aren't enough. Although all employees play a part in sustaining a high-performance culture, leaders are the guardians. They set the proper tone when they visibly model the organization's espoused values. If they don't, the values won't take—or worse, the posters and laminated cards will fuel employee cynicism, seen merely as a meaningless "flavor of the month" change initiative or the CEO's pet project that will fizzle out when that particular leader departs.

Unfortunately for executives, leadership has never been more public, thanks to the fishbowl of visibility created by the Internet. Everyone—employees, customers, shareholders, and the media—is watching or can quickly tune in when news of an executive blunder hits cyberspace. There's nowhere to hide.

Sobering Stats

Research indicates only about half of leaders at all levels do a good job of walking the organizational talk. According to an analysis of culture, scans from a wide range of organizations, the behavior of only 56 percent of senior leaders and 51 percent of middle managers is perceived as very or mostly consistent with the organization's values. These organizations may not be making headlines with egregious executive behavior, but they are still missing out on the benefits of a high-performance culture. If half of the leadership is perceived as adhering to the organization's values, that means you have another 50 percent behaving in ways that are disengaging to the employees.

There is a direct impact of this "talk/walk" disconnect on key employee engagement measures. In those organizations where less than half the leaders behave consistently in line with the organization's values:

- Only about a third of employees indicated they would recommend the organization as a good place to work.
- Less than half of employees indicated that they were proud to work for the organization.

In those organizations where senior leaders scored significantly lower than middle managers in modeling core values, the impact on the engagement measures was even more pronounced.

Are leaders that misaligned? Probably not. The challenge for many leaders is to *overtly model* what the organization stands for. They don't get credit for a lot of what they do that is off employees' radar screens. The workforce at large isn't privy, for example, to the passionate values-focused debates that produce controversial decisions. So it's up to leaders to manage those perceptions by connecting the dots for employees.

Showing the Math

Leaders can make explicit connections if they "show the math" for their decisions. Think back to middle school when your math teacher required you to provide not only the answer to a problem but also the process by which you arrived at your answer. This requirement enabled teachers to determine whether you were applying concepts correctly (even if you ended up with the wrong solution). In a high-performance culture, leaders show the math. They take the time to explain the process and rationale for decisions, to overtly illustrate how the organization's strategy, mission, and values are supported. Studies have shown that showing the math—or demonstrating *process fairness*—can help sell a decision that would have otherwise been extremely unpopular.

Ensuring Accountability

Hypocrisy at the top has an extremely negative impact on engagement. Senior teams, therefore, need to be vigilant in holding one another up to the highest standards of role modeling. One technique used successfully by some leadership teams is the practice of "discussing the undiscussables" in their meetings—raising and addressing the proverbial "900-pound gorilla that everyone sees but doesn't mention"—especially when it comes to team members not living the values.

What about managers in the middle? Managers may not feel they own the culture, therefore they may feel that they hold responsibility for the culture either. They may need education on the importance of their role or be equipped with the tools they need to be successful stewards of culture. They also need to know that they can't wait for the folks at the top to be exemplars of culture. Attention at this level of the organization is critical to achieving the momentum Kotter and Heskett describe: The organization must "motivate an increasingly large group of people to help with this leadership effort. These people must find hundreds or thousands of opportunities to influence behavior."[2] The authors point out that many an organization slid backward somewhere in between the executive suites and the front lines.

Inspire Employees

Leaders need to do more than relentlessly communicate and visibly model their organization's espoused values. A high-performance culture depends on the ability of leaders to inspire commitment to the organization's mission and values—as well as the notion of shared accountability for maintaining the culture. That task is easier said than done, as one managing director of a European bank describes the challenge faced by him and countless other successful business leaders: "A large percentage of us are left-brained—myself included. We tend to start with logic, move on to logic, and finish with logic. It's a struggle for us, even though we understand that logic doesn't inspire."

Blending Competence and Connection

A review of nearly a decade's worth of leadership assessment data supports this executive's view. In the preliminary analyses, senior executives scored highest on characteristics associated with traditional business competence such as job expertise, clarity of communications, and a focus on results. Yet the characteristics identified as most predictive of effective leadership represent what many might label as "soft" traits—such as trustworthiness and empathy.

These findings don't suggest that leaders should replace their business savvy with interpersonal skills. Rather, it means integrating business competence with personal connection. For leaders this involves:

- *Knowing yourself* and what motivates you. Leaders can't inspire others if they themselves aren't inspired or engaged. A recent employee engagement research indicates that 74 percent of directors and above are proud of their organization, leaving a quarter of senior leaders at a disadvantage for instilling pride in the workforce at large. It may be time to step back and consider why you come to work each day with a skip in your step. How do you personally connect with the organization's mission and values? Why are you proud?

- *Making yourself known.* Familiarity helps create trust. Research findings suggest that employees who think they know their manager very well score significantly higher in all key measures of employee engagement. One way to consider this issue: Employees will follow you through the sunny meadow based on your competence and title. But they won't step into the deep, dark woods after you if they don't know you as a person. They have to understand what you personally stand for and trust that you'll continue to stand for it when the going gets tough.

- *Knowing your employees.* Individual employees find meaning based on their unique personal career aspirations and values. In fact, there probably has never been a generation of employees more literate about their own passions and ambitions as the groups of employees at work today. (All those millions of copies of *What Color Is Your Parachute* are going home with people—some of whom are bound to be your employees.) The only way to connect the organization's priorities to theirs is to ask what's important to them. Give them the chance to tell you fully. Then you can communicate with relevant, meaningful, and empathetic messages.

One marketing director of a global insurance firm sums up the need to pull this all together: "To function as a leader your team needs to be able to understand what your values are, what you are here to do and the purpose of their role is in getting there. If as an organization and a leader you can be true to your values then you have something quite special."

Align Employees

More inspiring leadership goes a long way in creating a passionate community of employees. Regular coaching can help adjust employee behaviors to better align with values and business goals. Yet employee motivation and engagement remain largely in the hands—actually the hearts and minds—of employees.

Barry Posner and Warren Schmidt's often quoted 1992 study indicated that employees who "had the greatest clarity about both personal and organizational values had the highest degree of commitment to the organization."[3] The implication: As clear as you may be in communicating the organization's values, if employees aren't tuned in to their personal motivators, they won't necessarily be able or willing to engage fully and contribute toward the organization's goals. As Posner points out (with Jim Kouzes) in *The Leadership Challenge:* "Those individuals with the clearest personal values are better prepared to make choices based on principle—including deciding whether the principles of the organization fit with their own personal principles."[4]

Organizations with high-performance cultures recognize the power of individuals' personal values. It's not about making values clones, warns an HR manager at a hospitality/travel firm bluntly: "Employees can't be passionate about something that is mandated." The key is encouraging individual reflection and connection—and providing a framework for employees to discuss their insights with their managers.

One of Ireland's largest banks tackled this challenge when survey data suggested that 61 percent of employees could state the organization's mission but did not really grasp its meaning or importance to them. In addition to the usual corporate communications and leadership messages about the mission and core values, every employee and manager attended a workshop that helped them clarify their personal values. Employees at all levels also had the opportunity to consider how their jobs fit into the organization's definition of success. By identifying the sweet spot where their convictions and career goals intersected with the organization's values and goals, they achieved a higher level of satisfaction *and* contribution.

Align Business Practices

When organizations take the time to align their business practices with the core drivers of their culture, things run more smoothly. However, culture initiatives often hit major obstacles when aligning day-to-day operations (budgeting, fulfillment, recruiting, orientation, performance management, marketing, purchasing, and others) with their espoused values. Perhaps it's not surprising, because many organizations still struggle to more tightly link daily practices to their core business strategies. This culture link represents an advanced maneuver.

Yet it's worth the effort—especially with practices that influence the employee experience. Two examples are new hire orientation and performance management.

New Hire Orientation

Research indicates that only 40 percent of organizations hire and orient employees in a way that reinforces the organization's culture. That leaves the majority of firms missing a prime opportunity to create culture "owners" from day one and make new hires feel a part of something important.

Organizations with high-performance cultures focus on creating an emotional connection with their mission and values during orientation—some even start the induction process during the screening, selection, and hiring phases of the actual interview process itself. Some share company history, the founder's vision, compelling stories of core values in action, or accounts of lives powerfully touched by products or services. Others encourage new hires to experience their products or reinforce their brand in all orientation materials. Still others go a step further to ensure smooth assimilation by focusing on the cultural dos and don'ts. A director of learning and development at a global biotech firm explains that orientation includes tips for new hires to help minimize the "antibody response," where the organization's unique culture drives out well-intentioned new hires (just as the human body sometimes rejects transplanted organs).

Performance Management

Performance management systems are problematic business processes, period. HR is constantly changing the forms or technology and badgering managers to set goals and conduct reviews. Many organizations still struggle to identify which performance actually matters.

Research indicates that less than a third (30 percent) of employees believe that individuals who live the values and promote the culture of the organization are rewarded and promoted. That's hardly good news for organizations trying to build high-performance cultures. Yet increasing numbers of firms are incorporating their core values into their performance management systems to ensure the workforce is held accountable for behavior as well as results. The ultimate test, however, is what happens when an employee falls short on the values measures. Jack Welch was famous for explaining that he could work with a leader who didn't deliver results but did live GE's values (by looking for a position for that person where he could succeed)—but a leader who delivered results at the expense of the organization's values wasn't tolerated. That type of accountability in organizations is still quite rare.

EXAMPLES OF BUSINESS PRACTICES
Are yours aligned with your mission and values?

Organizational Mechanics

Budget process
Strategic planning process

Organizational structure
Decision making/authority levels
Performance targets
Purchasing

Employee Experience

Recruiting
Orientation
Development
Pay and incentives
Performance appraisals
Employee/management relations
Internal communications
Office layout

Customer Experience

Service delivery
Fulfillment
Complaint response
Marketing
Contracts
"Bricks" presence and design
"Clicks" (Web) presence and design

Other Stakeholder Experience

Supplier contracts and procedures
Field site or distributor relations
Other strategic partnerships
Shareholders
Community presence

Making It Happen

The steps outlined here, when taken together, might feel like too big of an initiative to take on all at once from a dead start. However, most organizations are already down the road toward creating a high-performance culture; yours is probably one of them. So you don't have to feel overwhelmed; you just have to feel a sense of urgency.

Don't delay in adding deliberation, attention, and intention to your pursuit of developing a high-performance culture. If you wait for the best time to address your organizational culture, your other employee engagement initiatives will be reduced to mere fire-fighting, and once you're done with one issue, another will pop up. You'll exhaust more resources trying to build engagement that way than you will if you tackle your organization's culture.

One CEO explained why a high-performance culture matters in his department:

The most fascinating aspect of this to me is that the organization has learned to draw strength, passion, and energy from within itself. It is no longer necessary to our very survival that I be available to offer my passion and energy. Not only has it dispersed itself among my leadership team, many leaders have emerged at all levels of the organization, with a newfound confidence and self-awareness of what we stand for and what we are capable of.

Sounds like that qualifies, using the Corporate Leadership Council's lingo, as the results of a "public good" engagement lever.

PITFALLS TO AVOID

Copycat Cultures

The mission and organizational values at the core of your culture need to be yours. Benchmarking just doesn't work. Your culture needs to be unique if it is to be a competitive differentiator—to engage *your* employees in *your* marketplace with *your* business objectives. There's nothing more demotivating than trying to be something you're not. Cultures that engage employees leverage their uniqueness while at the same time raising the bar with aspirational goals.

The Celebrity CEO on a Timeline

Beware of new leaders bent on promises of rapid culture change. The news is full of CEOs parachuting in to save a firm only to be spit out a year or two later by the very culture he or she is trying to change.

Communication Breakdowns

No news here. You can't conduct a few town hall meetings and call it a day. Just when you thought you've said it enough, say it again. Take a tip from the marketing department: Stay "on message." You may feel like a broken record, but remember that it's constant radio play that creates hit records—with everyone knowing the words and singing along. Leaders at every level have the opportunity to state and restate what the organization stands for as well as the organization's strategy and values.

Abstractions

Integrity. Respect. Customer first. Innovation. Risk taking. Who could argue with those words? But what do they look like in your organization? How can they be applied each day in every person's job? That's where two-way dialogue between employees and managers, not one-way corporate communications, matter. Engagement results when all employees understand why their jobs matter and how they can live the organization's values.

Missteps at the Top

Don't think that the failures of senior leaders to model the values will go undetected. Actions speak louder than words. And though research indicates that most employees don't feel safe challenging their leaders' decisions and behavior, findings also suggest that they'll take stock—and move on if there's hypocrisy at the top.

Missing Links in the Middle

Culture is too amorphous and large for senior leaders to effectively maintain it without help from the front lines. Yet most managers are squeezed between the urgency to deliver business results and the need to establish a high-performance culture. If they are held accountable for business results only, or if they see culture as a senior leadership responsibility, the culture will suffer. Give them the tools and support—and accountability—they need to succeed.

Misaligned Business Practices

All the elegant messages and well-intentioned leader behaviors will be for naught if the systems and policies that keep your organization running conflict with your culture's core drivers.

Taking Culture Too Far

It's rare (but possible) to focus so much on culture that you take your eye off your market. Consider Levi-Strauss—touted for its workplace breakthroughs but so internally focused that the firm forgot how to make a good and profitable pair of jeans. A solid business strategy translated into daily work priorities is a requirement for high engagement so that employees are not only enthusiastic about their work but also focusing their talents to make a difference to the bottom line.

An End Date

Culture is like a living organism that needs constant feeding and grooming. As your organization grows, recruits need to be assessed for cultural fit, new hires introduced into the culture, and employees reminded with vivid examples of the mission and core values in action. Leaders need to communicate and model. If you look away, your culture will continue to grow, but not necessarily in the direction you need to ensure the high performance and high engagement to sustain success in your market.

NOTES

1. John P. Kotter and James L. Heskett, *Corporate Culture and Performance* (New York: Free Press, 1992), p. 147.
2. Ibid., p. 101.

3. Barry Z. Posner and Warren Schmidt, "Values Congruence and Differences between the Interplay of Personal and Organizational Values Systems," *Journal of Business Ethics* 12 (1993): 172.

4. James M. Kouzes and Barry Z. Posner, *Leadership Challenge,* 3rd ed. (San Francisco: Jossey-Bass, 2002), p. 51.

Chapter 4

The Lost 20 Percent: Engaging the Almost Great*

Craig Mindrum

"If I know how to pick men, you have sales stuff in you. I dare you, Henry Woods, to get out of this office, right now, and come back tonight with more orders than you have ever sold in any one day in your whole life."

He looked at me dumbfounded. Then a flash came into his eyes. It must have been the light of battle. . . . He turned and walked out of my office.

That night he came back. The defiant look of the early morning was replaced by the glow of victory. He had made the best record of his life. He had beaten his best—and he has been beating his best ever since.

—*I Dare You*, William H. Danforth[1]

What if you have more top performers in your organization than you think you do—who simply need to be engaged at a very personal level to find themselves and live up to their potential? That's the implicit question posed by William Danforth's small book, self-published in 1942, and given away by Danforth—then the chairman of Ralston Purina—to a generation of young businesspeople as a means of inspiring them to greatness.

The book, presented to my father at some point and still carrying his signature on the first page, ended up on my parents' bookshelf, where I discovered it one day many years ago. I confess to being inspired as a young boy by the book's admittedly homespun stories. Danforth traces the "dare" mentality to his own youth when, as a "sallow-cheeked and hollow-chested" boy, he was challenged by a teacher to become the

---

*Copyright © 2007 by Craig Mindrum.

healthiest boy in the class. He rose to the dare and became a man who never missed a day of work from sickness and who "outlived and outlasted" most of his peers.

Another story he tells is of a talented mechanic who, forced by personal circumstances into working instead of going to college, eventually saw his career limited by the lack of technical college training. Dared by Danforth to return to school, he did, even though he had no money, and eventually became a prominent electrical engineer.

Then there is the story of Henry Woods, Danforth's underperforming and dispirited young employee. "I'm no salesman," Woods told Danforth that day. "I haven't got the nerve. I haven't got the ability, and I'm not worth the money you are paying me."

Some people are born to greatness, others achieve it, and still others have greatness thrust upon them. But the story of Henry Woods suggests a fourth alternative. Some people need a personal guiding hand, a short period of deeply personal interaction from a mentor or someone else they respect, to achieve the greatness that dwells within them as potential.

Such people are usually hidden within the system of the modern organization, public or private. A great deal of attention is paid to the top 20 percent of an organization's people. The rationalization for such an attitude is that an organization derives most of its productivity from that group. We do well, we say, to make sure the star performers are engaged and encouraged by the organization so they maximize their contribution and stay with the organization as long as possible. Certainly that attitude is appropriate, though our deeper and more personal motivation for focusing on them—something that often remains unstated—may also be that the top performers are, to an extent, easier to deal with. They are self-motivated and don't take us away from our other duties quite as often. The return on our investment of time we get from top performers is very high.

We also pay attention to the bottom 20 percent— those whose performance lags too far to the left of a standard bell curve. Such performers are eventually counseled out of an organization or, perhaps more often than we think, put in positions where they can finish out their careers while doing the least harm.

That leaves us the bulging part of the bell—the 60 percent of employees who are average performers or just slightly above or below average. Neither hot nor cold, they do their jobs without distinguishing themselves in any way. Yet embedded at various levels in that vast space of "lukewarm-ness" is another group—another 20 percent by estimate—who deserve attention. These are the ignored high potentials—people with as much raw talent and smarts as the top tier but who, for various reasons, are not rising to the performance level they are capable of attaining. Maybe they are high performers who are mired in a personal crisis, so their performance has slipped badly. Perhaps they have introverted personalities in a workplace of sparkling stars, and they struggle vainly to be noticed. Or perhaps they just need a few additional skills, a bit more self-confidence or someone's understanding to soar.

Too often in high-powered meritocracies, this 20 percent is lost amid the noise of daily tasks, the celebrations of the stars' accomplishments, and the million details competing for the attention of managers. Organizations really have no way of formally identifying the lost high potentials, and so all such performers get lumped together into a mediocre or average category. And that is part of the tragedy. They may appear to the untrained eye as undistinguished as the rest, but they are different. They can be top performers, but they need someone to get them over the hump.

Many workers in this category eventually leave their organizations. Others slide further down the negative side of the bell curve. That means that tremendous potential productivity is also lost to the organization, simply for lack of a kind word, a well-timed prod, or an expression of confidence at the right time and place. This does not include employees who can only perform well when someone is holding their hand. Those people probably need to be counseled out of the organization, into a different job or even career. But there are millions of people walking around today who could have been great for their organizations, but their supervisors were too busy or preoccupied to give them the level of personal attention they needed to take their rightful place among the top level of performers.

Today, as organizations from most industries and in many developed nations enter a period of talent scarcity, they can no longer afford to ignore the Henry Woods of the world. These workers are a great untapped source of productivity. Because it is a group that is commonly overlooked, it may be a source of competitive advantage.

In a series of interviews and conversations over the past months, I have tested my hypothesis about the lost 20 percent with a variety of business executives and researchers. I have yet to find anyone who did not resonate with the thesis at a very personal level. No matter what achievements we have enjoyed in our careers, it appears we carry with us at least one memory of an uncertain time when we wished we could have received a bit of temporary support and steady guidance that would have given us the confidence to leap into the unknown.

Yet many others also have their own Henry Woods stories in which they *were* helped or helped others rise to the dare to succeed.

PAUL'S STORY: STARTLING AN EMPLOYEE INTO BETTER PERFORMANCE

Paul Massih is global head of downstream procurement for Chevron, the global oil company. Bright and energetic, Massih can generate more ideas in an hour than many others can in a month. He combines managerial rigor with an acute sensitivity to people, as evidenced in this story.

Earlier in his career, Massih was leading a large global organization. On his staff, though not a direct report, was a man in his late 50s or early 60s. Very experienced and a great raconteur, the man carried himself in a "been there, done that, seen it all" kind of way. Perhaps because he took his position and stature at the company for granted, his work started to deteriorate as retirement loomed a few years away.

"All of a sudden," Massih says, "I started getting complaints—not only from his project managers but from customers, as well. He was coming in late, missing deadlines, and his work was shoddy." Massih followed the right protocol, speaking to the man's supervisor in an attempt to assess the situation and rectify it. The supervisor, like Massih, was also younger than this employee—and perhaps partly for that reason, the employee did not respond to attempts to get him refocused.

Finally, as the complaints mounted, Massih called the employee into his office one day. As he tells the story, "I had all the background paperwork prepared ahead of time, and the first thing I said to him was, 'If you want to leave the company, if you're ready to retire now, I've got the papers right here; all you need to do is sign them and we'll shake hands and part ways.'" Massih had the man's attention.

"But then I let him know that he actually had two doors in front of him, and he could choose which one to walk through. Leaving the company was one door. But then I said, 'The other door is if you're willing to talk to me about what's going on—what's causing you to act this way and to let your work deteriorate like this. If you talk to me and pledge to make an effort to fix things, I promise you we'll work through it together and we'll put you back in the saddle.'"

He chose the second door and confided in Massih. As it turns out, perhaps not surprisingly, the man was having a number of personal challenges involving his family that had led—again, perhaps not surprisingly—to the exacerbation of a drinking problem. "I told him," says Massih, "that we'd give him some time to work on the family issues, and that we had counseling services as part of our company benefits that would help him deal with alcohol dependency. But then I also told him that I would meet with him once a week, every week, until we turned this situation around. And that he could call me any time he was feeling overwhelmed. At first, we met for breakfast each week; then eventually we started meeting only once a month or so. It took four or five months, but finally the reports started coming back to me: This guy had turned it around. He was back to being one of our solid producers."

One day many months later, the employee stopped in to see Massih. "I just wanted to thank you," he said, "for investing the time in me. I'm close to retirement, and it might have turned out badly. I could have left with a bad taste in my mouth, and in the mouths of everyone I've come to know as colleagues all these years. But now I can leave, when the time is right, with my head high."

Why make such an investment in the "almost great?" Massih echoes the point made earlier that there are sound economic reasons for doing so. "These are the kinds of people," he says, "who fall to the bottom when you do your workforce rankings. And as you look through that list of people, you inevitably have to ask yourself who is salvageable and what kind of effort would be needed to salvage them—to turn them into productive, contributing members of the workforce. But you have to try in many cases."

Particularly in today's marketplace, it is difficult to find qualified people and develop them. "You invest a lot of time and money in them the first few years," says Massih. "It takes time for them to learn the company's mechanics and to become engrained in the culture. You can't just throw that investment out the door—and then add on top of it the cost of replacing that person with a new employee. I've always been a firm believer that it is much simpler to try to understand what is preventing an employee from reaching his or her potential and then helping them, instead of managing their career down a spiral and then eventually out of the company."

MIKE'S STORY: POLISHING THE DIAMONDS IN THE ROUGH

Mike Allison is director of learning services for Cerner Corporation, the U.S.-based supplier of health care information technology solutions. He has had several experiences in his career where some additional attention and effort on his part have made a difference to those employees he sees as "diamonds in the rough." In fact, Allison believes such attention is a responsibility of a good leader. "It is incumbent upon all managers," he says, "to ensure that marginal players with high potential are identified and cultivated."

In one case, an employee on Allison's team—we'll call her Janice—was performing not just at a mediocre level but so poorly that she had received written warnings and was on the verge of being managed out of the organization. "Yet I and several others could see her talents and potential quite clearly," says Allison, "so we began spending more time with her, coaching her, getting her the training she needed, helping her to understand what our expectations were for her performance and how specifically she could do better."

Allison noticed eventually that the time spent with Janice was making a difference—not only in her behaviors, but in the bond she felt with her co-workers and the entire organization. "Janice ultimately progressed to the point where today she is one of our most reliable and dependable employees," Allison concludes.

Another employee Allison worked with—we'll call him Jeremy—was suffering not from poor performance so much as an unacceptably low level of confidence. "Jeremy has always had a great work ethic," Allison says, "but when I first observed him he was fumbling through an intern interview. He was nervous and clearly struggling with his communication skills. He also wasn't sure of his place on the team."

In Jeremy's case, the interventions that worked involved training in communications and public speaking, as well as opportunities to shadow more experienced managers. As a result, Jeremy's confidence grew steadily. "We took him out of his comfort zone on some things—public speaking, networking with key executives, client engagements, and so forth—and he worked on those skills so diligently that they eventually became some of his greatest strengths," Allison says. Jeremy's personal and professional growth have been astounding. He is now a confident, articulate leader who no longer fears the spotlight and was recently accepted to Cerner's Fast Track Program for promising young leaders.

RAQUEL'S STORY: MENTORING THAT MAKES A BUSINESS IMPACT

Raquel Suarez's story is a bit different, though just as important. Hers is a tale not of overcoming underperformance but of simply needing to be noticed. When she was, she was propelled more quickly than she might have been otherwise into a position of leadership—helping her make a greater contribution more quickly to her company. Raquel is the director of DDB University (a learning organization) at marketing communications company DDB Worldwide, one of the most prestigious and awarded advertising firms in the world. She and her family immigrated to the United

States from Cuba when she was a young girl, enduring the hardships of making a life in a new country, learning the language, and working up the ladder of education and career. Following her university training, Suarez began her career in 1978 at Young & Rubicam, assuming various roles in human resources, training, and development.

Following a series of mergers and acquisitions, the subsidiary to which Suarez was assigned at one point in her career eventually became a tripartite venture led by French, Japanese, and American interests, and headed by a CEO named Tim Pollak. Suarez and Pollak had never worked together on a common project and had met only briefly prior to the new configuration of the business units. But Pollak had done his homework on Suarez's background.

One of the most urgent and also most difficult tasks in any merger is analyzing where redundancies in staffing exist, and then reconfiguring management teams to eliminate overlapping duties. Pollak immediately put Suarez in charge of this important task. As Suarez relates the story, "Almost as soon as we had our first meeting, Tim said, 'Raquel, I need you to get on a plane to Los Angeles tomorrow. Interview everyone out there, perform an assessment, and then come back to me with a recommendation about what the optimal leadership team should be for the office.'

"How did he know I was ready for that kind of responsibility, when I wasn't even sure myself? He simply believed in me and, by entrusting me with the task, he made me believe in myself. I had the potential, I had the smarts, I just didn't have the experience yet. So I really needed someone like him—a leader who trusted me and could see that all I needed was a bit of encouragement and a little direction. Then I could apply my own experience and resourcefulness. I didn't need him to hold my hand through performing the work itself; I could figure things out on my own. What I needed was someone in that kind of executive position who believed in me, and who recognized I simply needed the hands-on experience."

Then, says Suarez, Pollak followed up with the right level of guidance and coaching as time went on. "Tim could be very specific," says Suarez. "He would occasionally give me a steer or a brief word of advice—'Have you considered this or that?' But he always gave me the freedom to figure it out for myself."

Equally important was the encouragement and reinforcement he gave on an emotional, human, even heartfelt level. "I'm just delighted you've taken this on," Pollak told her at one point. "You're doing a fantastic job." Over time, she, Pollak, and the company's chief financial officer became a sort of three-legged stool of leadership during this challenging but exciting time in the company's history. "Tim has always been a very real, very accessible person. We would sit in his office sometimes with our tuna sandwiches on the coffee table, planning together what we were going to do with various issues in our offices around the world." As Suarez puts it, the experience was "like being invited to an important conversation."

"When I look back to the one moment in my career," she concludes, "where there was a rite of passage, a real turning point, that was it. I had been given some management responsibilities prior to that, but this just catapulted me into a different realm, one where I could see the business impact of what I was doing. Perhaps I would have achieved what I have at some point anyway, but who really knows? That one leader had a huge impact on my entire life."

COMMON THEMES IN TAPPING INTO THE POWER OF THE LOST 20 PERCENT

Several common themes emerge from these and other Henry Woods stories—experiences shared with me by executives, as well as my own personal experiences.

A Shock and a Stretch

One might surmise that the work of turning an average performer into a great one involves long, plodding efforts involving training, performance reviews, and the like. In fact, however, many turnarounds seem to come down to defining moments: Danforth's "dare" to Henry Woods, Tim Pollak telling Raquel Suarez to get on a plane to Los Angeles, Paul Massih telling his underperforming employee that he could sign the papers and leave the company that moment if that's what he wanted to do. These moments, involving either danger or a real stretch goal, come as an emotional shock to the system—a shock that in many cases appears to be necessary to induce behavior change. As Richard Pascale wrote in *Surfing the Edge of Chaos: The Laws of Nature and the New Laws of Business*, "Adults are much more likely to act their way into a new way of thinking than to think their way into a new way of acting."[2]

Bruce Fisher, director of the Leadership Academy at Illinois Institute of Technology and director of an organizational psychology consulting practice, says that "the threshold for a person going from an average performer to a superior performer is often crossed through what is sometimes called a 'transformational life event.'[3] Something occurred in the individual's work or personal life that knocked the wind out of him, prompting him to new insights and the motivation to do things differently."

Fisher notes that the research into corporate leadership suggests that the highest performing leaders and the most successful executives report significantly more transformational life events compared with all the others that don't quite make it to that superior level. Steven Jobs at Apple was reported to have been the kind of tyrannical executive who makes people's lives miserable—behavior that eventually got him fired. That experience led him to new personal insights into the importance of being respectful and tolerant and more trusting of people. Partly as a result of that transformation, Jobs's second go-round at Apple has produced significant success. Lee Iacocca's departure from Ford, Fisher says, can be seen in a similar way. Most of Iacocca's best work as a leader lay ahead of him at Chrysler. Who knows if it would have happened had he not been fired?

Warren Bennis and Bob Thomas describe these transformational events as "crucible experiences." A crucible is a vessel in which materials are melted and blended at high temperatures, producing a new substance—an apt metaphor for the kind of transformation being attempted. A crucible experience can be an apprenticeship, an ordeal, or both. Whatever it is, it is "both an opportunity and a test," Bennis and Thomas write.

"It is a defining moment that unleashes abilities, forces crucial choices, and sharpens focus. It teaches a person who he or she is. People can be destroyed by such an experience. But those who are not emerge from it aware of their gifts and goals, ready to seize opportunities and make their future."[4]

The challenge for managers is how to induce the shock-and-stretch crucible experiences in underperformers without being merely manipulative and without having to let the person go. Danforth's dare is one such approach. Another, as Fisher notes, is 360-degree feedback evaluations, where one receives candid appraisals from superiors, colleagues, and direct reports. "We can often be quite surprised and even taken back," says Fisher, "by the power of what we get from the 360-degree feedback process, where people have the freedom to express exactly what they feel."

Investment of Personal Time

Another common theme emerging from these stories is of a leader who is willing to invest more than the minimum amount of time in guiding the work of employees, helping them realize their potential. Consider Massih's willingness to meet weekly with the man underperforming because of challenges at home or Pollak's investment in guiding and encouraging Suarez's career.

As noted earlier, investing time in people is comparatively easy for good managers when it comes to their top-performing subordinates. Only rarely, however, do leaders receive the kind of training and behavior modeling necessary to provide effective guidance to the lost 20 percent. Yet it's precisely that group that needs personal interaction the most. One of the inherent risks in what is being proposed here, in fact, is a misunderstanding by executives who not only do not have the patience to deal with the less stellar performers but actually see that attitude as a virtue, that it's their job to provide the tough standards that produce exceptional performance. One executive told me, "It's not my job to play 'armchair psychologist' with my employees. They need to find their way." Yet as Fisher says, this is not about being a counselor. "It comes down to caring for your people and being honest and constructive in your relationship with them."

Reinhard Ziegler, now a retired partner from management consultancy Accenture, notes that the real question managers and executives need to ask themselves is whether they have the capacity to encourage both the top performers and the average ones. "This is an 'and' proposition," Ziegler says. "No one would say you should stop paying attention to your best people; you need to hang onto them. The issue is whether you can do both. How can you continue to engage the best ones, while also being willing to invest time in people who are in the next tier down in terms of performance? I don't know that every leader necessarily has a heart for that."

The effort and sacrifice required to spend needed time with average performers should not be underestimated. Ziegler, for example, was well known for his ability as a mentor. As a consequence, however, he often found it challenging to find the right balance himself—dealing with the considerable demands placed on him to produce revenues for the company while also providing personal guidance to the many employees who found in him a compassion and understanding rare in corporate environments.

People would sometimes tease Ziegler about his group of "funny friends"—employees who were not necessarily flagged as the absolute top performers—but he was able to recognize the value of those employees to the company. They were individuals with specific talents and abilities that didn't always match the profile of a top performer. Some of them were classic geeks, others were "idea guys," others were full of energy but had little practical experience to distinguish them.

In one case in particular in the late 1990s, Ziegler gathered this group and formed a leadership team in what was then a relatively new area—designing and delivering improved workforce performance. "That turned out to be some of the most significant work that any of us ever did. We set forth a roadmap for how our company could be a market maker in several key areas—a roadmap that very few people even understood at the time. And yet if you look at what Accenture is doing and selling now in this area, much of it came from the pioneering work that came out of that group. That wouldn't have happened if I hadn't been willing to spend the time to see the actual value that dwelt inside that group of 'funny friends.'"

Coaching + Mentoring

One key to improving the performance of the lost 20 percent is in a mix of coaching and mentoring. That mix can be seen working particularly well in Raquel Suarez's story, where Pollak served the wise mentor role, while also offering specific, ongoing coaching that provided helpful guidance without becoming overwhelming or heavy-handed.

Coaching can be an effective way to help the diamonds in the rough—those who appear to have potential but who are underperforming for one reason or another. David Joyner, who is executive vice president of sales and account services for pharmaceutical services company Caremark, occasionally sees employees who are, he says, "a bit rough on the edges. In many cases they are incredibly talented people, but they need refinement in a few specific areas that are holding them back. The 360-degree feedback tool is one way to get them to notice those areas, but then they also need the personal coaching and modeling that shows them the right way. I've had some cases where we've had middle-of-the-road sales people become our top performers year in and year out. It's because they got that coaching and feedback early on in their careers."

Fisher makes an important distinction between the objectives of coaching and mentoring. "Coaching is to a great degree targeted around specific developmental opportunities, or even behavioral issues with employees," Fisher says. "It's driven primarily by the organization's agenda and needs. With mentoring, on the other hand, the employee or protégée takes on a role almost like a client; it's about his or her needs and career development. Mentoring takes more of a whole person approach and thus is highly personalized to an individual."

That need for personalization becomes a challenge in designing and delivering leadership development programs, however. Coaching is something that has generalizable lessons and thus can be incorporated into leadership training. Mentoring, on the other hand, can actually suffer if it's treated as a "program." Says Fisher, "You can't structure a mentoring experience, match people up willy-nilly, and tell them to go do it. Research suggests that mentoring is not effective when administered that way. An authentic mentoring experience is based on chemistry, charisma, and mutual values; it happens or doesn't happen as part of the natural workings of a relationship."

Can mentoring be taught? Maybe. "I think that there are certain types of leaders who have it in them to mentor effectively," says Fisher, "and there are others who just don't care about it and who aren't good at it. I don't think it's necessarily impossible to turn those people into effective mentors, though certainly it's difficult."

IDENTIFYING AND HELPING THE LOST 20 PERCENT

If organizations and their leadership are to be successful at mining the potential productivity of a group of performers they are currently ignoring, they need the right means to identify those performers and then to provide the right kind of guidance for the right causes. This is easier said than done because, as we shall see, there is no single, common reason for underperformance. A variety of personal and organizational influences can come into play, in a large array of combinations and permutations.

One overarching lesson: Not everyone can be "saved," nor is that really the optimal outcome. As Massih puts it, "It's important, to the organization and to the individual, to save as many underperformers as we can, given that they have the ability and have demonstrated at least at some point the potential to deliver. But at the same time, you cannot save everyone. Some people just don't cut it, and you have to have the respect for yourself and for your organization to help boost those you can, but also to counsel others out of the organization, where they might be able to find a career path that matches their true desires and interests."

Presuming, however, that there is a substantial portion of underperformers who can be motivated to higher levels if dealt with the right way, here are some key questions to ask.

Are You Measuring the Right Things?

If significant portions of the workforce are not measuring up, are you certain your measuring stick is accurate and relevant and that it is measuring multiple important things, not just a single factor?

Tom Kraack, currently a senior executive in the financial services practice with Accenture, tells the story of a financial institution with which he consulted several years ago. "The CEO told me one day that he had a problem on his hands. It had to do with one of his bank presidents. He didn't know whether to give the guy the biggest raise he'd ever doled out or fire him. 'This guy is amazing, Tom' he told me.

'He exceeds his performance targets every time. From that standpoint, he's the best executive we've ever had. Yet something isn't right, we can tell.'"

Indeed, something wasn't right. The bank president had become a top performer only at enormous cost to the company. Morale at his bank was low, and attrition was high. "It was a classic case," Kraack says, "of a worker with great results, but terrible behaviors. The CEO eventually made the decision: He fired the president." In this case, the president was superior according to one set of measurements—business performance. But he was utterly failing according to another set of measurements—engaging leadership. In its decision to terminate, management eventually chose to honor the leadership metric. The CEO knew that he would suffer a short-term hit in performance and profitability. But the long-term value of creating an engaged culture overruled other considerations.

If a company only emphasizes short-term performance—which the lost 20 percent might be weak on—it might lose out on long-term benefits if it terminates those people. Ziegler's story suggests that organizations may often have short-term performance blinders on that prevent them from seeing the true potential of some employees. "Let's suppose," says Ziegler, "that you have a list of 10 traits on which you're going to measure performance. If you look at your employees generally acknowledged to be the top performers, many of them actually don't excel at all 10. More likely they are truly superb at three or four of them, and that's what sustains their reputation. And if you're in a profession where there is relentless quarterly pressure on performance, the traits that produce short-term performance will stand out. But is that really all your organization needs? Probably not."

In addition, says Ziegler, employees who don't stand out on the radar of performance may actually, on closer inspection, exhibit a breadth of abilities that the stars do not have. The second tier of employees may not excel at some of the 10 performance traits, but their distinctiveness might actually come from being very solid at all of them, while the top performers may have severe deficiencies in a couple of areas. "So if you invest in that employee with better breadth you could yield great results, and at the same time cover yourself in areas where some of your star performers might be a bit underperforming themselves."

Is This Role the Right Fit for the Employee?

Paul Massih tells of another experience he had with an employee several years ago while working for a different organization. The person had been one of the best traders for the company, highly respected for his commercial mind. During the first couple of years working for Massih in the procurement organization he did extremely well. Then his performance began to languish. "I kept working with the individual," Massih says, "and I also brought in a third party to work with him. Nothing seemed to make much of a difference."

What did finally make the difference? Massih moved the employee into a different role with a smaller team. "One of the issues," he says, "turned out to be that this employee had really made his reputation as more of an independent operator—a wheeler and dealer. Then we took him out of that environment and put him in charge of a large organization—a job that just wasn't a good fit for his skills and, more important, his interests. In those kinds of managerial roles, you're dealing with administrative and people issues perhaps 50 to 60 percent of the time. That wasn't his sweet spot. Today, in his new role, he is absolutely a star; he's happy and we're happy. We could have made everyone's lives miserable had we attempted to force fit him into something that wasn't right for him. His new role is not graded quite as highly as the previous one. But it's better to shine at the level you're good at, rather than struggle at a level not right for you."

A misfit between a person's working style—or thinking style—and his or her role is both the most pervasive and most perplexing of reasons behind a person's underperformance. Thinking styles, according to Robert Sternberg, a professor of psychology and education at Yale University, describe something different than a person's "ability." "An ability," Sternberg writes, "refers to how well someone can do something. A style refers to how someone likes to do something."[5] Some people, for example, prefer to think at high or global levels; others prefer the details. Some people think and learn better in groups; others prefer working independently.

In the corporate world, the mismatch between job role and thinking style is often so widespread as to be epidemic. Certain kinds of companies and certain kinds of jobs value certain ways of thinking over others. People who do not conform are usually perceived to be underperformers. Although there is no pure consensus on the issue among psychologists, Sternberg believes that ability alone probably accounts for no more than 10 percent of the variation among workers in job performance. Variations in thinking styles—and especially a mismatch between role and style—accounts for a large portion of the remaining 90 percent. As with Massih's procurement employee, if managers can take the time to understand the unique thinking style of underperforming employees, they might be able to match them more effectively with appropriate roles.

Are This Organization and This Career Right for the Employee?

People sometimes make career decisions for all the wrong reasons, with disastrous results—the waste of time and money or the loss of self-esteem and self-confidence. Admissions committees for graduate and professional schools often see evidence that an applicant may have been (or may still be) living someone else's idea (usually Mom and Dad's) of what his or her career should be. These kinds of people also show up in the workplace with some regularity.

Career decisions can be made for other kinds of wrong reasons, too. When Sternberg was getting his undergraduate degree, he writes, law was the prestigious career choice, seen as the ticket to wealth and the good life. More than half of his graduating class, in fact, pursued a law degree. Not surprisingly, when Sternberg returned to his 15-year class reunion, there were a lot of lawyers present. What was surprising, however, was the large number of those lawyers who were not happy with their career choice. They were making good money, but that had in fact trapped them. They couldn't ever be truly happy at what they were doing, nor could they afford to quit and do something else.

Many of the unhappy lawyers, Sternberg concludes, "had chosen their career not because it was a good match to either their styles or their abilities, but because it was the road to riches at the time. The result of this less than reflective choice was a lifetime of career dissatisfaction."[6]

It doesn't have to work out that way for underperforming employees in that position—those who made a bad career choice—if managers take the time to get to know such people better. The transformational or crucible experience such people need, especially if it comes at a relatively early point in their careers, is to be guided through a difficult but ultimately rewarding journey of personal exploration—a journey that might well take them eventually away from the organization for which they currently work, in search of a better fit.

Sternberg tells of one such success: a woman who had worked for him as a researcher but who was not a stellar performer. She simply didn't have the creative thinking styles necessary to succeed in that career. Eventually the woman left to start her own business. Some might have viewed that outcome as a failure—that is, she didn't make it as a researcher. "I viewed it as a success," says Sternberg. "She found something that was a better match for her styles of thinking."[7]

Is Your Organization Designed to Help Your People Succeed?

Some employees learn quickly how to use an organization's structures and hierarchies to their advantage, while others do not—a fact that may relate, in fact, to the point just discussed about styles. Two people of similar ability may not "play the corporate game" equally well. As Caremark's David Joyner notes, a big part of the coaching that the "diamonds in the rough" need is really about how to use the organization properly to their advantage. "Even with some of our most talented people," Joyner says, "our biggest challenge within the sales organization is getting the rest of the business to support our sales people to be successful. Some of my employees need to learn the lesson that they really have two customers. They have external customers they are actively selling to, but they also have internal customers—colleagues and functions whose support they need to be successful. Those are things they cannot pick up from a 'training' class; they need to be learned as part of the experience of working closely with a supervisor-mentor."

In other cases, performance environments have grown so complex, with multiple barriers to success, that almost all the employees have difficulty performing well, not just the ones who are somewhat tentative or uncertain in various ways.

Consider the well-known hierarchy of needs posited by Abraham Maslow, which forms the basis of so much work in employee motivation today. At the top of the hierarchy sits "self-actualization," which we could describe as the fulfilling of one's potential. Maslow himself summarized self-actualization as "the intrinsic growth of what is already in the organism, or more accurately, of what the organism is."[8] In other words, people have an *instinctual* need to make the most of their unique abilities.

They have been given innate potential simply by being born; what they then strive to do is to reach the fullest extent of that potential so they can be the best they can be.

In complex, confused organizations, the lost 20 percent are often stuck between what they feel they can (or want to) accomplish and what the organization seems to be telling them that they have not accomplished. Yet the organization often does not do enough to help. Today's sales force, for example, is coping with rapidly expanding product catalogs and an environment where they are supposed to do more than sell widgets. They are supposed to get to know their clients and sell solutions that cross and combine a variety of products and services. In such a complex environment, one where employees encounter what is technically termed *cognitive overload*, they often feel less inclined to take risks. Instead, they will pull back into the realm of what they know. That's hardly an environment conducive to innovation and top performance.

That's really the context for understanding the importance of performance support tools for today's critical workforces. In a sales environment, for example, various kinds of knowledge portals and sales workbenches can put information at a salesperson's fingertips, even prompting them with advice of what to sell to a client, based on what other clients have purchased in similar situations. In other words, helping and motivating a workforce is not only about personal interaction. Structure and tools go a long way, too.

Resources and services that help employees overcome temporary challenges—for example, counseling to deal with addiction, grieving, or significant life changes—are important. As we've seen, such personal challenges and traumas can often be a factor in an employee's underperformance. By providing supportive services, companies stand a chance of getting such employees back up to speed more quickly.

Some innovative companies are even putting in place the structures that can help them take a more comprehensive look across the performance of their total workforce, helping identify the unique needs of those who may not yet be top performers. At telecommunications giant Nortel, for example, leaders have defined a process for conducting an extremely individualized review of sales force performance. According to Dion Joannou, Nortel's North American president, "Every quarter we do what's called a 'session one review' with our CEO, Mike Zafirovski. The preparation takes several hundred man hours, but we end up looking at a very detailed level at our people and their development, which results in extensive discussions about sales enablement and our organization structures. With that level of detail we actually have the opportunity to go down a level, beyond the very top performers, to find those who aren't performing to standard. Then we can take more focused steps, either to give them the training and support they need, or to put them in roles where they can perform up to their potential."

Does Your Organization Measure and Reward Leadership Mentoring and Development Activities?

You get what you measure and reward. Any organization is going to say that it prizes the dedication of its senior management to developing people. Yet more than one executive with whom I have spoken has bemoaned the fact that an organization rarely puts its money where its mouth is. At performance review time, what dominates is financial performance; everything else takes a back seat.

What are the attributes one would look for in doing performance management that includes attention to a manager's mentoring capability? Generosity of spirit is one—the ability to read people well, notice hidden potential, and simply listen. That's how Raquel Suarez summed up her mentor, Tim Pollak's talent: "Tim was different in that he cared about you as a total person, not just about the professional side, or your particular work responsibilities. He was a good listener and very generous in a way that many other leaders are not. It's a competitive world, and many in management positions are primarily concerned only with their own advancement."

The ability to listen lies at the heart of many of the attributes discussed here of those who are able to identify and help the lost 20 percent. "One of the things I look for in other people," says Ziegler, "is what excites them. Some of that may be selfish on my part, because my interest and my opportunity to learn something goes up all of a sudden when people start to show more energy and passion about something that I may know less about."

"As a leader," Ziegler notes, "you've got two choices when you're talking to an employee. You can talk about yourself—which is a terrible leadership trait—or you can find out what interests the other person. When you do the latter, interesting things can happen not only for them but also for me and the entire company. I might know someone else with complementary interests and can help them establish a connection that makes a difference to their careers. Or maybe I will have an insight that they might be better suited to a different role than they now have. If you're sensitive to these things, and if you're really able to listen to a person, you can make a difference in their lives, both personally and professionally."

The use of 360-degree feedback results during performance evaluations, as noted earlier, can certainly help here. As such tools grow more sophisticated, they might even be parsed so that one can distinguish the feedback from top performers from that of second- or third-tier players. That would give an organization a better sense of how adequately its managers are being attentive to the possibilities of developing the lost 20 percent.

THE POWER OF RELATIONSHIPS

Relationships are key to enhancing employee engagement and performance at every level—relationships with co-workers as well as with those in authority. Relationships take on a special power, however, when it comes to motivating and engaging the lost 20 percent.

Relationships are both promise and challenge. Because a relationship by definition is deeply personalized and unique, relationship building cannot be easily taught. This puts the burden on organizations to model those behaviors from the top down—from the boardroom to the everyday interactions a manager has with the newest hire.

At the same time, effectively developing second- and third-tier players is not only in the hands of individuals. As we've seen, organization structures, performance management approaches, and tools can help create an environment where more people have a greater opportunity to live up to their potential.

In his book, Danforth quotes H. G. Wells: "Wealth, notoriety, place, and power are no measure of success whatever. The only true measure of success is the ratio between what we might have done and what we might have been on the one hand, and the thing we have made and the thing we have made of ourselves on the other."

By and large, based on Wells's definition of success, most employees want to succeed. Yet for various reasons, personal and professional, the gap between what they could be and what they are remains too large. Helping those people close that gap can be one of the greatest successes we can enjoy in our own lives, as well.

NOTES

1. William H. Danforth, *I Dare You* (St. Louis, MO: William Danforth, 1941), pp. 2–3.
2. Richard T. Pascale, Mark Milleman, and Linda Gioja, *Surfing the Edge of Chaos: The Laws of Nature and the New Laws of Business* (New York: Three Rivers Press, 2000), p. 14.
3. James M. Kouzes and Barry L. Posner, *The Leadership Challenge* (San Francisco: Jossey-Bass, 2007).
4. Warren G. Bennis and Robert J. Thomas, *Geeks and Geezers: How Era, Values and Defining Moments Shape Leaders* (Boston: Harvard Business School Press, 2002), p. 16.
5. Robert J. Sternberg, *Thinking Styles*, New York: Cambridge University Press, 1997, p. 8.
6. Ibid., p. 82.
7. Ibid., p. 80.
8. *Psychological Review* (1949).

Chapter 5

Essential Building Blocks to Successful Engagement Survey Programs*

Nancy DeLay

So, you want to conduct a survey. *Why?*

The most common reasons for launching surveys are baseline measurement (to establish an accurate picture of the organization's condition before a large-scale intervention or initiative), measurement of progress, and organization diagnosis of a perceived people problem or weakness. Sophisticated survey techniques can lay the foundation for identifying current strengths and weaknesses of important organizational characteristics such as leadership, employee loyalty and attachment to mission-critical objectives, trust, intent to stay, reward and recognition, and job design, as well as predicting outcomes given those strengths and weaknesses. The distinguishing factor of any survey, *your survey*, is determining what you want to achieve with the results. The *what* of what you're measuring (the diagnosis) should be grounded in organizational goals and objectives. A good survey is useless if it does nothing to move the organization and employees forward. In fact, it's worse than useless in that a survey that sets up expectations inside an organization where there is no intent to follow through on the results can cause disenchantment among employees where there wasn't any before.

So ironically, the success of your overall survey process/program has to do with beginning by asking the right question. To be precise: Exactly what do we want to accomplish with the results of this data-gathering exercise? The answer to this question is the first essential foundation for success. After you decide what you want to accomplish with the survey's results, it's time to look at these three questions:

- How do we define success?

---

*Copyright © 2007 by Nancy DeLay.

- How do we know we have been successful?
- What processes and tools are required to support and ensure success?

Taking the time to answer these questions makes the difference between success and failure of a survey program. These questions should be answered both at organizational and programmatic levels.

The planning phases of this process are the most important and can be the most time-consuming. However, best results will stem from careful planning from beginning to end—specifically knowing what you want at the end from the very beginning.

WHO ARE YOUR SURVEY'S STAKEHOLDERS?

Begin the survey process by conducting a stakeholder analysis. Identify who the right individuals or positions are to answer the questions regarding what success means and how a successful process is designed. These individuals include but are not limited to executive and business line leadership, functional leaders, unions (if you have them), and all levels of employee representatives. Inclusion of input from various levels in the organization will ensure buy-in and acceptance of results following the data-collection phase.

The success of any survey program is significantly influenced by the executive sponsors. So one of your most important stakeholders, naturally, is the individual or department that ordered the survey in the first place. An executive sponsor is most likely paying for the survey program out of his or her budget and will have accountability for delivering results. This person needs to be visible and carry a significant level of organizational influence and persuasion to be able to remove barriers and resistance when they present themselves (and they will).

Input from stakeholders is crucial to determining answers to the many questions that will need attention as you embark on your survey journey. The culture of the organization will determine how much involvement, and from whom, will be needed to answer important questions, such as what will be measured, when you will measure, and how you engage the organization in the action planning process. Some organizations are consensus-driven whereas, on the other end of the continuum, you have organizations that are "command and control" in nature. Survey programs can enjoy success in both types of cultures and pretty much anything in between. However these different contexts can impact the timelines and processes of implementation. For example, it can take significantly longer to design the content of a survey in a consensus driven organization versus a command-and-control type of environment. These influences must be considered throughout the life of the project.

Conversations with stakeholders yield an understanding of the driving reasons for conducting a survey. Over the years, surveys have been conducted to do everything from achieving a better understanding of where unionization might be a potential threat to assessing employees' quality of life issues. Understanding the intentions for the survey process allows clarity in designing the process and content. Additionally, once the overall purpose is determined, you will be able to manage expectations for the outcomes of the survey, especially if it's the inaugural survey. It is unlikely that you will be able to meet all goals on your sponsor's wish list in the first year. A conversation with all your stakeholders will help the entire group come to an agreement as to what is a reasonable set of expectations for the survey's first iteration. Lay out a path that will allow the survey program to grow with experience.

Once the purpose of the survey is delineated the next big question is when to conduct the survey, and more important, how and when the organization will roll out the results to the entire company. There are important implications associated with employee expectations that are set up when a survey is introduced to them. If they're going to take the time—either paid time during their workday or (not recommended) their personal time—they're going to want to know that there will be a return on their investment of time and focus. This is a powerful psychological contract. Should you conduct a survey and not take action on the results, this contract is broken and will have a negative impact on employees resulting in distrust, disillusionment, and cynicism. So, no matter what the purpose of conducting a survey is, your sponsor must be committed to acting on the results.

TIMING

Once the purpose of the survey has been determined, the next logical decision is that of timing—how long it will take to develop the survey, how long it will take to administer it, how long it will take to assess results, and then how long it will take to report the results and support. Finally, how much time will you need to ramp up for the next round? (Some companies that allow their survey process to get out of hand discover that it takes them 18 months to complete the cycle of an "annual" survey—which has a variety of negative ripple effects, such as cynical employees. Up-front planning helps them anticipate and prevent this.)

As can be seen in Table 5.1, there are two types of considerations that impact survey administration timing: results rollout and survey administration. Both sets of dates need to be considered in tandem. As Stephen Covey say, "Begin with the end in mind." Are there naturally occurring executive meetings (executive committee meetings, etc.) that can be leveraged for the executive presentation? Are there HR processes (scorecards, etc.) that survey results need to become part of? How are results going to be rolled out—cascade down, rolled up, or mass distribution? These events and processes will have a meaningful impact on when results need to be distributed throughout the organization. In addition, there are some practical considerations with respect to the actual reports. First, the time required to conduct data analysis, generate a report, and perform quality checks on the reports is driven by the complexity of the reports themselves, so the rollout of reports will be impacted downstream.

The more complex either the data presentation or the calculations and algorithms required to generate the reports, the longer the period of time required between administration of the survey and delivery of reports. The second aspect related specifically to the report is how deeply the results will be driven into the organization. The more reports, the longer the period of time to generate, unless one standardized report format is being delivered at all levels. Be careful to not fall into the trap of thinking that electronic reporting is simply a matter of a click of the button. Even though reports

Table 5.1
Survey Administration Timing Considerations

Type	Results Rollout	Survey Administration
Practical	Naturally occurring executive meetings	Holidays or observances that will take large portions of population out of the office
	HR processes that may incorporate survey results	Cyclical busy periods
	Results roll-out process	Work shift patterns
	Report complexity	Amount of time required for preparing organization for survey/time since last survey
		Required length of time live
Strategic	Launch of organizational initiatives	Baseline measurement triggered by a specific event
	Depth of report delivery	Organizational crisis
		Organizational restructuring

can be generated electronically, there still needs to be a substantial QC (quality control) process to ensure the right reports have the right data and that all data are correct. The more complex a report is and the more of them there are, the longer it can take to deliver them into the organization.

Additionally, other strategic considerations may need to be thought through. For example, perhaps the rollout of results needs to be considered with respect to how they fit with the launch of other organizational initiatives. If survey data feed other types of reporting mechanisms, report deliveries need be considered in light of these other deliverables.

As you're considering the rollout scenarios and issues, you must also think about the administration of the survey itself. Several practical considerations will affect administration, such as something as seemingly mundane as holiday patterns—which can get quite complex if you're dealing with a global organization or a highly diverse employee population. You want to administer the survey when you will be able to access the most employees in the organization, so religious and local holidays are an important matter. When you add the complexity of conducting a global survey, this drives the timing of the survey to typically be in either the May or September timeframe. Additionally, one must consider the cyclical nature of the business in which the survey is being administered. Businesses such as accounting firms, manufacturing, and retail are quite cyclical in nature and have particular periods during the year when employees will simply not have the time to attend to a survey. (The May or September timeframe, for instance, may not be optimal for a hospitality company, which may be busy ramping up for and recovering from a busy—or hurricane—season.)

The length of time a survey is in the field will also impact on timing. The typical length of time employees are given to respond to a survey is two weeks, with most responses being received in the first week of administration. There are legitimate reasons for needing to have a survey active for longer than two weeks; however, this makes it more challenging to find the right time for administration. Some organizations have unique work shift patterns that can impact both the timing of administration and the length of time a survey is live. For example, in the oil business, crews spend a month at time out at sea on oil stations and then are off for the following month. Thus, administration would need to straddle the last two weeks of a month and the first two weeks of the following month in order to give all crew members the opportunity to respond to the questionnaire.

The final practical consideration when it comes to timing of survey administration is the length of time that has passed since the last survey was last administered. The average employee engagement survey is administered on an annual basis. However, the timing should be driven by need, not by what others do. (However, if you set the expectation among employees that the survey will be annual, then you will have to specifically explain the expanded cycle.) Consider how the cycle affected the success of your last survey. Did you have sufficient time to gather and analyze the results and then design and implement action plans from the last survey?

If you're administering a survey for the first time and using it for a baseline measurement of some type, then administration by definition must precede the introduction of the event expected to drive change. For example, if an organization is contemplating a major strategic shift or, possibly, widespread changes in leadership, then having an employee engagement measurement prior to those events occurring can be very valuable for tracking the resulting changes over time and their impact on the employees.

One other consideration with respect to the timing discussion is that of pulse surveys. It is common for organizations to want an idea of how they are doing on those dimensions measured on the survey, or on perceptions of action planning on survey results, prior to annual census survey. This is dealt with by administering a small sample survey (a subset of survey questions) to take the pulse of the organization. These can be either quarterly or semi-annual and are intended to be reported at a very high level within the organization.

Sometimes the timing is such that a scheduled survey collides with some kind of crisis. Do you continue with the survey or not? If your organization has a long history running an annual survey, it may be important to continue with the survey process because it could cause more harm to *not* do the survey. Just be sure to keep the context in mind when you're interpreting the results. On the other hand, if your organization is in the planning process for a survey and an *external* crisis occurs, then it can be most judicious to delay the timing of the survey, possibly for up to six months.

SURVEY PARTNER SELECTION

Even if you have a long-established relationship with an external partner, it's worthwhile to conduct a fresh search every three to five years to make sure both of you are still appropriate for each other. Your organization has changed in that time, your partner's organization has also changed. The methodologies have evolved as well, so you want to be sure that all players are up to date. Conduct a thorough review of your program in order to put forth a request for proposals (RFP); this provides an opportunity to reexamine your current program as well as your relationship with your provider.

However, if you are new to the survey process, the place you want to start is crafting an RFP and developing a list of potential survey partner companies. There are a variety of survey partners available in the marketplace today. So taking the time to find the right one for you will be worth the effort. Survey partners can offer everything from thought leadership to data analysis and everything in between (see Table 5.2). However, one of the most important things they can do for you is provide objective third-party oversight of your program.

The relationship with a survey partner is about fit. Each service provider will have its own engagement model. Understanding its model and how it fits with your organization is crucial as it is the foundation of the measurement. In addition to the content of what goes into the survey, you will need to understand the survey partner's processes and tools for implementation of the project. The survey space has become technology dependent; one set of tools will be more appropriate to your organization than another. Take time to assess your needs and what the companies are offering to serve those needs.

One of the keys to successful survey programs is the partnership between client and service provider—a philosophy and atmosphere of two or more people moving toward a mutually beneficial goal in concert. You and your service provider benefit tremendously if the view is that of working together collaboratively. There are decisions and details to be attended to throughout the process, doing this jointly sets a foundation for program success. The required process steps will run smoothly if the philosophy of collaboration is coupled with an atmosphere of honest, open communication. That's not to say there will not be bumps in the road, such as missed deadlines and miscommunications. There typically are, but getting over those bumps is easier if there is shared agreement on how to approach them. The final important aspect of the definition is moving toward a mutually beneficial goal—together. Defining realistic goals as a team sets everyone and the project up for success.

The characteristics of a solid partnership are close cooperation, specificity of process and timing, and clearly defined roles and responsibilities, as well as mutual availability. It is common during the survey process for daily communication between a service provider partner and client. This ensures that details are being addressed and the project is moving forward.

Before engaging in a search you need to understand what characteristics you are looking for in a partner. What fundamental characteristics must they have? Do they need to have a global footprint? Should they be experts in your particular industry? Must they be older and well established? Or can they be a young, fast-paced organization? How technology-savvy must they be? Must they be a rich well of accumulated data so you can benchmark your results against those of their other clients? How much personal attention can they give you? Understanding the answers to these fundamental questions provides guidance in the partner selection process.

For all the due diligence that goes into partner selection, sometimes things can go wrong in the partnership and derail the process. There are three major areas where a

Table 5.2
Survey Partner Services

Thought leadership (helping your organization understand the theoretical concepts and how they fit within your organization)

Project management expertise
- Process consultation and management
- Timeline and milestone management
- Day-to-day implementation support
- Technical support

Consulting expertise
- Sampling advice
- Content consultation
- Survey design
- Report design
- Action planning content design
- Executive presentation
- Linkage research design

Technology tools of the trade
- Electronic surveying capabilities
- Response rate tracking
- Organizational structure tools
- Electronic report delivery
- Action planning tools

partnership can go astray. The first is around goals and objects. A lack of clearly defined goals and objectives or inconsistent use of the project goals/objects as guidelines in decision making can throw time-consuming confusion into the experience. Both parties must not only clearly understand the goals/objects but also use them in the decision-making processes as you navigate through the process. The second major area where a partnership can go off track is in the area of roles and responsibilities. Inappropriately defined roles and responsibilities or a lack of understanding and embracing of them will waylay a survey project quickly. The final thing that can negatively impact a partnership is operating in crisis mode. Crises can be anything from technology failure in delivering the survey to inaccurate data in the executive presentation. Once a project is in crisis mode, it is very difficult to get it back into a smooth rhythmic pattern. The important thing to remember when a crisis happens on a project is not to make uninformed, emotional, and harried decisions, this will only perpetuate the cycle of crises. Take a deep breath, gather your wits, collect information, determine the possible solutions, choose one, and execute.

On the other hand, the following things will make the partnership a success. First, *get into the details.* It is easy to say and think "it's just a survey," and it doesn't seem like it should be all that difficult. But it can be, even with professional support from industry experts. Everyone on the project team must understand the nuances of every aspect of the survey project. This is the secret to successful implementation and resulting changes. The second key to a successful partnership—and, thus, a successful survey program—is to *be in front of the process*. Not only is it important to understand the details of what is required, it is also equally important that everyone on the team be two steps ahead in the process. For example while the team is working on survey design they should also be preparing for translations (identifying in-country reviewers, etc.). The last two aspects of a successful partnership go together and they are to *plan for the unexpected and have a plan when the unexpected happens*. If you and your survey partner attend to these four things, you can reasonably expect a successful partnership and a successful survey program.

SURVEY DEVELOPMENT

There are several sections to a survey. Typically, the first section is the coding section, followed by the core questions, and then demographic questions. In some organizations there are additional questions per geography or line of business that are specific to that region or area. These are referred to as *supplemental questions*. But too much customization can get quickly out of hand, leading to a less effective survey organization-wide.

The selection of questions should reflect both desired outcomes (i.e., employee engagement) and inputs—those things that lead to the outcome (e.g., leadership, the job, reward and recognition). These are sometimes referred to as *lead* and *lag* indicators. The content of the survey has to be a precision-engineered collection of just the right questions worded just so and just the right number of them. Not too few, not too many. Your survey partner should be able to help you with this piece of the design.

The coding section is a series of logistical questions that a respondent answers. These are questions designed to help an employee identify where they sit in the organizational structure, without specifically revealing their identity (confidentiality is essential for candid survey responses). For example, these are typically items that ask what region, country, geography, or actual department one is located within the organization. There are two ways to determine what options employees have available to choose from regarding where they are situated within the organization structure. First is a human resources information system (HRIS) data feed that can be downloaded and provided to the vendor. The second, if an HRIS download is not available, which is common, then the coding section (the available options for them to choose from) is developed through some type of organizational mapping exercise that identifies the structure of the organization.

The amount of work required to take an organization through the mapping exercise should not be underestimated. It requires representatives from each region or line of business, sometimes both, to properly document the structure. Additionally, if the organizational structure is a matrixed structure, special consideration needs to be taken in mapping the organization so that you will be able to understand the answers to the core questions in the context of where the respondents work and who their managers are.

The next section of the survey is the core questions. This is where you will find the *engagement index*, those questions that measure engagement, such as commitment, satisfaction, and intention to leave, along with various other grouping of items, such as the leadership, job, and development questions. Core questions are partially determined by the survey partner you choose, the model it has adopted, and its pool of available items. The majority of the items in the section are questions that are commonly shared across many organizations (allowing for normative data to be provided, which can help you compare your company with other employers' engagement experiences).

You decide which categories your organization needs to measure. You've already gotten a good idea of what these categories are as a result of the stakeholder interviews at the outset of the entire survey project. Additionally, while the research regarding drivers of engagement is substantial, there are unique aspects to every organization that impact selection of core items. Accompanying this core set of items that are typically shared items across multiple organizations there is often a smaller section of items (say 10–15 percent) that will be unique to your company. These items address specific topics of interest at a moment in time, such as corporate responsibility or the success of the introduction of a change initiative. The special topics may or may not remain the same from measurement to measurement and address current issues for the organization. A word of caution about these items: The topics to be covered in this set of items should be relevant to the entire organization and not just a subset of the it. If the questions are relevant to only a subset, then either a different vehicle of measurement should be used or the items should be collected into a separate section of supplemental questions.

Supplemental questions can be valuable for a variety of reasons. They can reflect differing needs within lines of business or geographic areas of an organization. Since these special interest topics are not applicable to the majority of the organization, it doesn't make sense to ask them of everyone. Sometimes they can help you capture historical data during a transition period (occasionally there has been a special event that impacted only that area of the business, or it could be that a change was introduced to a particular segment). Any of these are reasons to introduce the use of supplemental questions to the survey process. However, there are a few cautions with respect to allowing supplemental questions to be asked on the engagement survey. The first of these is that it increases the complexity of the survey process exponentially—administration and reporting specifically. The second is that it can increase the length of the survey beyond what is recommended (about 50 items including everything), thus discouraging employees from answering all questions.

The final portion is the demographic section, which asks individuals to categorize themselves in various ways that can be sensitive. These are questions about age, race, gender, and tenure to mention a few. (Often access to data segmented by particular demographics is limited to either very high levels in the organization or sometimes to specific positions.)

Consider carefully which of these questions are to be included and exactly how the data are going to be used once the survey is completed. The reason these questions are positioned at the end of the survey is to allow people to opt out of answering them should they choose, but still retain their data regarding the questionnaire. If trust is an issue in your organization, the fewer demographic questions asked, the better. If, however, employees fully trust that the data will be handled in a confidential manner, then examining survey data by these various demographics can be extremely valuable.

The last consideration is whether to have open-ended or comment questions on the survey. A comment question allows an individual to respond in a free-form way to a question being asked. This part always comes at the end of the survey. There are challenges with asking open-ended questions, the first being how to interpret the responses. Typical responses to open questions are either very positive or very negative. They can be confusing when the time comes to evaluate the comments overall. It's human nature to focus on a comment from one individual and ignore the remainder of the data, which may be in total opposition to that one comment. Thus the examination of responses to comments needs to be done carefully. One way of using responses to open-ended questions is to conduct a content analysis, which groups similar responses so that a body of evidence can be built. The challenge with this is that analyzing responses is still a very manual process (even though there is some software that can help with this) and consequently can be expensive. You can manage this by allowing respondents to *self-theme* their responses. Self-theming allows the respondent to choose from a list of options, typically the categories asked in the main body of the survey, which category their comment belongs in. This method speeds up the content analysis process, thus saving time and money.

Once the content of a survey is developed, the executive sponsor and various other key stakeholders in the process must officially approve of the survey before it's administered. The process of sign-off varies per organization and is driven by organizational culture. For instance, if the organization is a consensus-driven organization, then more individuals must be involved in the process and a longer period of time must be planned for to come to agreement regarding content. If an organization is more command and control and a steering committee has been empowered to sign off on content, then approval will be a relatively easy process. Regardless of organizational context and culture, the stakeholders in the process must be kept informed and engaged in the development process in order to ensure acceptance of the measurement tool.

BRANDING, MARKETING, AND COMMUNICATING

Because employee surveys are voluntary and companies depend on high response rates to get the most value for their survey investment, it follows that branding, marketing, and communicating the value of survey participation are essential steps to bring as many employees on board as possible. A well-branded and marketed survey program will create an excitement in the company and compel almost every individual to anticipate the coming of the survey itself. This is the employees' chance to give the company their feedback, a positive opportunity for them to make a difference. While the most effective way to do this is take action on survey results from the previous year (see below), you can and should still market the survey especially if it's the inaugural edition. When an organization does an excellent job of branding, marketing, and communicating its survey process, everyone from the CEO to the janitor knows what the survey is all about and is looking forward to both the administration and the subsequent report. A brand should last the life of the survey program and should be immediately recognizable and memorable. Employees need to know that what they think matters—and it does, they *are* the organization. Many large organizations have branding, marketing, and communications divisions that can be tapped to help appropriately develop these campaigns. If you do not, in the first year of survey process it is worth the investment to bring in professional support in these areas.

Communications plans need to be developed for two audiences. The most common communication plan that is considered is the plan for the organization. There are many events that occur, multiple communication vehicles and opportunities for communication within an organization. Vehicles such as corporate newsletters/magazines, intranets, podcasts, posters, and leadership forums should be identified and leveraged throughout the process—remember, communication should not stop after administration. The message delivered via the various vehicles will vary depending on where you are in the survey process. Early communications often communicate about actions taken given previous survey results, helping potential respondents connect the action to the source. Later communications are aimed at generating excitement about the impending survey and communicating timing and logistics of completing a questionnaire.

Communications regarding results, reporting, and action planning are as important (if not more so) than the presurvey administration communications. In addition to communication to the organization as a whole, a second type of communication plan (particularly in large global organizations), one for the survey team, should be developed and leveraged. Often extended survey teams can be upward of 100 people globally, and clear communication channels can make the difference between a smooth process and one fraught with turbulence.

By identifying communication channels and the flow of communication, one can easily see how information flows within an organization and can leverage these channels to effectively communicate about the survey. Developing a diagram such as this will illuminate who should own communications. The ownership of communications around the survey process is often multilayered, including corporate communications, local communications groups, and all levels of leadership and management. The role of senior leadership visibility, as with all organization-wide initiatives, cannot be underestimated. While the initial identification and development of the communications channels and communications plans can be labor-intensive, the payoff can be huge with respect to involvement in the process and ultimately employee engagement.

There are many considerations with respect to ensuring the survey's success. One of the first is response rate. Setting a target response rate is a common and acceptable practice. But be realistic. If your response rates are in the 90s, good for you! Strive to keep them in the 90s but don't waste time, energy and resources in trying to go from 92 percent to 93 percent. Your target should be determined considering organizational context, how deep you want to drive reports, and at what level will your leadership trust they have a true picture of the organization.

There are several appropriate communications and activities that can help improve the response rate to the survey (see Table 5.3). However, there is one often-used methodology for raising response rates that can backfire, take on a life of its own, and eventually damage the survey process—tying response rates to some form of compensation or bonus system for managers. Holding managers accountable in this way can lead to coercion of employees to not only take a survey but also provide positive responses, manipulation of headcount, and an inappropriate focus on high response rates, instead of pursuing what's really important—taking action on employee feedback.

ADMINISTERING THE SURVEY

While the branding, marketing, and communication strategy can have a direct impact on response rate; additionally, the actual administration of the survey can equally impact the response rate. The way an organization decides to deliver the survey can have a direct impact on the response rate. The most salient of these is whether the survey is going to be confidential or anonymous—which are actually two different concepts. Confidence that their data will be handled responsibly (specifically that there will be no reprisals as a consequence to their candor) can directly impact whether an employee chooses to respond to the survey or not.

A truly *anonymous* survey means that no one will be able to tie an individual's responses to his or her identity. Guaranteeing anonymity impacts the way your survey partner can treat the data and ethically binds them in the way they handle survey data (i.e., never allowing data to be examined in a way in which an individual might be identified). Handling data in a *confidential* manner, however, does not preclude an individual's responses from being tied to identity either by the survey partner or, in some cases, by the contracting organization. Dealing with data in a confidential manner means *never* divulging an individual's response. It is an ethical obligation of a survey partner and should be of the utmost concern to everyone involved with the survey.

The most important consideration is the level of trust within an organization. Perception is reality. If there is a low level of employee trust, then guaranteeing anonymity will be the only thing that will give employees confidence that they can respond to the survey in a forthright manner. If there is a trusting culture in an organization, then the promise of confidentiality in dealing with data might be enough. The advantage to being able to tie employee identities to data comes in conducting linkage research and the robustness of results when one is able to do this.

A couple of the more practical considerations are what types of surveys will you offer (typically, your choice is between electronic versions—such as Web-based surveys—or paper) and in which languages. With the advance of technology over the past

Table 5.3
Communications and Activities That Will Help Increase Response Rates

- Communicate how past survey feedback has been used
- Make the strategy and purpose of the survey clear
- Establish a strong brand for the survey process
- Ensure confidentiality or anonymity of survey results
- Leverage local leadership involvement and communication
- Be creative about the process to inspire participation
- Create entitlements
- Share and learn from internal best practices

decade the ways an organization can deliver surveys to their employees is only limited by its own capabilities and commitment to inclusiveness. However, one must keep in mind that just because you *can* doesn't mean you *should*. The sophistication and availability of one's technology is not the only thing that influences how you should deliver a survey (i.e., electronic, paper-based, or interactive voice response). You must also consider the comfort level of people responding. So, knowing your employees and the different types of employees will help tremendously in determining the delivery method to use. One delivery method is not inherently better than the other—it's all about fit and choosing which method(s) is the best fit with your employees. The goal is to give every employee the opportunity to conveniently respond to the survey.

The second practical consideration is which languages should be offered to employees. Again, the answer to this question is based in knowing your organization. Some have made a commitment to English as their business language and thus choose to administer the survey in English only. Other organizations are highly committed to providing communications and information in all languages spoken by their employees. I have supported survey processes that have provided upward of 40 languages. Still other organizations agree upon decision rules regarding which languages will be translated—for example, any language that has more than 200 native speakers represented in the organization. There is no true best practice regarding which languages should be offered. Whatever your choice, keep in mind that it will send a message to your employees about diversity/inclusiveness values and commitment to engaging everyone equally regardless of who they are and where their jobs appear on the org chart. However, if your organization is committed to English being its business language, this may take priority over the diversity inclusiveness argument.

The final general consideration is how long the survey will be live (the amount of time individuals have available to respond). The standard practice is to allow a two- to three-week window in which employees can respond to the survey. The majority of responses will come within the first few days of going live with the survey, and there will be a peak in responses following a reminder to take the survey. Monitoring response rates by line of business or area can help you target reminder communications in order to increase response rates.

POSTSURVEY ACTIVITIES

The final set of considerations for the survey process is by far the most important because without focusing on reporting and action planning, then everything preceding this stage is for naught. Because this is the final stage, and it can take a tremendous amount of effort to get here, these aspects of the process can sometimes be overlooked and underplanned. It is a shame when this happens because the actions you take post-survey will be the actions that actually drive the engagement you're trying to achieve. If you take no action at all, research show that this will actually drive engagement down. There is no neutral point here. There are two aspects to follow-up: reporting and action planning.

There is currently a trend in which client organizations are demanding to have reports generated quickly. It's important to remember that there are some time-consuming steps your survey partner must take that might not be readily visible to you, the employer. The process must allow time for building the database following the close of the survey and conducting all the required data checks. Following the development of the database, reports can be generated. The amount of time required to fully generate reports, including the quality control process, is determined by the complexity of the calculations within the reports, the number of reports required, and the sophistication of representation of the data within the report itself. It typically can take anywhere from two to four weeks. However, keep in mind that if an employee took the survey the first day it was available and the survey was live for three weeks, then it could conceivably be nearly two months before they hear about results.

The best way to manage this period of time is via good organizational communications, letting everyone know when the survey process opens, when it closes, and then providing news of progress at milestones along the way. If the employees go through the trouble of responding to the survey and then hear nothing from the organization for weeks or even months, they'll start jumping to detrimental conclusions. Knowledge is power—give them the knowledge they need to be reassured that the postsurvey activities are moving along, and you'll retain the power to control the grapevine.

Reports come in all shapes and sizes and should fit your organization. For example, reports in retail organizations are typically designed to be very simple and quick to read with little detailed data in the actual report. Reports in engineering or scientific organizations tend to be more detailed and provide more data. Reports have two sets of parameters: static versus dynamic and standardized versus custom. Static standardized reports are the most common format that go to large numbers of individuals; these are typically in electronic formats. Additionally, a smaller number of individuals in the organization will have access to dynamic report manipulation tools that typically generate standardized reports of some type. Customized reports typically go through a dynamic development process but are invariably delivered in a "static" format, often via a presentation. The selection of which types of reports to be used is determined by who will be receiving reports, balanced with the organizational tolerance for length of time to report receipt.

The final and most important step in the survey process is *action planning*. This is the response phase, where the organization has the greatest opportunity to enhance employee engagement by acting on the feedback they have just given. Successful orchestration of this phase of the project can have a huge impact on the organization. Having many people doing one thing right can drive cultural change, which can be a rather illusive ambition. There are different ways to roll out reports and set down the path of action planning, but all of them are rooted in thorough planning prior to getting to the action-planning phase. In many companies, managers receive not only their scores but also guidance that helps them understand those scores and what it means to them—especially specific behaviors they can take to improve conditions in their departments. Some companies even produce training programs to walk the managers through the reports, urging them to select only a couple of the most important action items and focus on those, rather than taking on a whole spectrum of behavior changes.

The most important and first decision regarding action planning is at what level it is going to take place and who is responsible for developing and delivering on the plan. Finally, decide how you want to hold managers accountable to following their action plans. Once this is decided, preparing managers for how to act on their data is key to making progress in the engagement initiative. Keep the action plan basic and as simple as possible. But make sure that everyone understands that action planning is mandatory. When managers and employees perceive the action-planning phase to be an add-on, they can become disinterested, demoralized, and overwhelmed at the prospect and become paralyzed.

The visibility of action planning is important in many ways. Be sure not to overlook tying actions that are being taken to survey results in communications. If employees can see results are being taken because of their responses, it encourages them to continue providing feedback to make the organization better. Additionally, by tying actions to survey feedback, the foundation for the next survey is laid. It is important that the process remain alive and visible between action planning and the next survey. This is done through communications and keeping interest in the survey alive for the next go-round.

That next survey will come around before you know it.

Chapter 6

Spirit: A Vital Key to Engagement at Work*

Pat McHenry Sullivan

> "I want to ask you something about spirituality, but don't tell anyone else here. They wouldn't understand."
> —Senior VP of a large commercial real estate company during one of eight similar conversations at the firm with the author, summer 1976

> "A new trend is springing up . . . Companies that have some recognition of the spiritual side of life say that they tend to have employees who have greater loyalty, lower absenteeism, and higher creativity."[1]
> —CBS News, *Early Show*, April 19, 2007

Less than two decades ago, only a rare executive would admit openly to spiritual values at work. Today, that same executive would be able to find kindred spirits, information, and inspiration at work. Most major business magazines have tracked the spirit and work movement as a legitimate trend to watch. There have been several dozen large-scale spirit and work conferences in the United States and Canada since 1990. More than 30 MBA programs offer courses in or related to spirituality. Despite the impression that the word *spirituality* gives this discussion, spirituality at work isn't necessarily about the practice of formal religion on the job. It's about the larger issue of how people bring their whole selves to work and how businesses can benefit from it.

Patty Flaherty, director of Human Resources at Ford Motor Company (which offers its employees the Ford Interfaith Network [FIN] affinity group), says, "If everyone

---
*Copyright © 2007 by Pat McHenry Sullivan.

can bring all of themselves into the workplace and leverage the best of themselves, and feel appreciated for all who they are, then you get the best from your employees."[2]

Companies benefit from improved customer service, heightened creativity and innovation, increased productivity and profits, plus decreased turnover and other costs. When spirit effectively connects with work, all tasks can become more purposeful and satisfying. The stage is set for compassionate and ethical conduct. Decisions are made on a wiser basis. Stress and symptoms of burnout ease. Individuals can go home with more energy at the end of the day than they had at the beginning. This sets the stage for a satisfying personal life, a good night's sleep, and another productive day at work.

Any person, anywhere in the corporate ladder, can bring spirit to work and let the benefits ripple outward.

Many CEOs openly speak about their faith. William George, retired former chairman and CEO at Medtronics, publicly credited his daily meditation and other spiritual practices as impacting the company's consistently high profits. He often said,

If we serve our customers well, provide products and services of unsurpassed quality, and empower our employees to fulfill themselves and the company's mission, we will provide an outstanding return for our shareholders. . . . Spirituality unlocks the real sense of significance of the organization's purpose. People of many faiths, or no faith at all, can join together in a common cause of service to others through their work.[3]

One of the most dramatic company initiatives to integrate spirit and work occurred at the Methodist Hospital System in Houston, Texas, which reported results including significantly reduced turnover and vacancy rates and the highest patient/employee satisfaction levels in the hospital's history. When polled, employees said that "About 90 percent of the time, the values that they want to see in their workplace are largely the ones they do see," reported Cindy Vanover, project director for spiritual care and values integration at the hospital.[4]

The success of Methodist's initiatives won it a Spirit at Work award from the International Center for Spirit at Work in 2002. The case is considered by many spirit-and-work consultants as a model for integrating spirit at work:

a. Begin with clarity about your vision as well as your current reality;
b. Engage employees in every part of the initiative, from initial information and idea gathering to planning through implementation and review;
c. Be prepared to deal not just with people of every spiritual persuasion but also with every level of comfort with spiritual practices, ideas and language.

UNDERSTANDING SPIRIT AT WORK

Spirit (from the Latin *spiritus*, meaning "breath") is often defined as aliveness; connections that go beyond the physical plane; reality you can't see or measure with the immediate senses. For many, *spirit* means a connection to one's source, usually called God. *Spirit* often refers to an eternal essence. Even those who do not believe in an afterlife will commonly say the spirit of the person lives on because their impact on others remains.

Difficulty often occurs, however, when spirit is mistaken for religion. *Religion*, from the Latin *religio*, "to bind," typically means an organized set of beliefs and practices common to a particular group. In spite of the rapid growth of "faith at work" interest groups, many still feel that organized religion has no place in corporations.

Ian I. Mitroff and Elizabeth Denton's *A Spiritual Audit of Corporate America* is perhaps the most widely respected study of attitudes toward spirituality and religion in business. Their respondents shared a common consent that

> spirituality is a basic desire to find ultimate meaning and purpose in one's life and to live an integrated life. . . . [Respondents] viewed religion as dogmatic, intolerant, and dividing people more than bringing them together. In contrast, spirituality is largely viewed as . . . universal, non-denominational, broadly inclusive, and tolerant, and as the basic feeling of being connected with one's complete self, others, and the entire universe. . . . People are hungry for models of practicing spirituality in the workplace without offending their coworkers or causing acrimony.[5]

Judi Neal, founder of the Association for Spirit at Work (later the International Center for Spirit at Work) says:

> Spirituality in the workplace is about people seeing their work as a spiritual path, as an opportunity to grow personally and to contribute to society in a meaningful way. It is about learning to be more caring and compassionate with fellow employees, with bosses, with subordinates and customers. It is about integrity, being true to oneself, and telling the truth to others. Spirituality in the workplace can refer to an individual's attempts to live his or her values more fully in the workplace. Or it can refer to the ways in which organizations structure themselves to support the spiritual growth of employees.

In the final analysis, the understanding of spirit and of spirituality in the workplace is a very individual and personal matter. There are as many expressions of these concepts as there are people who talk or write about them. The interpretations of spirituality as it is applied to management education are just as varied. They can range from quietly practicing one's own spiritual principles in the teaching process without ever mentioning the word "spirituality" to actually offering courses on spirituality in the workplace.[6]

Sue Howard and David Welbourn, authors of *The Spirit at Work Phenomenon,* note three common themes that form the basis for definitions of spirit and work:

- The basic feeling of being connected with one's complete self, others, and the entire universe;
- Underlying principles, for example, virtues, values, emotions, wisdom, and intuition;
- The relationship between a personal inner experience and its (positive) manifestations in outer behaviors, principles, and practices.[7]

John Sullivan, research director for *Spirituality and Work Resource Guide* and cofounder with the author of the Spirit and Work Resource Center in Berkeley, California, defines spirituality as "that complex of thoughts, feelings and desires, that reach beyond the immediate needs of food and shelter."[8]

"Everyone searches for truths that bring deeper satisfaction to their lives," says Sullivan, "whether or not they (1) belong to a formal religious organization, (2) like the term 'spirituality' and (3) feel comfortable discussing spiritual issues. Organizations also have spiritual needs, to the extent that we think of spirituality as including values, vision, creativity and a sense of purpose."[9]

The spirit and work movement is a natural outgrowth of many social movements over the past five decades.

- **Diversity and inclusion.** In the early 1950s, races and creeds tended to be segregated at work. Today's diversity environment has allowed people of different cultures to share spiritual concerns while working together.
- **The women's movement.** The growing presence of women in the workplace has fostered such values as communication and cooperation.
- **The human potential movement.** The trends of self-discovery and self-actualization have increased acceptance of intuition, meditation, and various forms of consciousness expansion.
- **The environmental movement.** Concern for the world around them has made people more aware of the impact of their choices on others and the natural world.
- **The ecumenical religious movement.** Religious tolerance and inclusion now involves dialogue and common activities among people of all faiths. Religion is being openly discussed and debated in the public square. Increasingly, people want spirituality that is relevant to their lives, and they don't mind crossing religious lines for useful practices they can adapt to their own beliefs.

Unfortunately, the majority of clergy in many faiths have had little or no training in how their faith relates to business other than economic justice and ethics. John C. Haughey, S.J., wrote in 1989, "The fact that God is not often experienced in the workplace is not evidence of God's indifference to it or absence from it. Rather, it is a sign of poor religious education and of the superficiality of our discernment."[10] In *Church on Sunday, Work on Monday: The Challenge of Fusing Christian Values with Business Life,* Laura Nash and Scotty McLennan define a religious disconnect in American business as "Spirituality Goes to Work, the Church Stays Away."[11] Numerous interviews with business leaders portrayed a common perception of a church that didn't understand business needs or values and that was suspicious of their motives. The religious disconnect has led businesspeople to seek answers to spiritual questions in the secular world.

Even though spirituality in the workplace might be a relatively new phenomenon, the role of the workplace in spirituality has a long and honored tradition. A few religious groups, including Mennonites, have always expected their clergy to hold traditional jobs and bring the wisdom they learn from wrestling with work issues into their ministry. Individual clergy and people of faith have eloquently written or spoken about spirit and work. And every religion folds commentary about work into its teaching about how to thrive in this temporal life.

One loss from the common religion-business or spirit-business split has been the lack of common knowledge about the wisdom for work in all faith traditions. Listed in the order these major faiths became established, this wisdom includes the following.

- **Primal people** throughout the world have long had models for working harmoniously with each other and the natural world. They typically blend spiritual practices (such as blessing tools) with tasks.
- **Hinduism**, the oldest of the major religions, offers the model of *yoga*, meaning "pathway to God." Work can be a yoga when it is done with integrity and consciousness. Through the concept of karma, believers appreciate how their actions impact others. The faith's emphasis on engaging fully in activities while relinquishing the results to God (nonattachment) is a powerful antidote to typical type A executive behavior. Krishan Khalra, CEO of Biogenix, saved his marriage and led his company to increased profitability after immersing himself in Hindu scriptures and practicing nonattachment.[12]
- **Taoism (the Way)** has become best known in the workplace culture for the yin-yang symbol, signifying the balance of opposites, in which the essence of one is shown as the heart of the other. Taoism's basic text, the *Tao Te Ching*, has inspired numerous business codes on leadership or professional practices. Its emphasis on not forcing has often been popularly expressed as "go with the flow" and a call to spend more time *being* and less time *doing*. Taoism is much richer than these often simplistically stated concepts, so studying its texts in relation to work could be a rewarding practice.
- **Judaism** celebrates the covenantal (solemnly divine contract) relationship between God and humans. Judaism provides many foundations to our legal system. There is an emphasis on doing good works, both in charity to others and in *tikkun*, or participating in the ongoing need for "repair of the Earth" and its inhabitants. The Hebrew word *avodah* means both work and religious service (which could include worship and prayer).
- **Buddhism** has influenced people of all faiths at work because it offers a wide variety of practices that can be done silently, alone, and in the midst of workday pressures. The Buddhist concept of right livelihood embraces both the concept of vocation and the call to do any task with integrity and compassion. Meditation practices still the mind, making room for new wisdom and compassion. Because the faith is among the least dogmatic, many books by Buddhist authors are used by people of other faiths as a starting point for clarifying their own workday visions and values.
- **Christianity** provides the model and wisdom of Jesus for how to work with integrity and meaning anywhere, any time. Stories about him promote a leadership model that has often been imitated. They also promote models for people in all walks of life on how to live with faith and trust in the goodness of God. Whether believers take the Bible literally or metaphorically, Christianity at its best is known for workers and leaders who are ethical, kind, and trustworthy. Many CEOs and higher executives of large companies openly express their Christian faith.

- **Islam,** the newest of the major religions, is also the fastest growing. Founded by a businessman, Mohammed, Islam calls believers to be Muslims in the marketplace as well as in the mosque. This is not a commandment to proselytize at work but to keep ethical principles and stop working several times daily for prayer. Prayer and other practices, such as washing before prayers or fasting while the sun is up during the month of Ramadan, challenge Muslims to be true to their faith while meeting work demands.

Additionally, workplaces are filled with people who consider themselves spiritual but not religious. There are also atheists who define the mystery of life, death, and creation in nontheological terms. All these groups need to be considered when implementing spirit and work activities.

Numerous demographic trends and current events increase the calls for spirit at work.

- Ethical lapses from individuals and corporations have disgusted many workers and caused many companies to avoid joining the ranks of cautionary tales of leaders driven by greed and hubris.
- Outsourcing and increasing economic instability (or the fear of the same) have led many to reconsider their values and the meaning of their work.
- Growing social responsibility concerns by consumers, backed by their increasing willingness to invest their money where their values are, has increased individual and corporate desires to do well by doing good.
- Workday stress and burnout, which intensified with the 24-7 culture and the dot-com fallout, have sent many on a search for deeper sources of connecting their work with meaning.
- Aging Baby Boomers and younger generations increasingly demand more meaningful and purposeful work.
- The popular and business media are increasingly reporting on topics relating to spirit at work, to the point that it has become easier to address the subject in corporate settings.

Kenny Moore, a former monk who became the corporate ombudsman for the New York energy company Keyspan, sums up the problems very simply when he reports on three trends he noticed in many years of studying employee surveys: "Nobody trusts. Nobody believes in top management. And people are too stressed to care."[13]

Moore's characterization of "nobody" is only slightly exaggerated. The lack of trust, particularly in top management or in company integrity, has increasingly been reported over the past five years as a significant problem for many companies. Trust is also a major concern in entire industries (e.g., health care, the building trades, and financial management), the government, and indeed the entire economic system. People are definitely so stressed that even when they care, many believe they have no time to look at the problem or possible solutions.

Fortunately, the nature of spirit is that it allows us to tap into deeper and wider wisdom that can generate trust, vitality, harmony—and profits. Although the variety of spiritual applications to work challenges is apparently limited only to people's imagination and willingness to experiment, five major trends represent the diverse roles people play when they integrate spirit and work. Many workers fit in two or more of these trends. Even a small company is likely to exhibit all five trends.

1. Individuals bring spirit to work, with or without company notice or permission. For example, a file clerk studies Torah on breaks and blesses everyone she serves. A CEO takes frequent retreats at a monastery and regularly volunteers at a food bank. A Buddhist manager and Muslim engineer are prayer partners at work.

2. Leaders lead from the heart and soul. Probably the most impactful of the many spirit-based leadership books and articles has been a 1970 essay by Robert Greenleaf, "The Servant as Leader." It has influenced many companies, including Southwest Airlines, Starbucks Coffee, Men's Warehouse, and ServiceMaster.

Servant leadership principles are practically a recipe for engaging employees, including listening intently to others and self; empathy and respect, even when there is disagreement; healing for self and others; awareness; persuasion that guides rather than forces compliance; stewardship; commitment to the growth of people throughout the organization; and building community.[14]

3. Organizational development and HR professionals engage employee spirits in the company's mission and vision. These pros have long been at the forefront of the spirit and work movement after finding they could not do change management without engaging more than employees' bodies and minds. Newer managers (primarily Baby Boomers) sought much more of a teamwork approach to management.

By the mid-1990s, the popularity of spirit at work led to concerns about its misuse, which consultant Mike Bell of Yellowknife, Northwest Territories, satirized as "We take three ccs of spirituality, or have a spirituality 'power lunch,' and we believe we'll compete more effectively and be happier doing it. When all else fails, try prayer."[15]

4. Professionals express the heart and soul of their field. If it's honest work, it has a purpose. But how can you know and serve that purpose in the midst of business demands? People in many professions have wrestled with questions like these individually and in special interest groups. Often, they create new approaches to old professions.

"I began my sales career at an organization that lived and breathed big numbers," writes Carol Costello in *The Soul of Selling*. "They didn't care if you burned out, if you operated with integrity. . . . If you didn't deliver, you were toast. . . . Driving to work one morning, a booming voice in my head asked, *Is life worth living this way?* The answer was *No,* and I gave notice that afternoon."[16] Eventually Costello learned how to sell more effectively by selling with integrity in a way that brought her and her clients great satisfaction.

One of the best books on spirit and work, *Transforming Practices: How to Find Joy and Satisfaction in the Legal Life,* was sponsored by the *Journal of the American Bar Association*. Among the stories are lawyers who meditate at work and the Contemplative Law Society, which holds regular retreats for attorneys, judges, and law students. Kim Wright, founder of Renaissance Lawyer Society, connects purposeful and spirit-based legal groups to each other and promotes such movements as restorative justice.

5. People of faith seek ways to practice their faith at work. Faith-based groups meet in private homes or other noncommercial sites, business offices, or conference rooms. David Miller, a former business executive and author of *God at Work: The History and Promise of the Faith at Work Movement* acknowledges that bringing faith into the workplace invites legal or other problems. "I don't think it's appropriate for a public traded company to be *faith-based* because you are then privileging one religion over another. In contrast, a *faith-friendly* company tries to accommodate on an even playing field the spiritual dimension of people."[17]

Employers can incorporate spiritually nourishing practices into their workplace in inclusive and voluntary ways. Spirit and work practices are increasingly diverse and evolving. They are often ad hoc (not to mention private). The most common of these is meditation or prayer, usually done silently, alone and during work. Many companies provide meditation rooms where people of any faith (or none) are welcome. Other common practices that are commonly found at work (with or without the employers' knowledge) are as follows.

- **Blessing** is the practice of wishing self and others well, invoking the best for them, then relinquishing the results to God. Blessing may be combined with affirmation or forgiveness. It can be given silently, or spoken in nonreligious words appropriate to a business setting. At the least, such a practice shifts consciousness from blame or hostility to one of humility and receptiveness to the insights or wisdom of others. At best, it helps creates a state of grace.
- **Daily rituals**, which often begin at home, can also find a place at work. Throughout the day, there may be moments of reflection or recommitment to purpose. At the end of the day, there may be daily review and a relinquishing of the day as preparation for sleep.
- **"Practicing the presence of God"** (a Christian practice with equivalents in every other faith traditions) means to do a task with full consciousness and caring, as if it were being done in the presence of the divine, for the divine, and by the divine. Variations include treating a job like a ministry or any task as a spiritual practice (e.g., Costello's *The Soul of Selling*).
- **Creating sacred space** can involve bringing objects to the work space that remind the worker who he or she is and what he or she is called to do. Because of workplace laws, sacred symbols or objects (such as prayer beads) may be limited to a desk drawer or to the section of a desk that does not face a more public space. Sacred consciousness may be created by blessing the space and dedicating it to good work.
- **Deep listening and storytelling** have long been the heart of the spirit at work movement. Through listening we connect with the heart and soul of ourselves and others. Through storytelling we deepen the connection and inspire each other.
- **Affirmations** anchor visions of what we are called to create and do. They help us reframe a victim consciousness into one in which we are fully present, ready, and willing to add our gifts to the common good. They help us attract the best to our work and positively impact others.

- **Studying scriptures or other wisdom literature** can be done in formal groups, on or off site. It is often done by individuals quietly, before or after work, or on breaks. Many people place a passage a day by their computers. Others place spiritual insights in files for cherished or difficult projects, or in the daily calendar.
- **Honoring joys and concerns of fellow workers and the world.** The joys of new babies, the concerns over a co-worker's illness have traditionally been times where employees share deeper feelings with each other. In a Mountainview, California, apparel firm, a board in the lunchroom invites employees to note particular joys and concerns. Underneath, a candle is ready to be lit as desired. In many firms, the receptionist is unofficial keeper of the spirit, helping spread good news and informing employees when others need a little extra support.

Dealing with grief and major change offers special opportunities for employees to come together respectfully across religious boundaries. When a man who was estranged from his family died, members of the firm where he worked decided that they must be his family. Many in the firm gathered at a park, where they built a temporary altar amid blooming tulips. All who wished were invited to speak their blessings and prayers in whatever form was most comfortable to them.

A Fortune 100 company faced a special challenge when one of their East Coast staff was murdered, and many of her colleagues and friends worked on the West Coast. The West Coast contingent called the woman's family and discovered her faith. With the help of local clergy of that faith, they planned and held a local memorial. Attendees included employees and family members who could not make it to the East Coast funeral.

More than any other happening, the terrorist attacks of September 11, 2001, brought home the fact that work is a major community in our lives. It takes up the major part of our waking hours (88,000+ hours over the average lifetime). It is also where we have a strong impact on others. Workplace rituals can go a long way to creating a community that truly supports the best in each other.

Because the workplace is such a major community, people recently have begun to recognize how important it is to grieve not just the loss of a job by an individual but also the impact of layoffs on job survivors. Joyce Orecchia, planning manager at Agilent for 25 years, recognized the need to deal with several years of downsizing and offered to lead a book study group using David Noer's *Healing the Wound*. All interested employees were invited. As people discussed concepts in the book about the impact of downsizing, they found it easier to deal with their own pains and hopes.

Grief, fear, anger, and other painful emotions are also common during and after other major transitions, such as the conversion of Brooklyn Gas, a monopoly, into Keystone, an energy company that had to compete in the marketplace. To help employees deal with this transition, corporate ombudsman Kenny Moore held a funeral that invited people to write on index cards what was dying for them, for example, "lifetime employment" and "monopoly," then place the cards in an urn. Moore blessed the cards. Participants then wrote on other index cards what they needed to keep for their journey into the new reality, for example, "great people," and "dedication to the community."

These cards went into a steamer trunk. A stork symbolized the birth of the new company. People drew their visions for the company's future on poster paper.[18]

Over the last few decades, the public has increasingly honored the power of symbols and ceremony to help people grieve, deal with tragedy, bond, and anchor new hopes or visions. The ceremony Moore conducted apparently worked well at Brooklyn Gas because it was anchored both in Moore's ease with ceremonies (he is a former priest) and whatever goodwill existed toward him and the company. Thus, a ceremony intended to engage people in dealing with a common problem began with engaging them in a willingness to join together in the ceremony itself. Without such engagement and permission, the ceremony could easily have backfired.

THE LAW AND SPIRIT AT WORK

The biggest fears about connecting spirit and work are often focused on fears about the law. Understanding the law can help ease many of these fears and prevent problems.

Federal and state laws prohibit discrimination on the basis of religion or creed in the workplace, unless the business or nonprofit organization in question is itself a faith business, for example, a mosque or a Christian education association. Absent reasonable business considerations, businesses must accommodate religious practices. Since everyone's ideas of "reasonable" is different, the field of employment law in this area is growing.

So far, courts have made it clear, for example, that employers generally have to allow Muslim women to wear scarves at work and accommodate prayer practices throughout the day. However, Whirlpool won when assembly line workers complained they should be let off the line for prayer. Whirlpool argued successfully that this would require shutting down the assembly line, which would incur unreasonable costs to the company.

No matter how committed leaders may be to a particular religion, they cannot hire only followers of that faith or infuse company documents and activities with their religion's precepts. Doing so has invited winning lawsuits from employees of other faiths and the displeasure of employees and customers. When an American Airlines pilot asked Christians on board to raise their hands, then suggested non-Christians were crazy and should spend their flight time talking to Christians, the protest was loud and immediate.[19]

For most managers, the important question is "Will my or others' actions be viewed as beneficial and hospitable to all employees, or will employees feel my actions or failure to act as hostile to them?" Employment law attorney Gary Gwilliam of Oakland, California, who has been successfully litigating plaintiff employment claims for over 40 years, says managers are wise to stop worrying about being sued and instead deal with people issues honestly and kindly. "In the medical profession, doctors who have good bedside manners—who communicate with patients—are far less likely to face malpractice issues. If you speak from the heart with employees, most of the problems will go away."

Gwilliam is adamant that managers should deal with serious employee issues around religion or spirituality (and other personnel issues) face to face. "Too many people blast out emails without thinking, and those emails can lead to a lot of problems. To nip problems in the bud, treat employees according to the Golden Rule, with the same kindness and respect you want yourself."[20]

IMPLEMENTING SPIRIT AT WORK AT YOUR COMPANY

>Imagine a workplace,
>Where open hearts and compassion thrive,
>Where passion is cultivated and innovation soars,
>Where everyone is your ally and competition is obsolete,
>Where leaders empower, inspire, and motivate you to grow,
>Where serving and supporting employees is a management priority,
>Where gratitude and recognition abound,
>Where work-life balance is a reality,
>Where meditation is a productivity tool,
>Where Diversity is all-inclusive,
>Where integrity flourishes,
>Where community service is a company value,
>Where Earth preservation is practiced,
>Where Work & Spirit are united,
>I Imagine such a workplace![21]

What would spirit at work look like in your workplace? When Joyce Orecchia wrote the above vision, she had been planning manager at Agilent for 22 years. Most of the things she envisioned she saw happen at Agilent, though meditation and other practices were typically done informally and quietly. Her vision of "meditation as a productivity tool" is based on a trust that true spirit cannot be coopted but will take people past the realm of ego and wishful thinking into a deeper consciousness where everyone benefits.

How does Orecchia's vision spark yours? What are your own spiritual hopes and needs? What are your fears about it? What practices and ideas can you discover by talking with people in your own faith community, your profession, and work colleagues?

These and other questions need to be explored before you begin implementing a spirit at work program. As with all visioning exercises, it's always a good idea to dream a while without any concern for feasibility. Mine the examples and the books or articles mentioned in this chapter for inspiration.

For further inspiration, consider reviewing the vision and values of other companies. Here is one from *Motto* magazine, a bimonthly publication dedicated to purpose, passion, and profits.

- We believe there is a spirit of each business that shines into communities, employees, and customers. That spirit can be as positive (or negative) as the leaders choose to make it.
- We ardently believe in capitalism. Profitability drives possibilities.

- The "soft stuff," as it's sometimes derided, is as important as technology investment or financial structuring. When companies and individuals get it right, the power is remarkable.
- You can change your company into a place that will attract people you want as teammates.[22]

Spirit and work cannot be installed by decree—unless you are determined to invite trouble into your workplace. Begin by practicing it yourself alone and quietly, then explore the subject carefully with others.

Remember the quote at the beginning of this chapter? Many people at all levels of the corporate ladder still fear that no one else would understand their spiritual concerns at work. There are also many other fears and concerns.

- Is combining spirit and work flaky?
- Will it disrupt efficient business and waste time, money, or other resources?
- Will it drive away employees and customers?
- Will it lead me away from my current spiritual path?

Many fears and concerns ease quickly with information. Give a nervous executive evidence of how many others understand and share her concerns, and there's a good chance her fears will quickly turn into excitement as she discovers a world of new opportunities. Or she might never agree that bringing spirit openly to work is a good thing.

Even people who want to bring more spirit into work will rarely agree on who, what, why, and how. Some crave silence in a group; others start feeling twitchy after two seconds or less of group silence. Some people would love a ritual at work like the one Kenny Moore led. Others would feel embarrassed.

Fruitful dialogue about spirit and work can come informally from many sources: friends, family, workplace colleagues, people in your faith community, or any group of kindred spirits. There are also many models for organized discussion groups:

- For over 10 years, individuals have met monthly at the San Francisco Chamber of Commerce for open-ended brown bag discussions. After an opening meditation, a talking stick is used to facilitate dialogue, with a moment of silence after each sharing to reflect on what was said.
- Spirit at work consultant Sarah Hargrave has conducted monthly spirit at work breakfasts for about 15 years in three locations throughout the San Francisco Bay area. She announces the topic before meetings, based on information and preferences of previous participants.
- Special interest groups (SIGs) can be created easily in your professional or faith group. Many of these have flourished over the years among organization development and HR professionals, lawyers and other groups. The International Center for Spirit at Work (spiritatwork.org) offers SIG meetings over telephone bridge lines.

OD, HR, and other specialists who have worked with spirit in the corporate setting have commonly found that rather than define spirit at work for any group, it's wise to invite members to ask themselves, "What does spirit at work mean to me?" Such a discussion will often generate many flip-chart pages of images and practices, such as

- Working from my values, not leaving them in the parking lot;
- Working with meaning and purpose, which becomes work with joy;
- Bringing my whole self to work;
- Putting my faith to work every day.

Inevitably, any discussion about the meaning of spirit at work will elicit questions that help turn concerns into workable challenges. How can we bring spirit (including, if desired, the essence of one's religion) to work without causing religious wars or business upheavals? How do we talk about values and other meaningful topics without insulting others or invading their privacy? With further discussion, the group will help generate ideas for answering those questions in a way that is appropriate to your group.

However or wherever you talk about spirit and work, the key is *hospitality*. That means the same kind of hospitality you would practice if hosting a diverse group of people with different food tastes, dietary need, social preferences, and ease in social settings.

Linda Huey, chairperson of the Ford Interfaith Network (FIN) West Coast chapter under the Ford Motor Company's Diversity and Worklife Program says that "faith and spirituality are very private. A lot of people are so private they don't want to disclose what faith they are," or if they are not members of an organized faith. What makes the FIN work, she says, is that each faith respects others' faith and helps them with activities that all employees are invited to attend. The FIN works within the framework of education, with activities held over lunchtime, not during normal business hours.

The training field has long discovered that participation has to be voluntary whenever people are asked to speak about values and other personal subjects. Participants need to feel invited into dialogue. Dr. Mary Wagner, director of the Center for Education and Human Services Research at SRI International, understands that people in any on-site discussion about spirituality and work could have concerns like, "Can you talk about your own boss? Can you really talk about problems or conflicts about ethics with people who know your work group?"

Wagner never pushes her beliefs or spiritual practices on anyone with whom she works. "What works for me is to stay as truly and honestly in touch with my own faith as I can. Everything grows out of that. If your faith is different and I am centered in mine, I will treat you as someone sacred and divine. If you can reach other people from that place, then hospitality naturally flows. Respect naturally flows."[23]

There are already many recognized paths where spirit and work already have a natural home in your company. Diversity activities offer a natural place to open the dialogue about differences and connections among various spiritual beliefs and practices. In many companies, particularly as Muslims become more prominent in areas where they were previously rare (e.g., in Tennessee), the cafeteria offers foods that respect dietary laws and special foods to celebrate cultural holidays. Work life, stress release, and employee assistance programs in many firms create a fertile ground for exploring matters of meaning. Company newsletters offer an outlet for employees to speak respectfully about how their faith impacts their work and share bits of inspiration for the workday.

Many executive coaches discuss spiritual issues with their clients. Corporate chaplains, who until recently were primarily seen in the South or in smaller, privately held companies, are now becoming welcome across the nation in companies of all sizes, including Coca-Cola and numerous fast-food chains. Tyson Foods, the largest processor of chicken, beef, and pork in the United States, offers chaplains as a way to care for employees. The result: "Morale and worker retention have improved at participating plants." Tyson's use of chaplains has not been without controversy, particularly after chaplains publicly praised the company's charitable work when the company was under investigation by the government for labor and immigration law violations. Though Tyson was later acquitted of these charges, there are calls that chaplains not be used in any way for corporate public relations purposes.[24]

Coaches and chaplains now come in all religious denominations. Some are non-denominational or omni-faith.

Before you implement any program, discern that it is likely to make you glad (not regret) you did it. You and your colleagues are the only ones who can discern what works for you, because you know your company. As a manager, you already have many discernment tools at your disposal. Spiritual practices, such as meditation and prayer, help you access deeper sources of wisdom. The Quaker Clearance Committee model employs half a dozen or so trusted friends to pray with you and listen—without giving advice—as you explore the pros, cons, challenges, and dreams of a possible program.[25]

Spiritual practices are meant to augment, not replace common business planning and discernment tools such as listing the benchmarks and goals that would make you and others delighted that you created a program. Some questions to consider include:

- What could go wrong with your possible spirit and work program? How could you reframe potential problems into action steps that could lead to satisfying success?
- What needs to be cleared away so you have space in which to create your program?
- What foundation do you need in terms of research, dialogue and/or alliances with others?
- How can participants stay true to themselves and their faith while engaging in spirit at work activities with others?
- What will help you create something of lasting value rather than just another flavor of the month?

For all branches of spirit at work, humor and blessing help. There's nothing better than humor to break tension and challenge personal or group foibles, like idealized spiritual images. Unfortunately, it's not nearly so easy to find humor about spirit at work as it is to find advice about it.

Mike Bell's presentation to the 1995 OD Network National Conference, "Top Ten Reasons Why Managers Don't Like to Get into the Realm of Spirit," is still a laugh generator. Some excerpts of his satire are:

- *The language is too airy-fairy*: Can't shoehorn this kind of lingo into a policy statement or a management directive.
- *Too difficult to control:* Too unpredictable to be of any practical value.
- *Sounds too much like "jock-talk"*: With all the downsizing and layoffs, and the flattening of structures and the casualties . . . too many "teams" have been wiped out. And this spirit stuff is just a bit too close to telling people to "get out and win one for the Gipper."
- *It is too much hard work*: You can't delegate it. You can't do it part-time. Too much personal accountability. You've got to live in spirit and walk the talk, day in and day out.[26]

As for blessing, keep it simple. As you explore how best to bring spirit to your own work and your company, may you easily see clearly what is yours to do and what is not. May each step of building your vision be filled with integrity and great joy, for yourself and for all who are impacted by your work.

NOTES

1. cbsnews.com/stories/2007/04/19/earlyshow/main2707047.shtml.
2. Ibid.
3. George now teaches leadership at Harvard Business School. His best-selling books are *Authentic Leadership: Rediscovering the Secrets to Creating Lasting Value* and *True North: Discover Your Authentic Leadership.*
4. Matthew Gilbert, "True Believers at Methodist Hospital" *Workforce Management* (February 2005): 67–69. This comprehensive article, which provides extensive information on how the initiatives were accomplished, is available online with free registration at www.workforce.com.
5. Ian I. Mitroff and Elizabeth Denton, *A Spiritual Audit of Corporate America* (San Francisco: Jossey-Bass, 1999), pp. xv–xvi.
6. Judi Neal, "Teaching with Soul: Support for the Management Educator," adapted from "Spirituality in Management Education: A Guide to Resources, " *Journal of Management Education* (February 1997).
7. Sue Howard and David Welbourn, *The Spirit at Work Phenomenon* (London: Azure, 2004), p. 36.
8. J. Sullivan, ed., *Spirituality and Work Resource Guide* (Point Richmond, CA: Spirit of Health, 1996), pp vii–viii.
9. Personal interview, July 19, 2007.
10. John C. Haughey, *Converting 9 to 5: The Spirituality of Daily Work,* (New York: Crossroad Publishing, 1989), p. 60.
11. Laura Nash and Scotty McLennan *Church on Sunday, Work on Monday: The Challenge of Fusing Christian Values with Business Life* (San Francisco: Jossey-Bass, 2001), p. 3.
12. Khalra's story has been reported often since he was featured in Jim Braham, "God and the CEO: Does Spirituality belong in the Board Room?" *Industry Week* (February 1, 1999).

13. Linda Tischler, "Kenny Moore Held a Funeral and Everyone Came," *Fast Company*, http://www.fastcompany.com/magazine/79/firstperson.html.

14. http://www.greenleaf.org/leadership/read-about-it/Servant-Leadership-Articles-Book-Reviews.html.

15. Mike Bell's paper for the national 1995 OD Network. Bell is a former Passionist priest who is now principal of Inukshuk Management Consulting in Yellowknife, Northwest Territories (Canada). He specializes in helping aboriginal tribes deal with governments and corporations.

16. Carol Costello, *The Soul of Selling* (Dallas, TX: BenBella, 2005), p. 1.

17. Marc Gunther, "Finding God at Work: Companies Become 'Faith-Friendly,'" Fortune .com (January 17, 2007). See also David Miller, *God at Work: The History and Promise of the Faith at Work Movement* (Oxford University Press, 2007).

18. Tischler, "Kenny Moore Held a Funeral."

19. CNN.com/2004/TRAVEL/02/09/airline.christianity.index.html.

20. Interview by the author, May 8, 2007.

21. Joyce Orecchia, "Imagine a Workplace," used with permission. Ms. Orecchia is now a consultant on spirit at work and the coordinator or the corporate chaplain program for Newperspectives.net. For permission to reprint this piece, contact her at pandajoys@sbcglobal.net.

22. http://www.whatsyourmotto.com, copyright © 2007 dash30 Inc. *Motto* cannot be over-recommended as a source of stories, quotes, statistics, inspiration and tips for integrating spirit and work. Used with permission.

23. Interview by the author, about 2000.

24. Kerry Hall, "In a Time of Change, Tyson Turns to Faith," *Charlotte* (NC) *Observer* (January 8, 2006). http://www.religionandsocialpolicy.org/news/article_print.cfm?id=3692. See also http://www.csmonitor.com/2005/0901/p12s03-lire.html.

25. Parker J. Palmer, *Let Your Life Speak: Listening for the Voice of Vocation* (San Francisco: Jossey-Bass, 2000) offers examples on how a clearance committee works. You might also call a local Quaker meeting for further information.

26. Used with permission from the author.

Chapter 7

No "Best Practices"*

Tamara J. Erickson

Approaches to employee engagement based on best practices just don't work. High levels of engagement must be based on what your firm is distinctly good at—what you uniquely can offer to your employees. This requires developing a sound understanding of what your employees want and *signature processes* that make it clear what it means to work in your company.

Imagine that you're in the job market, with offers in hand from three firms. All three are attractive—the type of opportunities you've been looking for with competitive compensation packages. After an extensive round of interviews, you decide to meet with each firm one more time, specifically to talk about what your entry experience might be like and what you can expect in the first six months on the job. Which job would *you* take based on the following answers?

Company A: "Actually, your first three months will be a probationary period in which you'll get to know and work closely with your assigned teammates. They'll see how well you work with the group and contribute to its success. At the end of that period, your teammates—your peers—will vote on whether or not you will get to stay in the organization. Management has no influence in the final decision."

Company B: "We can't tell you what your exact role will be—or who you'll be working with. For the first three months, you'll be in our 'fishbowl'—performing a series of weekly challenges, perhaps designing new products or marketing campaigns, under the close scrutiny of our CEO and other senior executives. At the end of the time, depending on what we observe, we'll help you find the right position for your skills."

---

* Copyright © 2007 by Tamara J. Erickson.

Company C: "Your first three months will be spent learning our way of doing business. We have a specific way of operating, and we expect you to follow our processes closely. We're convinced that the ways outlined are the most productive and successful. After an extensive training program, you'll get a chance to apprentice with one of our strongest performers."

If you're like most people, these ways of starting work at a new company are not equally appealing. In fact, depending on your personality and preferences—depending on how you view work and the role you want it to play in your life—you'll probably have a distinct preference for one over the others.

If social relationships at work are important to you, if teamwork is something you enjoy and believe you excel at, the first offer will sound pretty good. The entry process certainly drives home the point that this is a company that puts a high priority on team behavior!

On the other hand, if you love the challenge of creating new things and see work as a platform to express yourself—and if you have a high tolerance for ambiguity—the second company might be for you. Again, the entry process sets a clear tone—intense challenge, high visibility, and chance to show what you can do.

If clarity and definition are important to you—if you want a well-defined path to succeed at work—the third company probably sounds like a dream come true. Clearly they have thought about how to do their work well—and are prepared to invest significant time and resources in helping you learn the ropes.

From your perspective as an employee, getting it right—finding a company whose values are closest to yours and where the experience of work within the firm matches your personality and preferences—is key to your ultimate enjoyment of the work. In the end, the realistic demands of the job need to be in line with the role you're prepared for work to play in your life. By choosing the company that is best suited to your needs and priorities, you increase the likelihood that you will be highly engaged in your work.

From your perspective as an employer, it's just as important to get it right for your employees. As the available workforce tightens, and the options for work proliferate, individuals are increasingly choosing what they would like to receive from the work experience at any given point in time. More and more, people are actively considering the trade-offs they are prepared to make. For example, they may want to go for a low-risk growth in their financial assets and are willing to forgo options for creativity in the work itself. Or they may want to develop or maintain important social networks and relationships, and are prepared to forgo other potential benefits of promotion and career advancement in exchange. The emphasis here is on the intelligent, informed candidate actively making choices—and deciding whether their priorities match your offering.

For companies, helping employees know what your firm stands for—what it's like to work for you—is critically important to attracting the type of workforce that will ultimately be "engageable" in the work you do and satisfied with the options you can realistically offer. If you try to be everything to everyone, especially by copying the so-called best practices of wrong companies, you will have little that's substantial, authentic, or valuable to offer anyone.

EMPLOYEE ENGAGEMENT . . . YES, BUT HOW?

Over the last five years we at the Concours Group have actively researched the path to employee engagement—ways to create a strong emotional connection between the employee and the corporation and its work. We have looked closely at what highly successful companies actually do with regard to their practices and processes. We have also surveyed many thousands of employees about how engaged they feel and what truly switches them on. Our aim was to develop a checklist of the best practices that companies need to develop to build a context in which employees are highly engaged.

The initial results of our research were mystifying. At first blush, the practices within each company seem surprisingly diverse! Rather than building a checklist of best practices based on common themes and principles, we discovered a whole world of variety. Successful companies do not all do the same things. In reality, companies with highly engaged employees took very different approaches to almost every aspect of the employee experience—compensation, performance management, the structure of individual jobs, management styles, availability of flexible work options, and virtually every other touch point.

Not only were there differences among companies, there was also a tremendous amount of diversity of practices and processes within the companies. Across highly successful companies, we found enormous variety in the fundamental relationships with employees. This variety reflects very different underlying philosophies about the role of work and of corporations in employees' lives, from the paternalistic to a virtually complete contractor-like hands-off approach to managing goal setting, achieving objectives, and creating a community of employees focused on a common mission.

The more we looked, the more we realized that the variation in practices was more than the noise in the system—the variation, in fact, was *the key to the engagement success of each company*. So the notion of a set of universal best practices for employee engagement is a myth. Companies with strong employee-employer relationships go far beyond treating everyone fairly or having good managers—the best also do something, well, *different*.

The best companies—those with high engagement, high customer satisfaction, and high productivity—share several important characteristics:

- They know who they are—and are completely comfortable that it's not all things to all people.
- They understand their target audience (current and future employees) as clearly as most companies understand their target market (current and future customers).
- They demonstrate who they are vividly, with stories of actual practices or events—not through slogans and posters.

The bottom line: Engagement is not about best practices. Going to conferences to see what other companies are doing, finding best practices and bringing them into your company, may get you to a level playing field. But it does no more. You can't benchmark your way to high levels of engagement. Extraordinary engagement lies in the heart of a leadership culture that is based on its own particular authenticity. The key is finding *and expressing* your company's core values and distinctive attributes in ways that are unique and memorable—in ways that draw employees who share those values and seek those attributes to you.

So how do these high-performing companies, with highly engaged employees, go about expressing their core values and distinctive attributes? Underlying this success is an extraordinary understanding of and relationship with employees. The excellent companies' distinctive practices match a clear target audience. Each firm's personality and the leadership's values are expressed clearly in tangible and memorable ways that go far beyond slogans on the wall or laminated values cards on each desk. They are embedded in tangible practices that illustrate and demonstrate the type of firm each is and aspires to be. These is what we call *signature processes*.[1]

BRINGING DISTINCTIVENESS TO LIFE

Let's go back to those three job offers. The first is loosely patterned after a powerful signature process at Whole Foods. Every store is divided into teams, and employees have control over who becomes part of their team. New employees are hired into one of the teams on a provisional basis. After four weeks of work, the team votes whether the employee gets to stay. To join the staff permanently, the newcomer needs a two-thirds yes vote.

This is not a popularity or beauty contest. The way they work together directly impacts financial prospects. So they are very careful about whom they vote in. For instance, additional pay (beyond base wages) is linked to how well they do as a team. Whole Foods's profit-sharing program calculates the performance of each team in every store 13 times a year. Teams that do well share in the profits. Those that don't, don't get a cut. People don't want buddies; they want workers—teammates who are going to help them make money.

This unique entry process undoubtedly serves a very valuable purpose of creating effective, productive teams. It also provides a powerful story about the firm's most important values. It's easy to imagine that candidates, considering a job offer from Whole Foods, would base some of their decision on their comfort with and enthusiasm for teamwork after hearing what their first four weeks will be like.

The second job offer example is based on the practices of Trilogy, a rapidly growing software and services provider. There, new hires are put in an exhausting and exhilarating three-month in-house immersion process run by top management, including the CEO. The company believes that the process plays an important role in developing the company's next generation of strategic ideas and products. It also, however, provides a powerful, palpable example of the type of environment an employee can expect at Trilogy, and the values that someone would have to have to be successful there—tolerance for ambiguity; enjoyment in the challenge of proving oneself in high pressure, competitive situations; willingness to learn new skills quickly and innovate frequently; and confidence in one's ability to perform successfully.

Our work would say that the induction experience sets the tone for behavior throughout the new hire's career with Trilogy—and serves as a powerful story to tell new recruits what life in the firm will be like. Candidates who would prefer a clearer cut, better-defined work environment would almost certainly decline after hearing the details of the rapidly changing, multitasked, fast-paced, learn-as-you-go first three months. On the other hand, candidates who are attracted to intense challenge and tolerant of risk would be likely to jump at this opportunity.

The Container Store is the model behind the third example. The Container Store is a Dallas-based retailer of storage solutions ranging from plastic containers to sophisticated shelving systems. The firm credits its steady growth and financial well-being to its ability to attract and retain—and very carefully train—a highly capable and fiercely loyal workforce.

An extensive and ongoing investment in employee training and indoctrination is central to The Container Store's business model. To ensure that new recruits understand the complexity of many product lines, training is both immediate and intense. Only after the completion of five full days of training can an employee get on a regular schedule. During their first year with The Container Store, all employees receive at least 235 hours of formal training, versus an industry average of about 7. For a retail workplace that generates its revenue only when its people are on the floor actually selling, this represents a tremendous investment in a new employee. In addition to the time away from the sales floor involved, the company pays trainees their regular salary during the training process.

The process for training employees in approaches that have been proven successful, coupled with The Container Store's continuing commitment to career development, is highly attractive to some individuals. Although the wages are lower than those available in other industries, the opportunity to succeed is clearly defined and thoroughly supported. The Container Store's training approach serves as a clear signature process, signaling to candidates what life will be like within the firm.

The three examples are very different entry processes, reflecting different business requirements and management philosophies. Comparing these three orientation approaches should give any candidate a very palpable sense of what it would be like to work at each firm. The stories should help *them* select the company that would be most likely to engage their energy and enthusiasm—where they'd prefer to invest their time and intellect. The signature processes should give each new hire a clear signal of the type of behaviors that are desired longer term.

Slogans on the wall don't do it. The core of the success of extraordinary companies is the creation and "legendization" of a signature process, one that is

- A highly visible, distinctive element of the employee experience
- Valuable to the firm in and of itself
- A powerful symbolic representation of the firm's human capital values
- Tricky for competitors to copy
- A convincing mechanism for prompting self-selection.

Companies with highly engaged employees each do very different things, things that are as unique as a signature. Compelling signature processes serve as effective models to influence employee behavior on an ongoing basis and powerful stories to attract the right new candidates. Signature processes are the essence of how great companies attract and retain employees who fit—employees who ultimately are engageable in the activities and values of the firm.

A number of progressive companies have begun to recognize the importance of hiring people who fit the company. Some have invested in elaborate screening processes to help judge the compatibility of the candidate's values with the company's culture. These are undoubtedly important steps. However, research would show that a much more effective route is to encourage the *candidate* to select the right company.

THE ROLES WORK PLAYS IN OUR LIVES

Why are signature processes so important to employee engagement? Because "work" does not mean the same thing to everyone.

People value different things from the work experience. Some care deeply about the social connections and friendships formed. Others care about the opportunity to express themselves creatively. Still others want to make as much money as possible in as flexible, low-commitment a way as possible.

We like to work in very different ways. Some prefer open-ended tasks, others highly structured tasks. Some like to work on teams, and others independently. Some people need and enjoy a great deal of day-to-day guidance. Others work best when left alone to solve an ambiguous challenge.

We are excited and intrigued by different values and goals. Some have high tolerance for risk and love the rush of a high-reward environment. Others crave the steady dependency of a well-structured, long-term climb up the career ladder.

What causes people to feel engaged differs from individual to individual. The differences have significant implications for the types of processes that would cause individuals to self-select, and the environments that would be most likely to create high levels of engagement once they are on the job.

Our work has identified six fundamentally different archetypes of the relationship with work found within the workforce.[2] The six values that work plays in our lives today are:

- Expressive Legacy—Work is about creating something with lasting value.
- Secure Progress—Work is about the dream of upward mobility; a predictable, upward path to success.
- Individual Expertise and Team Victory—Work is an opportunity to be a valuable part of a winning team.
- Risk with Reward—Work is an opportunity for challenge, change, learning, and maybe wealth.
- Flexible Support—Work is our livelihood but not currently a priority in our lives.
- Limited Obligations—Work's value is largely its near-term economic gain.

These six archetypes are based on understanding the distinct values, traits, and preferences regarding work. Statistically valid, the segments are based on an extensive survey of individuals' psychodemographic characteristics and other drivers of engagement. Each segment has distinct work-related preferences. That is, each segment cares deeply about several aspects of the employee-employer relationship (and cares very little about others). Our proprietary segmentation model recognizes the different role that work plays in people's lives—ranging from the straightforward and immediate need for money to the longer-term desire to build a lasting legacy for the future.

Interestingly, while people may shift priorities over the course of their career, particularly with regard to the need and preference for flexibility, the research hints that many values and preferences may be consistent over time. For example, the archetypes are closely correlated with career choice—certain occupations are much more frequently populated by individuals in one specific segment, indicating that the preference was evident in some form as the individual made their earliest work-related and probably even educational choices. This hypothesis is consistent with research on the psychodemographics of consumer segments; most people do not shift significantly among segments over time.

Understanding and responding to these segments represents the foundation for improving engagement.

Expressive Legacy

For individuals in this segment, work is about building something with lasting value. Nicknamed *self-empowered innovators*, these workers are entrepreneurial, hardworking, creative, well educated, and self-motivated. They consider themselves leaders and frequently achieve the level of senior manager. Many are self-employed or heading their own companies. For them, work is a source of great personal satisfaction. They are the most likely to define success as being true to themselves and agree that a good deal of their pride comes from work and careers. They are the most likely of all employees to say they are impassioned and energized by their work and that time passes quickly on the job. Half say they will never retire. Individuals in this segment are not highly motivated by traditional rewards, such as additional compensation, vacation time, or even a better benefits package. Instead, they are looking for work that continues to empower and stimulate them, enables them to continue to learn and grow, and has a greater social purpose. Signature processes to attract individuals in this segment should be based on

- Individual latitude
- Entrepreneurial opportunities
- Creative opportunities
- Stimulating work that enables them to continue to learn and grow
- Work that will have a lasting impact.

Secure Progress

Nicknamed *fair and square traditionalists*, work for individuals in this segment is based on the goal of upward mobility—a steady, predictable path to success. These individuals are highly reliable and loyal workers seeking traditional rewards. They got where they are by putting their noses to the grindstone, working hard, and being team players. In return, they want to be fairly rewarded for their efforts through concrete, traditional compensation like good benefits and a solid, predictable retirement package. The group is slightly below average in terms of education but above average in household income. They are pleased with their success and often describe themselves as family men and women, high achievers, and leaders among their peers. They have less interest in "softer" work benefits like stimulating work, enjoyable workplaces, work that is worthwhile to society, or even flexible work arrangements. They are the least drawn to riskier compensation like stock or bonuses. They seek stable and secure environments and have the longest average tenure with their employers. Signature processes to attract individuals in this segment should be based on

- Fair, predictable rewards
- Concrete compensation, benefits, and a solid retirement package
- Stable, secure work environments
- Work with structure and routine
- Career-related training.

Individual Expertise and Team Victory

Individuals in this segment, nicknamed *accomplished contributors*, view work as an opportunity to be part of a winning team. They care deeply about being highly competent at the work they do and contributing to the organization's success. They take pride in their work, are willing to put in extra effort, value teamwork, and seek an atmosphere that is cooperative and stimulating. To them, "contribution" is the name of the game, and they like to do work that is worthwhile to society. This group is loyal, hard-working, reliable, capable, and typically very experienced. They place less value than most others do on individualistic rewards such as more money or vacation and express less need for flexible work arrangements. Instead, they place strong emphasis on work that is personally stimulating, work environments that are congenial and fun, colleagues who cooperate, and employers who provide stability and job security. Signature processes to attract individuals in this segment should be based on

- Work that involves teaming with others
- Fun
- Collaboration
- Stable and structured environments

- Competence
- Work that leverages their personal strengths.

Risk with Reward

These *maverick morphers* seek lives filled with change and adventure—and see work as one of multiple opportunities to achieve these goals. These individuals tend to be well educated, successful, and restless. They thrive on exciting work and personal success. They're not afraid to take chances, try new things, and shape the rules to fit their lifestyles. Frequently working for smaller organizations or self-employed, they are often senior-level managers, despite their relative youth. Growth and opportunity and variety are what drive them, and they value organizations where they can work with other bright people and do work that is inherently worthwhile. They own their careers and pioneer new ways of working. They are the most likely to want flexible workplaces and schedules that enable them to work on their own terms and pursue their own interests. Confident in their abilities, they are the most likely to seek out bonus compensation and stock to reward accomplishments. Organizations need to work hard to retain them, as they actively explore their career options and their tenures with employers on average are brief. Signature processes to attract individuals in this segment should be based on

- Opportunities for personal financial upside: bonus and stock
- Flexible workplaces and schedules based on their own terms
- Opportunities to choose tasks and positions from a wide menu of options, to own their career
- Open-ended tasks and approaches
- Frequent exposure to other bright people and recognized thought leaders.

Flexible Support

For individuals in this group, nicknamed *stalled survivors*, work is a source of livelihood but not yet (or not currently) a very satisfying part of their lives. For a variety of possible reasons, work for these individuals is largely "on hold." The youngest workforce segment, many are just starting off in their careers, getting married, having children, finishing their education, or otherwise pursuing interests and priorities outside of work. They are busy trying to balance their lives—personally, financially, and emotionally. They tend to feel that they are pulled in too many directions and often describe themselves as stressed out from their many obligations. At this time in their careers, they are looking for employers who can make it a little easier to cope. They frequently seek out an improved work-life balance through more flexible work arrangements, and they value additional pay and vacation and family benefits such as child care and maternity/paternity leave. They also value employers who offer environments that are more congenial and fun. They tend to view their current challenges as a temporary phase, and many are seeking new roles and positions at work that will enable them to get more in control of both their careers and lives. Signature processes to attract individuals in this segment should be based on

- Flexible work arrangements, including, to the extent possible, options for self-scheduling
- Vacation or options for leave
- Family friendly benefits, preferably in a cafeteria-style offering to allow the choice among child care, elder care, and other options based on the individual's specific needs
- Work with well-defined routines—the ability to "plug in" and out again with ease
- Work that can be done virtually and does not require direct personal interaction
- Work environments that are congenial and fun.

Limited Obligations

Not surprisingly, these are individuals who see work primarily as a way to make the money necessary for survival and would prefer to do it by expending as little energy or taking on as few obligations as possible. Nicknamed *demanding disconnects*, these individuals view work as generally frustrating and see its value largely in terms of near-term economic gain. They derive the least satisfaction from their employment and return the least commitment to employers. Although they wish for stability, security, and greater recognition and reward, many are frustrated by the nature of their work, lack of opportunity, or perceived unfairness in their employment arrangements. Some are simply disgruntled. Many feel at dead-end—that they have gotten as much as possible out of their current positions and want to move on. They admit they are not high achievers or leaders. Most feel that their organizations do not bring out the best in them. Some are struggling with low income, more focused on making ends meet than on deriving personal fulfillment from their work—or helping employers prosper. They expect a lot in return for their labor and place high value on traditional compensation and benefits packages, while expressing less interest than other segments in work that is enjoyable, personally stimulating, or worthwhile to society. We believe some could be more highly engaged with different work designs. Although most companies probably would not care to design processes to attract or retain these individuals, the demanding disconnects comprise a viable and valuable workforce segment in some instances, such as seasonal work. Signature processes to attract individuals in this segment should be based on

- Low barriers to entry—hiring processes that are quick and easy; jobs that are relatively easy to come by and learn
- Work with well-defined routines
- Traditional compensation and lucrative benefits packages
- Stability and security
- Recognition.

Employees clearly want different things from their work experience based on the extent to which they fall into one of these segments. Even more significantly, *there is a significant correlation between the extent to which specific employee preferences are met and their engagement levels.* Different people are engaged by different types of experiences as employees.

More money does not, by itself, produce higher engagement levels—nor does any randomly chosen set of deal elements. In fact, the existence of a potpourri of elements of the employee experience, even if each one in and of itself is a best practice, does not create high engagement. Our work has found that the reasons why people are more or less engaged vary by segment, and high engagement occurs only when the specific factors that are most important to each type of employee are met on a consistent and coherent basis throughout the life cycle of the experience with that employer.

These results are significant and very encouraging. Just as with the psychodemographic segmentation of consumer markets, employers can develop models to understand the motivational distribution in their workforces. They can target employees that are best suited to the nature of the work within their business and shape powerful employer brands to attract the desired talent. They can then adjust work situations and elements of the employment experience to meet the needs and expectations of key segments so as to bring out the best in terms of engagement and therefore performance.

As Jim Collins advised some years ago in *Good to Great*, "First, get the right people on the bus."[3] The most powerful (and practical) approach to engagement is to target employees for both attraction and retention that are best aligned with your firm's human capital values, management philosophy, and the type of work you need to do. There's simply too much potential energy, commitment, and productivity going to waste through employees who are not happy with their current employee experience not to consider crafting a fundamentally new relationship between employees and employers.

FINDING YOUR UNIQUE SIGNATURE

So how do great companies evolve specific, actionable approaches for strengthening the link between employees' needs and preferences and the business? How do they shape a signature process?

Most companies probably have the seed of a signature. Find and extend it. Protect and amplify it. Create a modern legend shaped to the needs of today's business. Ensure that everyone understands the firm's value proposition. Think of this like writing the chorus to a song that everyone will sing. Here is a practical approach.

Identify your current value proposition. What do you tell candidates who are considering joining your firm today? What is your greatest distinction? Are there any stories or examples you use to back up your claims of what working in your company is like? What company lore already exists? Perhaps most important, do your colleagues describe the same value proposition and know the same stories as you do?

Regularly discuss whether today's value proposition makes sense given the employees you need for the future and what you can realistically offer. How are both your business needs and business environment changing? How do the type of people your business, in all likelihood, will need tomorrow differ from those you have today? How might you need to begin shifting your value proposition to attract and retain a different type of individual?

Can you realistically continue to offer the value proposition that you may have been using very successfully over the past decade? Many firms undergo significant changes in the "deal" that they are able to offer employees, driven by changes in the industry conditions, competitive environment, or corporate structure. It's critically important to meet these changes head on—discuss them openly with employees and begin work to create a realistic employee experience that is strong and unique in its own way. Some of your current employees may not like it and may elect to leave over time. In most cases, having them depart would be better than having them stay in body only—with disastrously low levels of engagement under the new deal. Still others may have changed along with you, and so you will be able to update your deal with them.

Assess your current employees' values and preferences. Your employees are your customers as well—they are consumers of your employment value proposition. So it's essential that you conduct an internal customer service review. Just as your marketing colleagues regularly reassess the relevance of your external brand in the market and its ability to support the products and services your firm offers, you also need to reassess your employee value proposition. What do your current employees really care about? What is their psychodemographic profile? It's as important to your business to have solid research in this area as it is to know about your external customers' characteristics. This insight forms the critical basis for any efforts to increase engagement. It provides the opportunity to strengthen your signature experience. Can you identify an unmet employment need? Can you create ways to meet it in a powerful way—and strengthen your business model in the process?

Interestingly, this insight may also provide opportunities to do *less* in some areas. Many companies are offering deal elements that few, if any, of their employees really care about—certainly ones that do not contribute to high levels of engagement. Perhaps through better understanding you can shift resources to areas of higher impact.

Don't forget to extend this research to prospective employees. Is there anything unique about people who have a skill set or capability that is critical to your future success that you might be able to address in a distinctive and compelling way? For example, if you live in a college community where flexibility might be important, is there a way to offer significantly more flexible arrangements than any competitive employers and attract the top talent?

Design innovative new signature experiences. Sometimes you will need to create a new signature experience, rather than adapt one that already exists. Look for processes that are important to your firm and think creatively about the best way to demonstrate your values through the design of the process. For example, let's say that networking is critical to the success of individuals within your business model—you need people who are oriented to reach out and work in teams with others. At the same time, you also need individuals with an entrepreneurial bent. Perhaps rather than having an orientation process that is static—everyone sitting together in one room for a required period of time listening to a prepared presentation—you might turn your orientation into a treasure hunt format. You might give each new hire a list of clues that can only be met by seeking out and having conversations with a diverse group of individuals from around the firm. Through this process, you could not only give people a head start on a useful network, but also use the experience to talk about the behaviors you will value throughout their time with the company.

Once developed, talk about the signature process. Like all great stories, the lore stays alive—and becomes most powerful—when it is told and retold.

NO BAIT AND SWITCH

Signature processes define and illustrate your target intentions. But not everything can be a signature. What about the other processes that comprise your employees' experience with your firm? Building a brand requires a whole set of practices, processes, and ways of working—some that are truly unique, signatures, and others that are aligned and supportive of the overall brand.

You can't, however, choose these other practices in a patchwork fashion—pulling best practices from miscellaneous sources, with little regard to how they fit with and reinforce your primary messages. For example, a compensation system based on group rewards may be the best of its type, but it may be completely wrong for the type of experience you're creating. Think through every touch point with your employees, and ensure that there are no mixed messages being sent at any point.

To execute effectively, you need consistency among multiple elements of the overall employee experience:

- Your corporation's external image with your customers
- Individuals' need and values
- The corporation's values, as expressed by its leaders
- The human resource policies and practices
- The specific roles and tasks
- The day-to-day work environment: behaviors of colleagues, first-line managers
- What behaviors are encouraged, tolerated or excluded—throughout the organization, from the absolute top.

The alignment of all the elements of an employee's life within the company, anchored by legendary signature processes, is what creates a cohesive end-to-end employee relationship that becomes a signature experience, leading to a powerful sense of engagement. At Whole Foods, for example, the approach to team-based work goes far beyond their probation-based induction process. They have compensation practices, rewards and recognition, promotion criteria, and so on that are also strongly team-based. The pieces of the experience fit together and reinforce each other. Ensure you deliver on the value proposition consistently throughout the employee experience.

Our research shows that one of the most common problems triggering low engagement is a sense of something akin to bait and switch—a perception that some parts of the employee experience are inconsistent with expectations, promises, or other, more popular parts of the experience. Many times we have heard employees, six months into the job, say, "It's just not what I expected or wanted." It's not surprising that engagement levels drop sharply during the first six months after hire.

Several years ago a firm asked for help redesigning their orientation process but turned out to have a strong bait and switch issue instead. They initially felt the orientation itself was driving people away from the firm. But upon closer examination, it was clear that the existing process was actually a very accurate representation of what the work experience was really like at this company. The problem was that they were attracting people under a very different premise. The company either needed to change the hiring process, perhaps adding stories that would make it more clear to people what it would feel like to work in the company—describing signature processes—or they needed to change the overall experience—what it was actually like to work in the company, bringing it more in line with the expectations of most of the people they were currently attracting. The orientation program was the least of their concerns.

Alignment of the total employee experience is important in two ways. It avoids disengaging people who signed on under one premise, as in the example just given. It also provides crucial guidance for the company's HR investments. It is impossible to know whether improving one aspect of the employee-employer relationship makes sense (i.e., would have a positive impact on employee engagement and productivity) unless you also know the importance of that deal element to employees within the context of the overall employee experience. Having the overall design clearly in mind provides a set of criteria—a filter—with which to judge future investments.

This approach requires a fundamental change from the way most HR leaders have approached their work: from defining standards and ensuring consistency with industry best practice, to designing for maximum distinction, within the context of a clear employer brand. Going forward, HR needs to think like brand managers—to create employee experiences that are as powerful and compelling and differentiating—as great customer experiences can be.

It's critical to your business to make the switch. To develop a highly engaged, fiercely loyal workforce, you need to attract and retain the right employees—the ones that are right for your organization. Although better selection processes have a role to play, an even better option is to describe elements of the work experience in sufficient detail so that savvy individuals are able to make the choice that is right for them.

THE PARADOX: GREATER SELECTIVITY FOR A TIGHTER WORKFORCE

Perhaps it seems paradoxical to suggest being more selective at a time when the available workforce is tightening.

It is certainly true that it will be more difficult to find and retain a sufficient number of talented employees in the years ahead. Changing demographics and shifting job requirements will make the availability of potential employees with the desired skills and capabilities increasingly scarce. But the solution is not to scoop up as many individuals as possible if many of them end up being fundamentally unhappy with the nature of the employee experience at your firm.

You need to get the right people to choose you. There's no sense in investing the time and expense required to attract a new hire, only to find you have one who is wondering what he or she has gotten into after three months on the job.

- Do you know the type(s) of people that you need in your organization for sustained success—number, skill sets, *and* orientation toward work? Do you target your future workforce as effectively as you target your customers?
- Do you have a distinctive signature process that conveys and reinforces the human capital values of the organization?
- Do you believe the employee experience is coherent—or could some elements represent a bait and switch turnoff to your best people and those you most want to attract?

The challenge for corporations competing for a tightening talent pool is to get a distinctive message across—to create a signature experience. When investors make choices about where to place financial assets, they look carefully at the returns that various options are likely to afford. When selecting a consumer product, potential buyers make trade-offs based on their preferences and priorities, many influenced by the attributes embedded in the company's brand promise. Potential employees are no different. They also make choices based on the returns you are likely to provide and the attributes you most clearly communicate.

When it comes to creating employee engagement, there are no universal best practices that will work equally well for all corporations and all employees. The key lies in tapping into your own firm's best characteristics and strongest values, demonstrating them through memorable signature processes, and integrating them to create a distinctive signature experience for the specific employees you want and need.

NOTES

1. The phrase "signature process" was originated by Lynda Gratton and Sumantra Ghoshal at the London Business School. Much of the work on the use of these authentic, company-specific processes to create signature experiences for employees, and thus high levels of engagement, was done in collaboration with Dr. Gratton. For further reading, see Tamara J. Erickson and Lynda Gratton, "What It Means to Work Here," *Harvard Business Review* (March 2007).

2. These findings were developed by Tamara Erickson, Ken Dychtwald, and Bob Morison, based a statistical survey of the U.S. workforce conducted for the Concours Group and Age Wave by Harris International, funded by 24 major corporations as part of the research program *The New Employee/Employer Equation* (The Concours Group and Age Wave, 2004). For further information, see K. Dychtwald, T. Erickson, B. Morison, and D. Baxter, *Handbook of the New American Workforce* BSG Concours: www.concoursgroup.com (2007).

3. Jim Collins, *Good to Great: Why Some Companies Make the Leap . . . and Others Don't* (New York: HarperCollins, 2001), esp. Chapter 3.

Chapter 8

Managers: The Key to an Engaged Workplace*

Derrick R. Barton

It is commonly believed that when employees quit, they don't quit the company, they quit their bosses. No matter how elaborate a company's engagement program may be, managers make the real difference when it comes down to engaging employees. The reason: Managers have the most direct contact with employees. Managers influence how people experience their jobs, they set the tone for each day, and their actions and interactions all make a real difference. From high-tech to heavy manufacturing, financial services to health care, managers are the key to affecting each employee's decision to engage or disengage, to stay or leave.

Let's think about how managers impact an employee's work situation. Managers impact the work employees do each day by deciding who does what within operating areas. They also determine how much autonomy is allowed within specific activities. Managers influence the level of challenge and responsibility in a job and whether an organization capitalizes on each employee's strengths and capabilities. All of these manager actions and decisions help determine an employee's level of engagement and desire to stay.

Managers also impact the overall work environment through their direct actions. They create a team atmosphere that promotes the open exchange of ideas and builds trust. They model the way they expect employees to treat each other. Managers who provide employees with the time, information, and tools they need to do their jobs well will directly influence whether employees engage and perform at their best.

---

*Copyright © 2007 Derrick R. Barton.

Managers capable of engaging employees make the time to communicate, provide feedback, coach performance, ask for ideas, and give credit where credit is due. They also influence how organization processes and policies impact employees. Take pay, job security, and career opportunities—all key variables that have set processes and policies defined by the organization. Now think about how managers execute these processes and policies with employees. Giving pay increases, reviewing performance, determining an employee's readiness for their next career move are all affected by how a manager interacts with a team and individual employees. Once again, managers make a real difference.

In the end, the manager will impact an employee's overall work situation, and therefore create the greatest influence on an employee's decision to engage and stay. As a result, it is essential all managers understand the role they play in employee engagement and retention, and know what they can do to make a difference and cause employees to choose to engage and choose to stay.

Although many companies and consulting organizations are using the same term—*employee engagement*—there is not a clear agreement as to what this actually means. The Gallup Organization defines engagement as how "engaged employees work with passion and feel a profound connection to their company; they drive innovation and move the organization forward." The Corporate Leadership Council defines engagement as "the extent to which employees commit to something or someone in their organization and how hard they work and how long they stay as a result of that commitment." Watson Wyatt further defines how "Engagement is a combination of commitment and line of sight. Committed employees are proud to work for their companies and motivated to help drive success. But commitment alone is not enough. Employees also need focus and direction."

In the performance-based definition from the Center for Talent Retention, engagement is described as "the productive use of one's talents, ideas, and energy." Let's break this definition down into its key components:

- **Productive use:** To understand how engaged someone is, observe what the person does on the job, see what results the person delivers, and look at how the person impacts others.
- **One's talents:** The capabilities we all have lodged within our knowledge, experiences, skills, and abilities that equip us to perform.
- **Ideas and energy:** Our ideas and energy help drive our desire to perform.

The Center for Talent Retention has identified four levels (see Figure 8.1) of employee engagement, which have been used globally over the past seven years by thousands of managers to improve employee engagement.

To make sure the engagement levels resonate within an organization, managers should further define what engagement looks like within their own operating environments by answering these three questions for each level of engagement.

- What do you see employees *do* at this level?

Figure 8.1
Employee Engagement Levels. (*Source*: Center for Talent Retention © 2000–2007.)

Engagement Levels	Engagement Level Descriptions
Level 4 Fully Engaged	• Passionate about their work and the organization • Will do what ever it takes to deliver results • Feels like a true owner • Delivering consistent, high quality results is their trademark • Finds innovative solutions to the toughest problems • Seen as a role model and leader
Level 3 Engaged	• Focused on their deliverables, project, and individual responsibilities • Delivers good, solid performance • Always does their fair share of work • Works well with others and will help out when asked
Level 2 Somewhat Engaged	• Selective about where they put their energy • Spends a lot of time doing things that are not helping customers or the organization • Delivers when they have to, or when you are watching • Does what it takes to get by • A master at distracting others
Level 1 Disengaged	• Only works when they have to, they really want to be doing something else • Results are NOT meeting the standard • Has a "We"—"They" perspective • Negative about the organization, as well as in their interactions with coworkers and customers

- What *results* do employees at this level achieve?
- How do employees at this level *impact others*?

As the levels of engagement are identified for an organization, it becomes very clear how engagement impacts performance and how managers impact engagement. This is especially crucial as managers discover how important it is to retain their engaged and fully engaged employees, but also how possible it is to increase the "somewhat engaged" employees level of engagement.

In the Center for Talent Retention's database showing how organizations impact engagement, we find that managers can keep almost all employees who are "fully engaged" at this level of engagement. Just as impressive are the results seen when managers take action with "engaged" employees—managers are able to cause about 20 percent of the "engaged" employees to move to the "fully engaged" level. This movement in engagement nets the organization on average a 22 percent increase in performance for each person. When managers take action with "somewhat engaged" employees, they are able to help approximately half the employees to engage within a six-month period. The performance gained by this move is 25 percent for each employee. Finally, if employees are "disengaged," managers across organizations are only able to get about

10 percent to move all the way to the "engaged" level. However, this improvement results in a 45 percent increase in performance.

ORGANIZATION RESULTS REQUIRE EMPLOYEE PERFORMANCE

Managers are under considerable pressure to deliver results for the business, customers, and employees. Therefore they are most motivated when they can see a solid return on their investment of time and effort. It is essential to create a line-of-sight for how engaging employee talent fits into delivering organization results and to outline what managers need to do to make an impact on engaging and retaining talent.

Creating a line-of-sight requires organizations to link performance requirements with the drivers of engagement. To survive and grow, organizations must be able to deliver against three sets of needs: customer needs, business needs, and employee needs. Organizations that do not demonstrate the ability to deliver against all three needs suffer the consequences. Customers leave, business capital dries up, or employees disengage and leave.

- Customer Needs: Organizations must demonstrate the ability to meet customer needs or customers will go elsewhere. Customers expect a consistent service or a high-quality product every time.
- Business Needs: Organizations must demonstrate the ability to reach business objectives (profit, revenue, execute a business plan, and manage costs) or capital for continued operations and growth plans will not be available.
- Employee Needs: Organizations must demonstrate the ability to meet the needs of employees or employees will disengage and leave or, worse, disengage and stay.

EMPLOYEE PERFORMANCE (ACTIONS AND RESULTS)

Successful organizations are very clear on what results they must deliver. Everyone knows the key measures of success and how strategic initiatives will ensure the organization can deliver against the organization goals. These successful organizations also link employee performance to the key organization results and objectives. They make sure that each employee knows how his or her job directly serves the organization's long-term goals.

Employees must contribute to those objectives by performing critical work assignments in a way that delivers the desired results within their roles. Working hard every day and not delivering results does not equal success. Likewise, delivering results in a way that creates additional problems down the line for others isn't helping the organization succeed.

Employee performance (actions and results) has three main requirements: employees need to know what to do, employees need to be capable of doing it, and employees have to want to perform.

Know what to do. Employees need to understand the correct procedures and processes that must be performed, the goals that provide direction and focus their actions, as well as understanding *why* they must perform to those goals.

Can do. This second component determines that all employees must be capable of performing and contributing. Do they have the requisite knowledge, skills, and abilities? Do they have the required experience to handle the situations that arise within their role? Do they have the necessary technology and materials they need to perform successfully?

Want to do. Is there a desire to do what it takes to deliver at a high level of performance? Are the employees committed to delivering solid results? Are they going to go above and beyond what is called for? Or are they going to choose to deliver just enough to get by?

High-performing organization results can only be sustained over time when all employees know what to do, have the skills and capabilities to do it, and have the desire to perform. It's up to the managers to help each employee successfully deliver performance by achieving these three needs.

EMPLOYEES CHOOSE TO ENGAGE AND STAY

Employees choose to engage or disengage, and employees choose to stay or leave. Knowing it is an employee's choice allows managers to take action to influence it. It does not allow them to control it, however.

Although what may cause employees to choose to engage or disengage (or stay or go) may vary among employees, the impact on performance does not. When employees choose to be engaged and stay, performance increases. If an engaged employee chooses to leave for some reason, performance decreases. When employees become somewhat engaged or disengaged and choose to stay, performance decreases. If the disengaged employee leaves and an engaged employee takes his or her place, performance increases.

People choose to engage and choose to stay based on how well their most critical needs are met by their work situation (see Figure 8.2). Managers therefore need to make the time to understand the needs that will be core to causing employees to make these critical decisions.

It's important to keep in mind that not all employees stay engaged for the same reasons. Each person has a set of most critical needs, which when achieved within their current work situation, causes them to give their best to the organization. Some of these needs are directly related to the work they do every day. Others are impacted by a work environment that is ideal to satisfy their personal situation and working style. Finally, what the organization offers (pay, career opportunities, job security, etc.) can impact the decision to engage and the decision to stay.

Therefore, the management challenge is to understand each employee's most critical needs, determine whether those needs are being met, and then take action to make the appropriate improvements.

Figure 8.2
FIT Model. (*Source*: Center for Talent Retention © 2007.)

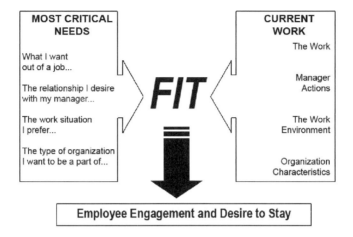

There is no set of universal variables that engage all employees. However there is one universal truth: Engagement happens one person at a time.

The Center for Talent Retention has identified 50 talent variables that make an impact on the decision to engage or disengage, stay or leave. The talent variables are organized into four main categories and defined at two levels of performance. One level captures the talent variable at a level that causes employees to join, engage, and stay within an organization. The other level captures the talent variable at the level that causes employees to pass up internal opportunities, disengage, or leave an organization entirely. This set of 50 talent variables can be used to select the characteristics that make a difference for *your* employees and organization.

The WORK talent variables represent the qualities and characteristics associated with the tasks, assignments, and projects an employee is responsible for in his or her role. Managers are able to increase engagement by providing challenging work, allowing for appropriate levels of responsibility, making sure employees work on projects they love to do, and capitalizing on employee strengths and capabilities.

The WORK ENVIRONMENT talent variables represent the qualities and characteristics associated with the employee's work surroundings and how organization practices impact the work environment. Managers are able to increase engagement by providing training and skill development, creating an environment where employees are appreciated and valued, establishing a network of people they can turn to if they need help, and making sure employees have a great balance between work and their personal life.

The MANAGER ACTIONS talent variables represent the manager actions and qualities impacting an employee's work situation. Managers are able to increase engagement by giving great feedback so employees know where they stand, actively listening to understand each employee's point of view, creating clear goals and performance expectations, and making time to ask for ideas.

The ORGANIZATION talent variables represent the qualities and characteristics associated with the organization's direction and the impact company policies have on an employee's work situation. Managers are able to increase engagement by providing competitive salaries, appropriate job security, making sure professional development and growth opportunities continually happen, and creating a sense of mission and purpose that is exciting and inspires employees to do their best.

Again, even though there are similarities among employees, an organization must remember that employees are also individuals with unique needs, capabilities, and ideas. Anita Roddick, founder and former CEO of the Body Shop, made a group of senior business leaders sit back and take note at a conference when she said, "We went to hire employees and people showed up instead."

This dynamic of creating a good fit for a person's most critical needs as a requirement to engage and retain talent is the core to causing employees to choose to engage and choose to stay. Review the top variables (Figure 8.3) selected by employees when answering the question, "What is most critical to engage you to perform at your best and creates a place you want to stay?"

Organizations cannot be successful unless managers take an active role in engaging and retaining great employees according to their most critical needs. The management challenge is to understand each employee's needs, how well their current work situation meets these needs, and then take action to make the appropriate changes to increase the fit between what is most critical and the current work situation.

The next section outlines two talent practices and a number of manager actions that make a difference in engaging all employees.

A FOUNDATION TALENT PRACTICE: ONE-TO-ONE DIALOGUE

One-to-one dialogue is the foundation for engaging each person to perform at his or her best. It enables managers to understand what is most critical to employees as individuals, and what actions both the manager and the employee can take to improve the employee's current work situation. Let's take a look at the components of a great one-to-one dialogue (see Figure 8.4).

The first component is identifying what is most critical to your employee.

The second component of one-to-one dialogue is learning why the need is critical to the employee. Understanding this will help you assess the priority of the issue, as well as the surrounding circumstances and unique situation.

The third component is learning what it is really like for the employee right now. To take action on an employee's most critical needs, you must have a clear understanding of how well those most critical needs are currently being met.

The final component of one-to-one dialogue is identifying the actions you will take, as well as the actions your employee will take, to make a critical difference in the current situation.

Even though the process is straightforward, planning and executing a successful one-to-one dialogue process with employees can be challenging.

Figure 8.3
Top Most Critical Needs. (*Source*: Center for Talent Retention © 2000–2006.)

	Top Most Critical Needs – Sorted by Talent Variable Category *What is most critical to engage you to perform at your best and creates a place you want to stay?*
WORK	☐ I can make a positive impact here. ☐ My work is very challenging. ☐ I have the necessary resources to do a good job. ☐ My job capitalizes on my strengths and capabilities. ☐ I love to do what I'm doing.
MANAGER ACTIONS	☐ I feel comfortable asking my manager questions & discussing important issues. ☐ My goals and performance expectations are clear-I know what it takes to be successful here. ☐ My manager gives great feedback—I always know where I stand. ☐ I get a lot of coaching from my manager and other knowledgeable resources. ☐ My manager often asks for my ideas.
WORK ENVIRONMENT	☐ I feel appreciated and valued. ☐ I get a lot of skill development and training—I'm developing new capabilities. ☐ I have a network of people I can turn to if I need help. ☐ I have a great balance between work and my personal life. ☐ New ideas are valued and supported.
ORGANIZATION CHARACTERSTICS	☐ My salary is competitive in the marketplace. ☐ This organization cares about its customers, employees, as well as making money. ☐ The organization's mission and purpose is exciting and inspires me to do my best. ☐ I can see a number of great career opportunities here. ☐ Our organization is on the right track—we will be very competitive.

Figure 8.4
One-to-One Dialogue Framework. (*Source*: Center for Talent Retention © 2007.)

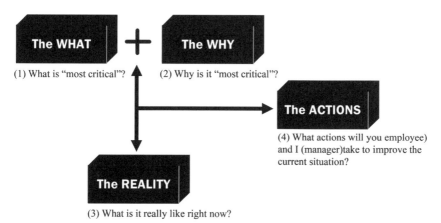

Before the One-to-One Dialogue

Introduce the one-to-one dialogue process to your employees by clearly describing the desired results you would like to achieve. Be sure to emphasize that you want to make the time to understand what's most critical to them as individuals, how they are experiencing their work within your organization, and what you and your employees can do to improve the areas impacting an employee's engagement and desire to stay. Create a plan and schedule the dialogues to ensure you and the employee are fully prepared to identify the areas where actions can be taken.

During the One-to-One Dialogue

The important part of a one-to-one dialogue is the actual conversation. Real dialogue focuses on listening, understanding, and learning the unique needs of your employee. Mutual understanding will not just happen—you must *make time* to talk with each employee. Be sure you are able to gain perspective of each employee's unique situation by understanding the *why* before you try and solve anything.

One-to-one dialogue is a critical talent practice to perform with all of your employees. Some managers focus on their low-performing or disengaged employees, while others spend all their time with the best-performing or fully engaged employees. Both are worth your effort.

Below are the desired outcomes of a one-to-one dialogue for each engagement level. Use the desired outcomes as a guide to plan your upcoming dialogue with each employee.

- *Fully engaged employees.* Identify what is most critical to keeping the fully engaged employee performing at a fully engaged level or understand what internal career moves would be a great fit for the employee's needs, interests, and capabilities.

- *Engaged employees.* The desired outcomes for engaged employees is to determine which most critical needs must be impacted to increase an engaged employee to the fully engaged level or continue meeting the most critical needs that will maintain an engaged employee at the engaged level.

- *Somewhat engaged employees.* Discuss the most critical needs that are not being met and determine how to increase a somewhat engaged employee to the engaged level or determine if there is an opportunity to transfer a somewhat engaged employee to another position that will meet more of his or her most critical needs and cause the person to perform at an engaged level.

- *Disengaged employees.* Finally, learn what is in the way of the disengaged employee performing at the engaged level or move the disengaged employee out of the organization and replace the person with an engaged employee if there is no improvement.

A FOUNDATION TALENT PRACTICE: TEAM MEMBER TALENT PLAN

One-to-one dialogue will get the right things on the table. Now you must determine what to do to engage and retain your employee. In a team member talent plan you will outline the most critical needs and determine which ones to address. Once you select the most critical needs that require attention, determine what you and your employee can do to make a positive impact on the current work situation.

As you assess each employee situation, you must determine the appropriate manager response for the employee's specific situation. Let's look at three different types of manager responses you can use to solve different team member situations: take action, involve, and manage expectations.

If *your* individual actions caused the situation, if *your* actions can solve the problem, or if *you* can directly impact whether your team or team members perform, then *take action*. Outline what you will do to solve the critical needs gap, by when, and then keep your commitment. For example, if an employee wants more feedback, then taking action to provide feedback will immediately make a positive impact for the employee.

If the situation is caused by you and the team member, you cannot solve the situation alone, or other people may be a better resource for this particular situation, then *involve*. To fulfill the involve response, you must identify what you *and* others will do to solve the critical needs gap, by when, and then, of course, keep the commitment. If "Adjusting my work schedule or work arrangements" is a critical employee need, the *involve* response will allow you and the employee to work together to figure out if adjustments to the shift schedule are possible. The last thing you would want to do is take this issue on yourself to solve for the employee.

If the issue is outside of your control or influence and will not change, the organization is moving in the opposite direction from the employee's desired situation, or the employee's performance is currently not meeting expectations, then *manage expectations*. Identify the critical needs gap, recognize the importance of the issue to the person, and discuss what can and cannot be done and why. Take the situation where a new employee thinks she is ready to move up to the next position. You know she is not ready. As the manager, you must manage expectations by clearly describing the situation to the employee, explaining why the employee's capabilities or experience level needs to increase, or how other employees have more knowledge and experience needed for the opening. As a manager, you should redirect the employee to build skills needed for future openings.

In many situations, you may need to use a combination of manager responses to impact the employee's situation. Choosing the appropriate response to a team member's current situation can quickly lead to an improvement in an employee's work situation and his or her level of engagement.

MANAGER ACTIONS MAKE A DIFFERENCE

There is a wealth of materials available to outline different management and leadership models. Certainly there is overlap between the models and a certain level of agreement and disagreement among experts in the field. Figure 8.5 is an outline of 7 manager capabilities containing 15 manager actions and 5 manager qualities the Center for Talent Retention developed over the past decade to capture what managers do to engage and retain talent. Again, it does not capture all management actions,

Figure 8.5
Engaging and Retaining Talent: Manager Actions. (*Source*: Center for Talent Retention © 2007.)

7 Manager Capabilities	15 Manager Actions			
Communication	#18 I feel comfortable asking my manager questions and discussing important issues.	#26 My manager actively listens to me and seeks to understand my point of view.	#32 My manager often asks for my ideas.	#40 My manager gets the facts before making judgments or taking action.
Supporting Work	#2 My manager stands up and supports me.	#10 My manager gives me the space I need to do my work.	#20 My manager understands my work.	
Credibility	#22 My manager tells the truth no matter what.	#34 My manager "walks-the-talk."		
Coaching Performance	#28 My goals and performance expectations are clear—I know what it takes to be successful here.	#30 I get a lot of coaching from my manager and other knowledgeable resources.		
Providing Feedback	#14 My manager gives feedback in a way that makes it easy to want to improve.	#24 My manager gives great feedback—I always know where I stand.		
Caring	#12 My manager genuinely cares about me as a person.			
Personal Actions	#16 My manager knows how to handle his or her personal frustrations.			

5 Manager Qualities	#4 I feel comfortable around my manager.	#6 I trust and respect my manager.	#8 My manager is highly qualified.	#36 I really like my manager.	#38 My manager and I have values which allow us to work very well together.

NOTE: The number listed by each manager action and quality corresponds to the talent variable number assigned within the Retention Cards--a tool from the Center for Talent Retention.

and it is not meant to be an exhaustive list of leadership competencies. It is simply a list of manager actions that have been proven to engage and retain employee talent.

Each of the five manager qualities is influenced by one or more of the manager actions. For example, a manager is "trusted and respected" by employees (a manager quality) because he or she "walks the talk," "supports employees during difficult situations," and is a "role model for handling pressure situations." Thus, the quality of "I trust and respect my manager" is achieved as a result of the actions the manager takes.

Each of the 15 manager actions fit into one of 7 manager capabilities. These capabilities represent the actions all managers must take on the job to engage and retain employee talent. Even though each manager may have his or her own style of managing employees, each of these capabilities is critical for all managers and can be demonstrated through a variety of managerial styles.

Manager capabilities are further defined into distinct manager actions describing what you would see a manager do on the job to impact talent results.

DEVELOPING YOUR MANAGER CAPABILITIES

Improving your ability to perform the critical manager actions needed to engage and retain employees takes focus and determination, just like any successful development effort. Begin by answering four key development questions.

Question #1: Do You Want to Develop?

This seems like a simple question, but it lies at the heart of the issue of how you want to achieve your own potential and whether you will increase managing capabilities. Have you made the choice to put forth effort, change the way you do things, and make time for your personal development?

Question #2: What Areas of Your Performance Will you Develop?

As you look to personally develop as a manager, it is up to you to make a decision about where you will put your development energy. You have three choices: leverage a strength, develop an average capability, and strengthen a weakness.

- Leverage a Strength. Choose something you do really well. Concentrate on continuing to do this well and see if there are opportunities to use this strength in other areas. Leveraging a strength can be a very effective way to enhance your impact with employees.
- Develop an Average Capability. There are things you do proficiently, but you have ideas about how you can improve your management performance. You can make great strides to increase performance by building your average capabilities into strengths.
- Strengthen a Weakness. There is great power in changing a weakness into a solid capability or a real strength. Managers must make a conscious effort to implement specific changes to improve current areas of weakness. It takes time and focus as well as persistence to pull it off.

When looking for what to improve, many of us naturally gravitate to an area of weakness. Though that is a natural inclination, it is not your only choice and may not be your best choice. The important thing is to take action and do something to improve your managing capabilities. It has to be something you *want* to improve.

Question #3: How Will You Develop Your Capabilities?

A development process based on on-the-job actions is recommended to build any of the manager capabilities. This type of development is built on the premise that people develop through doing.

Question #4: What's Your Development Plan?

It's commonly said that failing to plan is planning to fail. This holds true for development. It is absolutely critical for you to identify what specific actions will be taken to improve your capabilities. General development may happen over time, but targeted development rarely happens without a solid plan.

SUMMARY

The Center for Talent Retention has worked with leaders and managers within some of the best Fortune 500 companies, as well as those within good companies trying to become great. We always take a few standard measurements before we begin any intervention to understand the current employee talent situation and focus improvement efforts. When we ask front-line leaders the question, "Can you describe the specific talent results your organization is trying to achieve?," 93 percent say "no." Another 86 percent answer "no" to the question, "Does your organization hold you accountable to engage and retain your employees?" And "no" is the answer 73 percent of the time to the question, "Do you spend enough time and energy engaging and retaining your employees?"

This level of performance may have worked in the past when the employee talent supply was adequate and the talent demand was limited. Organizations can't afford to execute a passive plan to engage and retain talent. Managers must shift priorities and eliminate the barriers to taking action. They must turn each "no" response into a "yes."

Some CEOs, business leaders, HR professionals, and managers know it . . . they are focusing the organization to engage and retain 100 percent of their talent. Bill Whitmore, CEO for AlliedBarton Security Services, addressed his entire management team in 2007, accountable for leading 50,000 employees, with the following remarks to clarify how his managers are the key to and engaged workplace.

Managing our employees cannot be our second priority.

- It cannot be what we do when we finish our paperwork.
- It cannot be something we fit in when we can find the time.
- It cannot be shortcutting our employees, in order to meet an operational deadline.
- It cannot be our priority solely when there is a personnel issue affecting our client.
- It cannot be ignored.

What it does mean is that every one of our employees knows what is expected of them.

- It means that we have a responsibility to solicit input from our employees and listen to their ideas.
- It means that we must routinely provide feedback, so no employee wonders how he or she is doing.
- It means that through our actions, we really do believe that people are our most important asset.
- It means engaging and coaching employees, one person at a time.

We will only be great if we have great employees. We will only have great employees if they are engaged. We will only have engaged employees if we have great managers.

Chapter 9

Work-Life Means Business*

Kathleen M. Lingle

In today's work environment, where people are working longer and harder in more demanding jobs than 25 years ago, the economic principle of scarcity dictates that time has become as valuable as money. The traditional employment contract has dissipated, along with the mutual loyalty it fostered. According to the Bureau of Labor Statistics, by 1998, the median tenure that an employee spent with a single employer had dropped to 3.6 years, a dramatic shift from an average of 22 years in 1950. Pensions, retiree medical coverage, and heavy reliance on the security of base pay are relics of the past, supplanted by "the new pay,"[1] designed to encourage employees to fund their own retirement, contingent on successful performance. Cost sharing of benefit coverage and self-directed health care consumerism are rising tides; "paternalism" has become a pejorative term. Meanwhile, the compensation and perquisites of the chief executives of American corporations have multiplied handsomely in step with the growing pressures of their own increasing responsibilities.

One of their central challenges is to elicit engagement, which means finding effective ways to harness the discretionary energy of employees to go "above and beyond" toward achieving the organization's business objectives. Apparently, some realize the enormity of this task, because for the first time, a slight majority of senior leaders (55 percent) are indicating that they intend to spend more money on people than technology.[2]

Meanwhile, employees are beset with their own concerns and responsibilities. They are under increasing pressure to perform faster and to continuously higher standards,

---
*Copyright © 2007 by Kathleen M. Lingle.

to manage their financial options responsibly while paying for an ever larger share of the health and welfare safety net that supports themselves and their family, to not begrudge the relative stagnation of their own growth in earnings while their CEO might earn up to several hundred times what they do, and to build lifestyle habits while responding to work demands wherever and whenever they arise, even at home or on vacation. In fact, by 2002, almost half of U.S. workers (46 percent) reported that they were contacted about their jobs outside of work hours (which averaged 45 per week), and a quarter (26 percent) were working at least one weekend day on a regular basis.[3]

Not surprisingly, 44 percent of U.S. employees feel overworked, and a third (33 percent) can be categorized as chronically so.[4]

Working conditions, compensation strategy, and benefits philosophy aren't the only elements that have radically altered over the past several decades. The workforce has been transforming itself with equal vigor. According to 25 years of comparative data available from the Families and Work Institute's *National Study of the Changing Workforce*, a nationally representative study of the U.S. labor force that is conducted at five-year intervals, the following interrelated trends stand out when comparing the findings of the 2002 study with 1997 (and earlier) results.

- **The American workforce is more ethnically diverse**: 21 percent were people of color versus 12 percent five years earlier.
- **The workforce is aging**: Over half (56 percent) were 40 years or older in 2002 as compared with 38 percent in 1977. Over the same period of time, the number of employees under 30 years old declined from 37 percent to less than a quarter of the workforce (22 percent).
- **There are approximately equal numbers of men and women in the wage and salary workforce**: Women have attained higher educational levels than men, and now comprise more than half of the entrants into the traditional professions, most notably law and accounting. Reflecting their higher education, women are more likely to be managers than men (38 percent versus 28 percent). But women have still not completely cracked the glass ceiling, as their presence continues to be a novelty in the "C suites" across the country, in spite of superior education and expertise in management.
- **Dual-earner couples now comprise three quarters (78 percent) of the workforce**, up from two thirds (66 percent) in 2002, and rising.
- **Consequently, a single-minded focus on work is giving way to a "dual-focus."** The traditional "work-primary" employee, whose first obligation is to the job no matter what the personal sacrifice, is being supplanted by a predominance of "dual-focus" or "dual-centric" workers. These are now the majority of employees who place somewhat equal weighting between work and family or other personal responsibilities. Out of necessity, they develop the ability to fluidly shift their time and energy between priorities at work and home as needs arise in both domains. This is the inexorable consequence of the rising incidence of dual-earner couples, since there is no one at home during working hours to take care of the children or manage the household or participate in community events. The twenty-first-century reality is that everyone who works is juggling a dual agenda, one professional and one personal.

Dual-focus workers are proving themselves to be among the most valuable contributors to the workplace today. According to research by the Families and Work Institute dual-focus workers (1) are more engaged and therefore more productive than their work-primary colleagues; (2) are mentally and physically healthier; (3) experience higher levels of job satisfaction; and (4) are generally more satisfied with their lives. They are the new human capital.

Capturing the benefits that dual-focus workers offer their employers requires an understanding of the newest discipline within people strategy, *work-life effectiveness*. Given the changes we have described in the workplace and the workforce, work-life effectiveness is coming into its own as a vital component of proactive and integrative people strategies that go by such diverse labels as *total rewards, human capital, talent management,* and *employer of choice.*

WORK-LIFE EFFECTIVENESS DEFINED

The phrase "work-life" is problematic. Its concepts began as "work and family." In recent years, however, the corporate world has trended toward replacing "family" with "life" to acknowledge the fact that everyone who works has a life, not only parents or people who live with traditional families. As the definition of who and what is "family" has changed, and as the work-life portfolio has expanded well beyond support for child care where it began, so has the name for this human capital practice evolved.

The term *work-life* (whether separated by a dash, slash, or a space) has become ubiquitous, sometimes standing awkwardly alone, but it is most often used as an adjective followed by a noun, most commonly "balance." It does beg for a qualifier (work-life *what?*), since "work-life" is an invented term that inevitably raises more questions than it resolves. However, the notion of work-life *balance* simply doesn't reflect current workplace reality. Balance implies an equilibrium of two equal parts, which isn't really the case within the work world. Ever since Harvard economist Juliet Schor pointed out that Americans are working an average of one month more each year,[5] abetted by the unwelcome intrusion of the mechanistic notion of "working 24 /7," any illusion of achieving this kind of equilibrium has evaporated for most workers.

Balance may accurately describe an individual struggle for equilibrium, but it has not proven to be a useful business term. Ours is fundamentally an unbalanced world, a situation that now is becoming more prevalent around the globe. There is no such thing as a workplace in balance. In fact, there are still employers today who behave as if it is to their advantage to maintain disequilibrium, perhaps in deference to the archaic belief that the only good employee is an unbalanced, overworked one who consistently prioritizes work before family or personal responsibilities. Worse, as Thomson and Fitzpatrick observe,[6] *work-life balance* connotes a trade-off between the interests of the company and those of its employees, which is the exact opposite of the contribution that work-life strategy brings to the workplace.

As the professional association that represents the burgeoning work-life field, the Alliance for Work-Life Progress prefers the concept of *work-life effectiveness.* Effectiveness can be described and therefore measured. The term makes no value judgments and leaves it up to each individual (including the CEO) to define what success means, however "unbalanced" that scenario might be by the dictates of conventional wisdom. *Work-life effectiveness* refers to and aligns with workplace or organization effectiveness, which it measurably enhances.

New realities in the workplace are contributing to the rise of the dual-focused worker.[7] Strategies of proactive support for work-life effectiveness are taking root in response to the growing body of evidence that suggests it literally pays to treat employees with the levels of respect and solicitude normally reserved for external customers.

Work-life effectiveness describes a human capital strategy that centers on creative, customized ways of partnering with employees to become continually more effective (successful) both at work and at home, as a powerful catalyst for engagement and retention. It is grounded in the reality that everyone who works is simultaneously juggling at least two agendas, one personal and one professional or job-related. It recognizes that business and personal success are interconnected and do not automatically operate to the exclusion or detriment of each other. (Truly successful people, in fact, are often successful across several domains of life, and are great assets to their employer as well as their family and community. The opposite is equally true—successful companies provide valuable rewards to and enrich the lives of employees, families, and the communities in which they operate.) Work-life effectiveness is based on this exchange relationship (see Figure 9.1), a unique reciprocity of respect and support between employees and their employer. According to this strategic view of the workforce, the more success employees achieve in both the public and private domains of life, the more discretionary energy they will generate and devote to both, thus maximizing positive business as well as personal outcomes.

The employer's work-life portfolio encompasses a broad array of programs, policies, resources, and leadership practices that respect the "whole person"—an employee who functions simultaneously in multiple roles—as a contributor in the workplace, within a family (however personally defined), and in the community that the employee and employer both draw on for sustenance and resources. Overt acknowledgment of the importance of these multiple roles in the development of overall competence is highly motivating. It is therefore not a trivial pursuit, but as good for business as it is for the individual. As Ann Crittenden says,[8] leadership begins at home. Parents are generally better workers because of the transfer of skills from one domain to the other: emotional intelligence, persuasion, coordination, patience, teaching, organization, caring, teamwork, networking, community involvement, communication, and so on. The same is true for the amateur musicians, artists, cooks, writers, speakers, athletes, paramedics, and politicians who comprise the workforce because their talents and skills (many of which are the same as those of parents) can also be pressed into service for many corporate purposes. None of these "extra" or personal life contributions appear in the typical job description, but they nonetheless define who someone is and what they bring to the workplace in a more holistic, rewarding, enriching, fun, human, and therefore satisfying way.

Thus, it is the central premise of work-life effectiveness that the simple act of respecting people for *who they are* in the context of their entire life, in addition to *what they do* or *produce* for the organization that employs them, is a necessary

Figure 9.1
The Exchange Relationship in Work-Life Effectiveness.

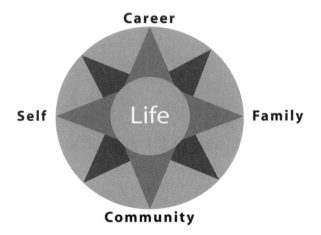

response to the new realities of the twenty-first century marketplace. It is the work-life field's contention that the organizational consequences of doing so are beneficial to *all* stakeholders—employers, employees, customers/clients, shareholders, families, and communities. Furthermore, these positive outcomes are measurable, using a combination of quantitative and qualitative techniques.

ORGANIZATIONAL SUPPORT FOR WORK-LIFE EFFECTIVENESS

So what does this new type of collaboration between employers and employees to optimize business and personal outcomes look like organizationally? Over the past several decades, organizational support for work-life effectiveness has clustered into seven major categories, each defined by a robust suite of responses that weave together a number of related policies, programs, and practices. What differentiates work-life responses from other aspects of people strategy is their anchor point at the intersection between the worker, his or her family, the community, and the workplace.

- Caring for dependents (policies and services for reconciling family obligations and employment)
- Creative uses of paid and unpaid time off
- Proactive approaches to health and wellness
- Workplace flexibility
- Financial support
- Community involvement—internal (caring for each other as a community) and outreach to the external community
- Managing cultural challenges

Each employer takes a somewhat different approach to addressing one or more of these work-life issues, based on the composition and needs of its workforce and clients, its business model and organizational culture. This is what makes being a work-life professional so endlessly fascinating and challenging.

THE WORK-LIFE PORTFOLIO

Each category has been shown by empirical evidence to provide differential returns on investment over different timeframes. But research also demonstrates that the power of the whole is greater than the sum of the parts. That is, as employees use more and more work-life options across multiple categories in response to the numerous and predictable work-life conflicts encountered in the course of a typical career, the greater the benefits that can be documented for the business, workforce, and other key stakeholders, such as clients and shareholders, families, and communities. (See *Categories of Work-Life Effectiveness: Successfully Evolving Your Organization's Work-Life Portfolio,* at www.awlp.org.)

It is also becoming clear that the categories are not linear, but powerfully interact with each other. For example, workplace flexibility is increasingly shown to exert a positive impact on health outcomes, and should therefore be widely regarded as an important part of the tools that HR has at its disposal to combat the rise in health care costs.

It should be noted that not all of these programs, policies, and practices typically reside in one neatly organized and appropriately resourced department or function. Nor does the work-life professional independently "own" much of the terrain in which she or he operates. The work-life function is therefore a highly collaborative endeavor that helps connect the dots between many other human resources efforts. At its best, it serves as a catalyst that helps drive the organization to measurably superior outcomes, such as maximizing employee engagement.

Category #1: Caring for Dependents (Children and Aging Parents)

This category of support encompasses policies and services that are designed to reconcile parenthood, other unpaid care giving, and employment, for men as well as women.

Prior to the mid-1980s, even though work-life titles didn't exist within employer organizations, in some large corporations, someone had been assigned the responsibility for investigating child care issues and solutions, in response to the large influx of women into the workplace over the preceding decade. The phrase *work and family* was in vogue, given the preoccupation with the very first work-family issue: Who was going to take care of the children of the rising tide of working mothers?

So the first work-life practitioners were (or became) child care experts: early education or child development specialists, teachers, or other caregivers who focused on children or childhood. Accordingly, one of the first work-life services made widely available to employers was childcare resource and referral, developed originally for

IBM in 1983 by Boston-based Work Family Directions (now WFD Consulting). Not long after, to help address the mounting pressures on what has become known as the *sandwiched generation*, this core service was augmented with support for elder care resource and referral. To this day, the work-life practitioner is often expert in a variety of dependent care issues and responses, including the ability to design and interpret dependent care needs assessments—skills and core competencies that continue to differentiate him/her from other HR specialists.

Business Impact

- A wide array of child care benefits enhanced retention at 94 percent of companies offering them;[9] on-site child care enhanced retention and performance among knowledge and service workers;[10] backup child care services for well children saved one company 6,900 work days in one year, and netted a return on investment of 115 percent and a net savings after expenses of $803,000.[11]
- Employees of Bristol Myers Squibb report having better relationships with their supervisors and feeling more positive about company policies as a result of being users of the on-site child care centers (Sloan Work and Family Research Network Newsletter, Winter 2004).
- A 2003 study by Circadian Technologies[12] found that when child care is offered, absenteeism, turnover, and overtime are reduced. Absenteeism costs went down by an average of $300 a year per employee.
- A 2001 General Services Administration[13] study found that child-care subsidies offered to low-income workers helped more than half (55 percent) to better concentrate on work, a fifth (19 percent) experienced lower rates of absenteeism, and 75 percent of recipients felt the subsidy program had improved their job performance.

Category #2: Creative Uses of Paid and Unpaid Time Off

Now that time has become the new currency, finding enough of it to spend with family, on one's self, and in the community is the most fundamental work-life need. This is especially true in the United States, which has no national family policy that supports paid time off for parenting, education, or even being sick. To make matters worse, ours tends to be a hard-driving workforce that takes perverse pride in not taking all of our allocated vacation time.

Some of the more innovative policies in this category include paid family leave for new fathers as well as mothers, sabbaticals, paid or release time for community service, responsive shift-work policies, paid time off (PTO) leave banks, extreme travel compensatory time, and after-hours email policies.

Given the prevalence of overwork and stress cited earlier in this chapter, the business advantages of providing (and enforcing) adequate time off for a variety of needs requires more attention.

Business Impact

- A 2000 study by the Radcliffe Public Policy Center[14] surveyed 1,008 male workers between the ages of 20 and 39 who reported that spending more time with their families was more important to them than challenging work or earning a high salary. In fact, 70 percent of respondents indicated that they would be willing to give up some pay in exchange for more family time.

- Aetna's extended maternity leave for new mothers resulted in an annual savings of approximately $1 million.[15]
- A cross-industry study by WFD Consulting demonstrated that managers who work more than 60 hours a week are not more committed to their organizations than those who work only 45 hours. But there was one significant difference. The group working over 60 hours experienced a 230 percent increase in burnout.[16]
- At a 24-hour command center of a pharmaceutical company, the staff monitoring a hazardous manufacturing process developed a schedule with more concentrated time off for each of the 30 individuals directly involved. After two years, the group had eliminated seven shifts, reduced error rates and overtime, and reduced shutdown time, in spite of an increase in the number of monitoring "hot spots" from 10,000 to 20,000 during the same timeframe. Productivity increased and the center became a magnet for transfers and new hires, given the availability of regular and predictable time off.[17]

Category #3: Proactive Approaches to Health and Well-Being

Reduction of stress is the central promise of work-life effectiveness. Since the negative impact of stress-related illness has been shown to eclipse the combined annual profits of the Fortune 100 companies,[18] a focus on this category of work-life support holds the most promise of contributing to the reduction in the escalating cost of health care. The work-life practitioner adds distinctive value because of a focus on the family and knowledge of family systems theory. Today, many employers are trying to encourage individual employees to engage in behavioral change that includes healthier options. Most of this is done with (or to) the employee at the workplace, with minimal attention paid to the influence of the family or significant others. However, if the major influencers in any individual's life are not also changing their habits, the employee doesn't stand much chance of sustaining their own behavior change.

Work-life professionals knowledgeable about family systems theory recognize that weight loss, smoking cessation, and other programs that involve the employee at the work site only are less effective than those that involve the spouse and other family members. When the employee goes home every night to a system that doesn't support his or her best intentions, the recidivism rate is high. Efforts to achieve the same goals through a work-life lens would incorporate the family, either through on-site health fairs, intervention programs that include/train the spouse as well as the employee, or even just mailing work-life-health information home so the whole family can consume it. The important family involvement in annual benefit selection decisions is often prohibited by corporate computer registration systems.

The return on investment in employee health and well-being may take somewhat longer to accrue than the implementation of several other categories of work-life support (i.e., child care and workplace flexibility), but it is powerful when it does kick in. It is important to note how many aspects of the work environment impact wellness, including the presence or absence of respect (as perceived by employees).

Business Impact

- A long-term evaluation of the financial and health impact of a large-scale corporate health and wellness program at Johnson & Johnson showed that participating employees had significantly lower medical expenses and achieved overall improvements in several health risk categories. The reduction in medical care costs averaged $225 per employee, resulting in an overall savings of $8.5 million annually.[19]
- As the result of a workplace health promotion effort, DuPont experienced a 14 percent decline in days lost to disability claims over a two-year period. The resulting savings offset the program's cost during the first year, and resulted in an overall return of $2.05 for every dollar invested.[20]
- A 2003 study of hospital workers in Finland found "attention to interpersonal treatment" decreased the risk of ill health. Male employees who felt they were treated unfairly were 41 percent more likely to take sick leave, and women who felt likewise were 12 percent more likely to take sick leave than those who felt respected.[21]

Category #4: Community Involvement

This is one domain where employers' and employees' interests are spontaneously in close alignment, since both the labor force and in most cases customers come from the community in which the organization operates. Corporate social responsibility is expanding to include not only new types of external community outreach but also a renewed internal focus on building a strong internal sense of community. Formal ethics programs, shared (or catastrophic) leave banks, and disaster relief funds are some of the creative ways of taking care of each other.

Business Impact

- In an internal study at General Mills, supervisors reported an improvement in teamwork and other interpersonal skills for employees who participated in the company's volunteer program.[22]
- According to a 2002 DePaul University study, socially responsible companies had more than a 10 percent higher sales, profit, and return on equity growth than companies not on the list of 100 Best Corporate Citizens of 2001.[23]
- A 1997 NYU Stern School of Business study of 216 socially responsible companies revealed that Fortune 500 companies with a good reputation are more profitable and enjoy higher stock prices.[24]

Category #5: Financial Support (Self and Family)

Providing financially for oneself and family from career entry through retirement is basic to work-life effectiveness. In this arena, benefits, compensation, and work-life professionals collaborate closely to create nontraditional policies where appropriate and find compelling ways to communicate the value of financial offerings. Some examples of programs and services of value to employees today include personal financial planning, adoption reimbursement, dependent and health care flexible spending accounts, discounted pet/auto/home insurance, mortgage assistance, group discounts on a variety of retail products, and workplace convenience services (dry cleaning, parking lot oil changes, etc.).

Business Impact

- CF Industries (a Long Grove, Illinois, manufacturer) has been offering financial planning classes and counseling for many years. They have found that employees who gain the ability to make personal financial choices are more productive, have a greater sense of ownership, and engage in minimal absenteeism.[25]
- While there is less empirical, publicly accessible research available here, work-life practitioners have much internal qualitative (anecdotal) evidence from employees who express gratitude and loyalty for such supports as adoption assistance and corporate-provided discounts on everything from cars to diamonds to clothing.

Category #6: Workplace Flexibility

Workplace flexibility refers to a leadership practice that facilitates the customization over when, where, and how work gets done by individuals and teams. This practice has been empirically shown to increase engagement, retention, productivity, and even wellness and is thus the keystone of the work-life portfolio. It is grounded in a business strategy that connects flexible management practices with the need to achieve the levels of speed, nimbleness, innovation, flexibility, and creativity increasingly demanded by customers in the twenty-first century.

Workplace flexibility holds the promise of creating an ideal work environment characterized by quick and efficient decision making, short cycle times, high levels of employee engagement and empowerment, flexible leadership and management practices, high-performance teams, and individual contributors that work well from anywhere in response to market demands. Thus, its implementation has as much impact on business outcomes as it does on the quality of life of employees.

Flexibility practices are proving to be the most powerful motivator in the work-life effectiveness portfolio, in large part because they fulfill a psychological need for what Robert Karasek[26] (specialist in the psychosocial aspects of work and work redesign processes) describes as *job autonomy*—an optimal sense of control over one's job and working conditions. Karasek's research has shown that job control lowers stress and even health risks while increasing job performance. This is shaping up to be the next frontier in management training—helping supervisors learn how to optimize the level of job control for teams and/or individuals in order to increase engagement.

There are many tools and approaches employed to enhance workplace flexibility, including flexible career strategies, flexible benefit options, management flexibility training, flexible work scheduling, and work redesign that streamlines essential processes and continually identifies and eliminates low-value work as an antidote to overwork—the nemesis of workplace flexibility.

In summary, workplace flexibility is a complex strategy that often gets confused with the tools that support it, especially flexible scheduling. Despite its advantages, opposition to flexibility is so deeply rooted in core beliefs about the nature of people and of work that it has become both the power tool and the conundrum of the work-life portfolio. Here is the dilemma: Flexibility is one of the most powerful drivers of retention and engagement today. It has no fixed cost. It is the work-life initiative most sought by employees (especially top performers). It is empirically linked to higher levels of productivity, resilience, and shareholder value. It is ubiquitous among "employers of choice," who are significantly more profitable than their less flexible peer group. Hundreds (if not thousands) of companies have policies and tools to support it. It continues to be the most popular topic at national work-life conferences and in the media.

Yet achieving workplace flexibility is the most difficult task the work-life professional and his or her employer mutually embarks upon, because success often requires an organization to reinvent its entire culture. The catch? It can only take root where trust and respect for the whole person are in abundant supply.

There is far more empirical evidence for this pillar of the work-life portfolio than for any other. The most robust, current evidence is contained in a November 2005 report issued by Corporate Voice for Working Families, researched by WFD Consulting and sponsored by the Alfred P. Sloan Foundation, titled *Business Impacts of Flexibility: An Imperative for Expansion.*[27] It draws on internal organizational research provided by 29 household name American companies. It also serves a primer for guidance about how to create a flexible work environment. Here are a few of the quantifiable business impacts cited in the study.

Retention

- Accenture's work-life survey showed 80 percent of employees said work-life effectiveness impacted their intention to stay.
- Deloitte calculates it saved $41.5 million in turnover costs in one year alone (2003). Additionally, retention of women in the pipeline to partnership via flexibility practices has helped increase the number of women in leadership from 14 to 168 over the past decade.

Commitment

- Deloitte's employees who agreed they have the flexibility they need scored 32 percent higher in commitment than employees who did not have adequate flexibility.
- AstraZeneca's survey findings echo Deloitte's, with commitment scores 28 percent higher for employees who have they flexibility they need.
- 95 percent of employees working for a manager sensitive to the need for flexibility are motivated to go the extra mile, versus 80 percent of employees with less supportive managers.

Reducing the Impact of Stress

- Bristol Myers Squibb employees on flexible work arrangement 30 percent lower in stress and burnout.

- An unidentified financial services company participating in the study reported that employees who have the control they need over their work schedules had burnout index scores less than half that of their out-of-control colleagues.

Financial Performance/Business Outcomes

- First Tennessee Bank branches with flexibility practices experienced 50 percent higher employee retention, 7 percent higher customer retention, and $106 million more profit over two years than branches without flexibility practices.
- Ernst and Young found that adequate flexibility is predictive of revenue per person. Business units scoring in the highest quartile of commitment scores had 20 percent higher revenue per person than business units in the lowest quartile, leading to the conclusion that flexibility is an important driver of performance and thus of financial results.
- Marriott experienced greater productivity by managers given more flexibility, even though the managers worked fewer hours. An analysis of pilot data indicated that this gain was largely achieved by eliminating low-value work. An additional bonus was that stress and turnover decreased among participating managers.
- Three specific cycle time improvements were logged at a PNC bank operations center during a seven-month compressed work week pilot program, at the same time customer service was enhanced. Absenteeism dropped to 9 days from 60. Turnover also decreased among the pilot group, resulting in savings estimated to approximate $100,000.

The ultimate standard that defines an enduring business practice is its ability to create economic value. The evidence for flexibility's prowess in this regard comes from several sources, one of which is reflected in Watson Wyatt's Human Capital Index research, which has established the link between superior human capital management and equally superior shareholder value. Excellence in five key human resources areas is associated with a definable increase in bottom line performance. One of these clusters is labeled "Collegial, Flexible Workplace," which centers on management practices and support for flexible work arrangements and the concomitant trust and shared values that are required for successful implementation. This cluster of eight specific human capital practices creates 9 percent of shareholder value, of which company support for flexible work options alone contributes 3.5 percent, which stands out as the one behavior in the cluster that is pulling most of the weight.

MANAGING CULTURAL CHALLENGES

If the benefits of providing support for any one of the major work-life challenges that employees encounter are measurably positive (not to mention the multiplier effect of implementing all of them), why doesn't every employer everywhere immediately get on board? After several decades of practice and the accumulation of more and more empirical evidence and demonstrated value, why does so much resistance persist to this particular aspect of managing human capital?

The answer lies deeply rooted in cultural norms—both corporate culture and the American culture. Thanks to the work of Bob Drago, Sandy Burud, and Marie

Tomolo, the mystery of why otherwise rational senior leaders are capable of turning their backs on even the most financially sound work-life business case is more comprehensible. Something else exerts a far more compelling influence than logic and numbers, in contrast to leadership behavior in response to most other workplace issues. In fact, creating organization-wide support for work-life effectiveness is often so complex and difficult an undertaking as to require strong leadership in culture change management.

According to Bob Drago,[28] three cultural norms govern our expectations of behavior. Norms run deep, are shared throughout the entire society, are not generally discussable, and help us make sense of new things and reach decisions about them. They carry penalties when they are violated. Unfortunately, these particular norms directly clash with the entire premise of work-life effectiveness.

1. *Motherhood norm*, which is the belief that women should be mothers and care takers for no or low pay.
2. *Ideal worker norm*, which is the belief in total commitment to career, with commensurate rewards (unless you are in violation of the first norm).
3. *Individualism norm*, which is the belief that the government should not help those needing care.

The impact of these norms is profound. "Our economy and society are rigged to create imbalance," says Drago. He explains how the three norms interact to create what we know to be a gender gap, but with a twist: The "new" gender gap he perceives is between those who care (i.e., engage in unpaid care for others) and those who succeed (i.e., work for pay). Because there is no government support for people who don't work, it comes as no surprise that women make up more than 60 percent of adults living in poverty. Poverty, Drago reminds us, "is often a result of caring for children, disabled adults, and elderly relatives."[29]

Enter the work-life professional into the typical boardroom (of ideal worker executives) to present the killer business case for supporting a specific work-life challenge of the dual-focus worker, a group that might include a preponderance of women. As any seasoned work-life professional who has been in that boardroom can testify, the outcome can be unpredictable, and the proceedings are guaranteed to differ significantly from a discussion about spending an equivalent amount of money on the purchase of a new software package.

Sandy Burud (former president of Alliance for Work-Life Progress) throws into the cultural mix three more spanners, based on extensive interviewing of senior executives about why they do or do not buy into the work-life perspective:

- The belief that workers are not motivated to work hard on their own; rather, they wind down like mechanical clocks; their natural state is inactivity (laziness).
- The belief that business is a competitive, masculine activity in which one party wins and the other must lose; it's basically a zero-sum game.

- The belief that work is not intrinsically engaging or rewarding; it takes a lot of energy and external incentive and pressure to get people to do it.

Needless to say, even if Drago and Burud are only half right about the number and nature of the norms they describe, they have shed light on why it is that the work-life practitioner fights the good fight primarily alone and at one company at a time. In order to combat these very real barriers to the full engagement and productivity of every contributor in the workforce, it is usually necessary to engage in specific culture change interventions to eliminate inequities. Thus, there is a strong link between work-life effectiveness, diversity initiatives, women's advancement, mentoring, and networking.

THE ROLE OF THE WORK-LIFE PROFESSIONAL

"They say that time changes things, but you actually have to change them yourself."
—Andy Warhol

The work-life professional's unique contribution is to create the overarching and effective work-life strategy, build the architecture, expand and manage the dynamic and ever-changing work-life portfolio, and assess the impact on all of these stakeholders. Since work-life is never a stand-alone function, its practitioners seldom have strong position authority, and the pillars usually have little correspondence to governance structure, the work-life practitioner must work effectively with and through all other HR functions within the organization. Therefore, power of persuasion, passion, the ability to create cogent business cases on demand, tact and diplomacy, and a sense of humor are essential characteristics of the job.

Given the broad and expanding charter, the role of the twenty-first-century work-life professional is dynamic, fun, diverse, somewhat risky, and challenging. For example, the implementation of workplace flexibility inevitably causes friction with existing cultural norms, since very few organizations were designed from inception to be flexible in all aspects of people strategy, leadership philosophy, process, and technology. Since flexibility keeps proving itself to be a vital link between business strategy and engagement of the workforce, the most seasoned work-life practitioners have learned firsthand that the primary value they add is as change agent. This role serves to differentiate them from some of their other colleagues in HR, who historically have been more focused on issues of compliance and risk avoidance.

Amplifying work done by the Boston College Center for Work and Family to define the competencies required for success as a work-life professional, these are some of the key elements:

- Change agent: Understanding the culture change process and how to manage it in an organizational context.
- Business acumen.
- Organizational savvy.

- Relationship building: mediation skills, networking, diplomacy.
- Strategic diagnosis and action planning: ability to paint a vision of the future that others can see and actualize.
- Technical knowledge of more than one category of the work-life portfolio.
- Analytical skills: measurement of effectiveness across different domains; specialized needs assessments.
- Exceptional communication skills (verbal, written, platform): persuasiveness; ability to influence key decision makers; work effectively with managers at all levels; spell-binding storytelling.
- Courage! Willingness to take risks and lead the charge to a better future.

CONCLUSION

This chapter has documented that treating people with respect for the juggling act they conduct on a daily basis literally pays. Commensurate with the growing recognition of its beneficial impact on business outcomes, work-life effectiveness should be appreciated as no mere repackaging of benefit offerings, but understood for what it is—a major restructuring of the employment deal in alignment with the new realities of the workplace. And does it mean business? According to the Great Place to Work Institute,[30] the *Fortune* companies recognized as great places to work enjoyed three to four *times* the stock value of their peer companies.

NOTES

1. Jay R. Schuster, and Patricia K. Zingheim, *The New Pay* (San Francisco: Jossey-Bass, 1992).

2. Wayne Cascio, SHRM data presented during a general session titled "The New Human Capital Equation" at the Conference Board/Families and Work Institute annual work-life conference, June 2006, New York City.

3. Families and Work Institute, *National Study of the Changing Workforce* (1997, 2002), www.familiesandwork.org.

4. Ellen Galinsky James T. Bond, Stacy S. Kim, Lois Backon, Erin Brownfield, and Kelly Sakai, *Overwork in America: When the Way We Work Becomes Too Much* (2005) http://familiesandwork.org/site/research/summary/overwork2005summ.pdf.

5. Juliet B. Schor, *The Overworked American: The Unexpected Decline of Leisure* (New York: Basic Books, 1991).

6. Harvey A. Thompson and Beatrice A. Fitzpatrick, *Flexible Work Arrangements: A Productivity Triple Play* (New York: BOLD Initiative, 2006).

7. Sandra Burud and Marie Tumolo, *Leveraging the New Human Capital: Adaptive Strategies, Results Achieved, and Stories of Transformation* (Mountain View, CA: Davies-Black Publishing, 2004).

8. Ann Crittenden, *If You've Raised Kids, You Can Manage Anything* (New York: Gotham Books, 2004).

9. A. G. Dawson, C. S. Mikel, C. S. Lorenz, and J. King, "An Experimental Study of the Effects of Employer-Sponsored Child Care Services on Selected Employee Behaviors,"

Foundation for Human Service Studies and CSR (1984), cited in Sandra Burud and Marie Tumolo, *Leveraging the New Human Capital* (Mountain View, CA: Davies-Black Publishing, 2004).

10. Sandra Burud, "Child Care Analysis for Bank: Executive Summary and Key Findings," 2000, unpublished paper, cited in Burud and Tumolo, *Leveraging the New Human Capital*.

11. Dana Friedman, *ROI: Making the Case for Chase with Arithmetic* (Watertown, MA: Bright Horizons, 1998), cited in Burud and Tumolo, *Leveraging the New Human Capital*, p. 368.

12. Circadian Technologies, *Cost Benefits of Child Care for Extended Hours Operation* (2002), cited in Work and Family Connection's December 2003 Report, *The Most Important Work-Life-Related Studies*.

13. General Services Administration, study findings published in the *Washington Post* (August 13, 2001), cited in Work and Family Connection, *The Most Important Work-Life-Related Studies*.

14. Radcliffe Public Policy Center, *Life's Work: Generational Attitudes Toward Work and Life Integration*, *Washington Post Online* (May 3, 2000), cited in Work and Family Connection, *The Most Important Work-Life-Related Studies*.

15. Burud and Tumolo, *Leveraging the New Human Capital*.

16. Sharon Lobel, in John De Graaf, ed., *Take Back Your Time* (San Francisco: Berrett-Koehler Publishers, 2003).

17. Ibid.

18. American Stress Institute. Most recently published in a Corporate Voice for Working Families Report, *Business Impacts of Flexibility: An Imperative for Expansion* (November 2005), p. 14, researched by WFD Consulting; http://www.cvworkingfamilies.org/flex_report/flex_report.shtml. This report draws on internal organizational research provided by 29 household name American companies.

19. Work and Family Connection, *The Most Important Work-Life-Related Studies*.

20. Ibid.

21. Ibid.

22. Ibid.

23. Ibid.

24. Ibid.

25. Ibid.

26. www.robert-karasek.com. Professor Karasek, now teaching at the University of Massachusetts Lowell, Department of Work Environment, is known for his job demand control model, the leading model in the field of work stress. He began researching this aspect of stress and its connection to wellness in the 1970s. Central to the model is the interaction between job demands and job control. Low job control in combination with high job demands brings on psychological and physical stress with various negative outcomes. The reverse situation (high demands and high control) results in well-being, learning, peak performance, and so on. All work-life needs assessments, beginning with and led by the Families and Work Institute, employ job demand/stress scales that come from Karasek's work. As a result, FWI's research (especially the National Study of the Changing Workforce, which now has 25 years' worth of longitudinal data) isolates job autonomy as one key element that defines the most effective work environments. Work-life research has empirically defined the major characteristics of an "effective work environment." Flexibility practices are a way of instituting job autonomy/control in high-demand/performance environments. One outcome when companies get this combo right is more engaged, healthier employees. Employers everywhere are scratching their heads, wondering why health care costs keep rising and rising and little is working to reverse

this trend, while the key is in their hands and it has no direct cost associated with it. See the interview with Karasek by the Research Institute for Psychology and Health, Utrecht University, the Netherlands, for the whole story about Karasek's career and the highlights about how all of these workplace elements intertwine: http://www.fss.uu.nl/penh/karasek.htm.

27. Work and Family Connection, *The Most Important Work-Life-Related Studies*.

28. Robert W. Drago, *Striking a Balance: Work, Family, Life* (Boston: Dollars & Sense, Economic Affairs Bureau, 2007).

29. Ibid.

30. Great Place to Work Institute, press release (February 15, 2005), www.greatplacetowork.com.

Chapter 10

Coaching for High Potentials to Become High-Performing Leaders*

Duncan Mathison

The biography of a great leader can be fascinating. When we witness the results of their leadership, creating new industries, facing down threats, galvanizing people to act together for a great enterprise, we want to understand how that great leader came to be. Was she born or made a leader? Is his ability to lead hard-wired into his personality? Was it the parenting? What childhood experience created the adult visionary? We believe if we could dissect and understand what creates a great leader we might replicate the success. (At the very least, maybe we could pick them out at the graduating class and put them into our management training programs.)

Born or made? It really doesn't make any difference because, let's be honest, no matter how they happen, we need more great leaders. There will never be enough top-quality leaders to go around. In fact, the shift of labor market demographics driven by retiring Baby Boomers clearly suggests there will be a shortage of even mediocre leaders. Organizations who understand this fact will quickly realize that investing today to both build as well as find leadership capability for tomorrow is not a luxury but a critical strategic imperative.

This can be a tough pill to swallow in an environment where quarterly results overshadow longer-term concerns and investments. There will always be the temptation to invest in hiring more people than invest in developing the people we have. That takes more time. But develop we must. Because developing people is an expensive proposition, whether it is through purposeful identification of "high-potential" employees and targeted leadership development efforts or the *really* expensive school

---

*Copyright © 2007 by Duncan Mathison.

of hard knocks. Just because you don't have a leadership development program doesn't mean you are not paying for it. The cost is there—in lost productivity, unwanted turnover, failed initiatives, and bad decisions. We need people to learn. And not from failure.

Developing good leaders has been shown to have significant return on investment. Although many think in terms of the potential damage a poor leader can do to the organization, it is more significant to note that the top 20 percent of executives in companies account for twice the profits and 40 percent less employee turnover when compared with the middle performing 80 percent. Increasing the effectiveness of the top half of your middle 80 percent of leaders has huge implications. Yet often development efforts fail to target the right population, dilute their focus, and miss the point. As a result, budgets for leadership development are pushed aside by merit raises, bonus plans, recruiting ad campaigns, and new cafeterias that appear to have a greater return on investment.

In today's global "flat" business environment, with lower barriers to technology, capital, markets, and talent, the only true competitive advantage resides in superior leadership to make better decisions as well as build and inspire a more effective workforce. If those of us responsible for organization performance can focus our efforts on those leaders with the greatest potential and invest in a development strategy that is highly focused and really builds leadership capability based on what we already know works (and avoid the common pitfalls), we will be able to realize the true potential of our organization's talent.

BUY THEM OR GROW THEM?

How often have we heard the story where the CEO wants a strong leader to take an operation to the "next level?" After a survey of the internal talent pool, the executive committee concludes that the talent does not exist inside the organization, or it cannot afford to take talent away from other functioning operations. So the CEO makes what seems to be a safe decision and seeks someone from the outside with a "proven track record," who had already done it before in another organization, even with a fierce competitor. Based on the hiring criteria to find an outsider, with the outsider perspective and the outsider experience, the offer is made with great anticipation by all parties. But after about 9 months, questions begin to surface about fit and style issues and after 18 months, when the leader fails to galvanize the promised business results, serious discussions about seeking a replacement begin. When asked what went wrong, the CEO cites examples of arrogant attitudes, political missteps, and missed opportunities.

Sometimes there is no choice but to bring in outside leadership talent. There are times when the transformational leap that an organization must make requires talent that has a clear vision and capability that may not exist internally. Yet like experimental organ transplants, the rejection rate of new leadership hires is staggering. Some estimates place the failure rate north of 40 percent with early signs of failure within the first 90 days. When recruiting top executive talent, it is not uncommon to spend more than a half million dollars with recruiting fees, relocation costs (including the buying and selling of homes), hiring bonuses, and more. It is also common for new outside leaders to bring in their own people, resulting in even more recruiting and on-boarding costs. Then, when the leader fails, the prenegotiated separation package must be paid and the revolving door of outside talent spins again, quickly adding up to millions of dollars in costs with no discernible outcome.

Why do they really fail? Why do they get "rejected?" Some suggest it is culture. Some suggest it is a matter of bad hiring technique. In reality, it's both. It's the common failure to appreciate how essential it is for leaders to be native in the culture—no matter what the culture is. Effective leadership includes the ability to understand and interact with how a particular organization works—its systems, its processes, and most important, its social networks. Truly effective leadership is about the ability to lead people in *your* organization.

It is inevitable that any organization will need new leadership sometime in the future. New leaders will be needed to replace those who depart, or to support growth or to be deployed when addressing significant threats and opportunities faced by the organization. Therefore, organizations will eventually have to pay to acquire leadership talent. So why do we so commonly turn to outside talent, for which we pay a premium and for which we should realistically have such low expectations of success? It is far better to invest first in the people we have. Not *all* the people, necessarily, but the people who are now in leadership roles and in those who possess the highest potential to become tomorrow's leaders.

So the questions we need to ask are not, "Who are these people and where are they out in the world?" but rather, "Who are these people? How do we find them within our organization? What is the most efficient way to develop them?"

DEVELOPING LEADERSHIP SKILLS IS DIFFERENT THAN OTHER SKILL DEVELOPMENT

Today's managers in their late 30s or early 40s might possess anywhere between 16 to 18 years of formal education. Add to that to an average of 10 to 15 years in a specific industry, and it can be said that they are subject matter experts in their function and industry. They have acquired most of the knowledge they need to do their jobs. They understand the problems and challenges. They may even know—quite accurately—what needs to be done to address those problems and challenges. But being skilled leaders takes real leadership experience, not just classroom training.

If we were to use a sports analogy, this type of knowledge might be called the *rules of a game*—a game that could be taught by an inspiring instructor in a classroom with some quality game reviews thrown in. After such training, we would know the boundaries of the playing field. We would know what constitutes a goal and how to keep score. We might even learn a playbook along with a few basic skills, all from an instructional approach. But we would never get good at playing the sport without being on the field, where we can be observed, coached, and allowed to build confidence through real experience. In fact, we would at best become much like a rabid sports fan—experts on the sport, deeply knowledgeable on every nuance of the game, but as players never competitive ourselves. We see this type of capability in our organizations today. Stand by the water cooler. Every organization is full of rabid sports fans discussing who is the first draft pick among the high potential leaders in your organization.

What makes a great leader is the same thing that makes a great athlete. It is the raw material of potential talent, tested on the field when winning truly counts. They are given feedback about what they are doing right as well as what they need to improve. They are challenged intellectually and emotionally to move beyond their comfort zone. They work with someone who understands how they learn, as well as what motivates them. Someone who is a true partner vested in their success who will have in-depth discussions with them about how they can approach challenges differently and seize opportunity.

When great leaders are asked, "How did you learn how to be as good as you are?" the answer is quite consistent. They talk about crucible experiences, when there was a lot at stake and their performance was key to success. They talk about having a guide that gave them valuable insight at the right time. They talk about moments of truth, where they learned about who they are, and what it is about themselves that others respond to. They talk about times when they truly saw what they did or said that caused people to perform or turn away.

These most effective leaders rarely point to leadership seminars they attended. They don't talk about management retreats. They don't talk about the classroom or online training they received. But they are intellectually bright and demonstrate an ability to be curious enough to learn from many different and unexpected sources and apply what they learn to the challenges at hand.

If we truly want to develop the kind of leaders who will inspire others, make better decisions, and bring the best out in our organization's human capital, we must create a more workable approach. It has to be more efficient, accessible, and customized to both the needs of the executive as well as the demands of the organization. Finally, it must be targeted to the right people. Once we think we have those people, we must provide four key ingredients that have been regularly linked to executive development.

1. **Awareness:** Provide assessment and feedback to help them understand who they are and how they operate today.
2. **Analysis:** Identify their developmental gaps in the context of specific business leader challenges they are facing in their current and next role.
3. **Action:** Place them in challenging "crucible" developmental situations, tied to the organization's success. Provide them with focused coaching to help them integrate their experience, their potential, and their learning into new, more effective actions as leaders.
4. **Achievement:** Assess their degree of achievement in three areas. The ability to (1) meet developmental goals, (2) apply new capabilities to influence critical business metrics, and (3) improve their readiness to advance to the next level.

The goal with this approach is to provide the executive with deep insights into who they are and develop those capabilities needed that will specifically help them meet the business challenges they face. Sustainable change comes about only when the executive actually experiences the direct payoff from their efforts to improve as leaders.

To facilitate this transformative process, a coach plays a critical role converting potential for talent into sustained performance through a collaborative effort with the executive. Good executive coaches naturally work within the framework of what has been demonstrated repeatedly as the key drivers of effective leadership development. Individual executive coaching is unique compared with other broader brush developmental approaches because the coach begins with the leader as they currently are—accomplished, smart, and capable high performers—and helps them become more effective leaders using today's crucibles that demand real business results.

The challenge, of course, is to find the right employee who has the true high potential to be a leader and then pair them with the right coach.

WHO ARE THE HIGH-POTENTIAL LEADERS?

High potentials are employees who have the ability to become leaders in your organization if they are given the right opportunity, development, and support. They may be not quite ready for the next level of leadership today, but in time, with development, they will be. High potentials are almost always high performers in their current jobs and are regularly promoted to higher levels of responsibility. This pattern of promotion continues, as it has been so often observed, until the person is no longer viewed as a high performer (a phenomenon commonly known as the Peter Principle). In other words, they are promoted into management and leadership roles until the roles are more demanding than their capabilities.

Consequently, high potentials may be high performers, but not all high performers are high potentials. In fact it appears that among the very best of any organization's top performers, only about 30 percent could be considered as having leadership potential at the next level of responsibility.

Therefore, if we seek to develop and promote from our pool of high performers, there is a 70 percent chance we will choose the wrong person. The confusion between high performers and high potentials, plus the tendency to promote people beyond their capability, often contributes to disappointment in leadership development efforts in organizations.

Assuming that choosing the right people from a pool of high performers is important, we need to create a process to help us select the true high potentials from those who are merely high performers. One favored approach is to develop a nine-square model through a dialog with executive management to help management categorize employees into broad groups (see Figure 10.1). On the horizontal axis, employees are grouped by performance that might be, for example, the lowest 10 percent, middle 80 percent, and top 10 percent. On the vertical axis, employees would be distributed based on a number of factors that are *drivers of potential*. Again a forced distribution here is helpful such as a 10 percent–80 percent–10 percent, as it will focus the conversations needed for selection.

Specific factors linked to drivers of potential vary depending on the culture. The important thing is to build a set of factors to guide conversation and ensure that they

Figure 10.1
High Performance Selection Grid.

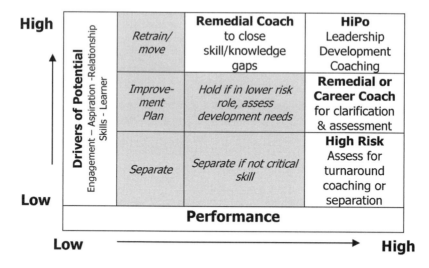

avoid unintended and inappropriate biases. However, the assessment of potential should have a number of descriptors linked to common differentiators between high potentials who are also high performers and those who are merely high performers. These factors can be lumped into four categories worth exploring.

Engagement. The degree to which the employee appears vested in the organization and can be relied upon to represent the values of the organization is the first factor to be considered. There is certainly an emotional quality to this that may be difficult to assess, but it should be evidenced in their day-to-day behavior. For example, the employees might indicate that they believe in the value the organization brings to customers. They might demonstrate their ability to apply the company's mission statement, and organizational values to constructive day-to-day decision making, particularly in ambiguous or novel situations. There is also a rational self-interest component to engagement—the extent to which employees believe it is in their best interest to work with the company to meet personal, career, or lifestyle objectives. If they see the organization as the best place to professionally advance or even meet a personal objective of raising their family in a particular community, employees who believe it is in their best rational interest to stay are more engaged.

Ability to learn and adapt. Being smart is important. But what is more important is the ability to draw lessons from experience and apply those lessons to new situations. In probing for this factor, it is helpful to ask to what degree a high performer looks for lessons from experience and applies those lessons to new situations.

Research has consistently shown that the most effective leaders are complex learners. They will draw from a range of sources, people, and situations to help them understand and adjust to a new challenge. They have inquisitive minds and tend to ask insightful questions to draw out the right solution as opposed to simply applying their own answer. This ability to learn and adapt is a form of street smarts, as opposed to education and credentials. They tend to be excellent observers but more important have the ability to apply the lessons to their own behavior and adapt.

Emotional/relationship skills. A bit more complex than the ability to play well with others, emotional intelligence is the ability to build effective working relationships and is a foundational component of leadership. Many smart, motivated, and talented executives will derail because of weaknesses in this area. A large percentage of turn-around coaching assignments are focused on helping an executive repair and develop relationships with peers, subordinates, and superiors. When assessing for strength in this area, ask to what degree the employee is able to build effective relationships outside of the chain of authority, how well they manage conflict positively, and whether they appear to understand and effectively manage people with diverse backgrounds and agendas.

Aspiration. Do they seek out new opportunities and challenges? Leadership and the work that it requires to get there demands more time and more effort to be successful than staying put in current roles. Having the desire for the added income, benefits, and prestige of expanded leadership roles is an important factor to consider. But ambition can be a misleading factor. An employee can be a high potential without possessing ambition. This may be because they have lower expectations of their own potential or believe it is beyond their grasp. Therefore, insight as to whether their lack of aspiration is because they have difficulty believing it is attainable or if they simply are unwilling to make the investment will be relevant.

This talent review process has many applications, and it can help a leadership team or any individual manager get clarity on the talent assets and gaps of an organization. Understand that these descriptors of potential are discussion guides to placing people on a performance/potential grid. Decide on an appropriate distribution grid to avoid overly generous ratings. Your goal should be to identify a group appropriately sized to fit the development resources and organizational need.

For the purposes of executive development and in particular executive coaching, three, maybe four target groups can be identified. With each group the approach to coaching will be different, the measurement for success will be different, and the expectations for return on investment will be different. It's also important to remember that there are a number of groups for whom we may be tempted to provide coaching but shouldn't for two critical reasons. First, it could be a waste of money as there will be a poor return on investment; second, it could subsequently poison any future efforts to use coaching as a leadership development tool.

Although there are some helpful tools, there is no universal assessment for leadership potential in *your* organization. Each organization and leadership role within the organization has unique needs. Sometimes a customized leadership competency model can be helpful. However discussions will get bogged down in competency assessments as opposed to assessments of potential. It is always better to hold interactive discussions with the leadership using identifiers of potential that fit a specific corporate culture and the language of an executive team. A second, no less critical benefit of these discussions is to engage leadership in the process of thinking through who of your high performers are high potentials in the context of organizational needs. This builds the foundation of support needed to make the decisions necessary to place high potentials in developmental roles. It is also important that the identifiers have been vetted to ensure better clarity and appropriateness to create a benchmark for discussion of individuals. Avoid the unnecessary burden of complex scoring schemes.

WHO SHOULD HAVE A COACH?

Coach Those Who Are the High Performers/High Potential-Driven First

The greatest return on investment will be with the group in the uppermost right quadrant. Members of this group often get passed over for development work because they do not present a management problem and tend to be promoted or passed along in the system quickly. As a result, they often receive very limited thoughtful and critical feedback and development. Often they hear, "You are doing great! Here is your next challenge." This creates a situation where the high performer overdevelops or overrelies on few very core capabilities, such as drive for results, influencing, analytical or technical/functional skills. These are often the foundations of early success but then later derailment as they move to more complex and wider-scope executive roles. But this group, often characterized as high achievers, will often embrace the challenge a coach can bring to them as they realize both their developmental needs and the evolving demands of an executive role.

Coach the High Performers with Moderate Potential Second

The second coaching targets are the high performance, mid–potential-driver employees. This group typically takes thoughtful assessment of the issues surrounding their reduced potential. Their high performance makes them a critical asset. Further, because of their performance, they will have higher expectations for recognition and advancement that may be out of alignment with management's perspective. They may have the credentials, the experience, and job knowledge, but there is concern about the fit to the next level. The issues related to the reduced potential suggest that they run the risk of being seriously derailed in their careers or become highly frustrated with their lack of advancement.

There are two common characteristics that place people in this category. The first characteristic may be ambivalence regarding their career direction caused by lack of focus and aspiration. Career coaching can help people gain greater clarity, and it serves as a means to send a clear message to the employee about their value to the organization while asking them to resolve their ambivalence and take greater ownership of their career. The coaching can also help tease out the issues related to management's view of the individual. Development plans often include management of their image with more senior executives.

The more common developmental need for the high performers with mid-range potential usually grows from their ability to manage ambiguity and operate smoothly across functional lines. They may have overrelied on chain of command or sponsorship by a senior executive to remove barriers and create conditions needed to achieve results. As a result, their developmental needs require a coach to help them build the skills to manage ambiguous situations on their own, operate cross-functionally, and be more politically astute.

Coach the High Potential–Driver/Mid-Performer Third

Those at the top of the potential curve but average on the performance curve are your third most important group to coach. They may have been promoted too quickly, or they are faced with a job that is outgrowing them. Quick intervention is important, as it is unlikely they will improve on their own. Typically, skill gaps are the drivers for the fall-off in performance. Sometimes interpersonal problems are exacerbated when job stress is created by the gap between job demand and capability. A coach is well positioned to help them manage the emotional aspects while they build capability. An example of this is where a VP was in a role for a small company but as the company grew and was acquired, the scale in complexity outgrew the past successful style that was more hands-on. Or, in another example, a longtime operations leader was moved into a site general manager role with greater involvement in the more strategically focused corporate leadership group. While excellent at leading his operation, he lacked the strategic skills to be a high-functioning member of the executive team concerned most about corporate strategy.

High Performers with Low Potential Are High Risk and Can Be Very Poor Investments for Developmental Coaching

High performers with low potential are people most likely to be considered coaching candidates. While often valued for their results, they create a disproportionate level of noise in the organization. They may run roughshod over peers and subordinates in the pursuit of results and might even push cultural or ethical limits within the organization. These employees, particularly in manager roles, can represent a significant risk to the organization, deeply hurt morale, and create significant dysfunction in the organization. As a last-ditch alternative, executive coaching is often thought of as a means to "smooth out" the very rough edges of this problematic employee. But generally, these are not good candidates for coaching. Unfortunately, many employees in this group should be seriously assessed for separation.

Engagement and aspiration provide a rationale for an individual to improve for the sake of their career and the organization. But these employees can lack some of the fundamental characteristics that are the greatest motivators of behavioral change. Ability to learn and adapt is a necessary skill for change. Emotional and relationship skills are a foundation to explore behavioral alternatives. Coaching tends to rely on these motivators for improvement. In their absence, it is more challenging, maybe impossible, to win a high return on the investment in coaching.

There are exceptions, of course. A good coach will look for the right success factors before proceeding with the assignment with this group. To be successful, the coach must help the employee establish the WIIFM (what's in it for me) for sustained behavioral change at the outset of the assignment. This is more likely to happen if the manager is unambiguous about the long-term cost to the employee's career if he or she fails to change.

Because the organizational pain can be significant from this type of individual, coaching often gives peers and subordinates great hope that at last, "something" will be done to improve the coachee's interpersonal or leadership style. The unrealistic expectation that the employee will hear the feedback and immediately respond sets the stage for disappointment and loss of any support for both the employee and the manager (not to mention the coaching process itself).

Some members of this group of high performers with low potential can be helped. But they need clear and unambiguous messaging from their leadership and a coach who has the ability to work with derailed executives.

PICK THE COACH WHO WILL REALLY MAKE A PERFORMANCE DIFFERENCE

Q: How many coaches does it take to change a light bulb?
A: One. But the light bulb really has to want to change.

When viewed at a fundamental level, we think of coaching as one-on-one conversations where the discussion drives behavior change. Yet, as we see in Figure 10.2, others who may have different roles may be involved in such conversations to drive behavior change as well. They may also serve in a coaching type of role and may even call themselves an executive coach. These "helpers" could be a friend, a therapist, a mentor, a spiritual guide, a teacher, a consultant, or a boss. What makes executive development coaching different from other roles is grounded in the intent of the relationship, who is accountable for outcomes, who pays, who is the subject matter expert, and even how the problem is defined.

From one degree to another, all of these helpers have similar strategies in their work. They all have some means to assess and define the current state of the situation. This might include tests or written assessments, surveys, interviews, financial statements, or some kind of metrics. They all have a means to understand the desired state or goal and even a widely varying point of view on how to reach the goal. But, and this is a big *but*, given the same situation, the goal selection may be heavily influenced based on the bias of the helper. For example, the boss will be primarily concerned with the boss's goals. The consultant will be concerned with the goals that fit the consultant's area of expertise. This bias by the helper is not automatically a negative given the situation, but when developing high-potential employees, it can seriously derail the intent of a developmental program geared toward development of future leaders. As one HR executive observed about an internationally known personal development coach, "She has worked with some of our most talented executives, who concluded it was the organization holding them back, not their own developmental needs. So they left." The company had made the mistake of hiring a *personal* development coach who worked with executives when what they really needed was an executive development coach.

Figure 10.2
Shifts in Coaching Expectations and Performance Based on the Role of the Coach.

	Therapist	Personal Coach	Executive Coach	Consultant	Mentor	Boss
Relationship	Let me help you with <u>your</u> problem	Let me help you clarify and attain your personal/career goals	Let me help you be more effective leading through people and business challenges	Let me help you understand what's wrong in the organization and how to fix it	Let me help you learn how to get things done around here	Let me help you with <u>my</u> problem.
Types of Problems	Emotional pain, behavior dysfunction	Personal/life goals, values clarification, life choices	Business driven leadership/work relationship effectiveness issues	Organizational problems	Building social networks, influence	Boss's problems

Regardless of the kind of coach who is supporting high potentials, we have to ask, "Can people fundamentally change?" Many suggest people are hard-wired into a personality that determines their leadership style. This could be true, particularly if they rely solely on their first or instinctual reaction to a leadership situation. Experience and research tell us that some executives do fundamentally change as the result of developmental coaching. They can dramatically shift the way their personal style, often in reaction to a dramatic event in their personal or professional lives. More often however, truly talented executives create effective workarounds. They delegate tasks that they do not do well or select members of their own team who will complement their style. They discern the types of leadership situations where they are more effective and avoid ones where they are less effective. Finally they might add to their behavioral repertoire in leadership situations to provide themselves more options.

Coaching is about helping executives deploy themselves more effectively as well as expanding their capabilities. Coaching is helping an executive understand the foundation of his or her style and develop broader more flexible behavioral options to meet the leadership demands in the organization and his or her role.

BUSINESS-DRIVEN EXECUTIVE COACHING

Align the Way People Really Develop with the Urgent Demands of Your Organization to Sustain Developmental Growth

Any executive coach will have some means to create insight and awareness for a client. Most often, coaches will use some kind of multirater or 360 feedback tool. This might be a written or Web-based tool or even a series of interviews with directed reports, peers, or bosses. In addition, a number of leadership style assessments can also be used to provide insight for a client and their behavioral style while being perceived by the client as objective. Yet feedback and insight alone rarely drives sustained behavioral change (see sidebar, "The Myth of Feedback").

Because of their role as well as their expertise, executive coaches are the most effective professionals to develop the capabilities of high-potential leaders. But to be truly effective, they need to develop executives *exclusively* in the context of real and urgent business demands (see Figure 10.3).

1. The most powerful driver for development comes about when the executive is faced with a specific and challenging business situation.
2. Without focus on specific business challenges, coaching drifts and loses both relevance to the urgent demands of the business and a clear return on investment.

It is important to understand the bias that a coach brings to the work to ensure it aligns with the assignment. Ask coaches about the scope of their services provided in their professional practices. If the Web site lists that they also do consulting, their coaching may have a bias that focuses on their area of expertise. One informal survey of certified executive coaches found practices that included a single father's support group, marriage counseling, and spiritual guidance. If the coach cannot stay focused

Figure 10.3
Contracting and Managing the Coaching Process.

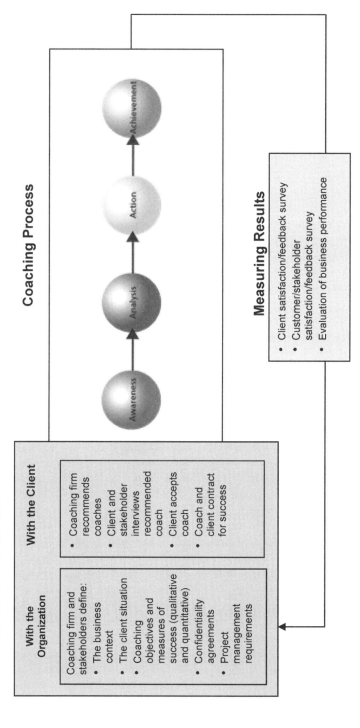

on how they present themselves to the marketplace, he or she probably will have difficulty staying within the boundaries of a corporate executive coaching assignment. Be wary of the coach who brings only one brand of tools or is wedded to one school of leadership. Just like hiring a handyman who only owns a hammer—every problem will look like a nail.

When we manage the coach selection and contracting process correctly, we will drive coaching effectiveness as a developmental tool for high potentials. The coaching firm should work with key stakeholders and the client to define the business context, the client situation, and outcomes for success. The firm, of course, should present *one* coach for client approval after an interview. Beauty parades of three or more coaches from which the client chooses will lower the effectiveness. In these cases, clients often choose the coach whom they believe would be least likely to push them outside of their comfort zone.

Making the coach-and-client relationship work well has a number of factors. There should be a well-defined process that has some version of the *awareness, analysis, action,* and *achievement* phases against which progress can be measured. Face-to-face sessions are important but in today's business environment, remote communications are both required and helpful. The psychotherapy model of one session per week should give way to a more practical combination of sessions, phone, and email contact that fit the rhythm and key events of the business environment.

Coaching allows a client to replace less effective responses to business and people situations with a more adaptive and effective set of behaviors. Sustained change occurs when an executive routinely recognizes the situational triggers for instinctive behavior and proactively chooses more effective leadership behaviors. Therefore, coaching is most powerful and sustaining when the coach works with a client long enough to help him or her see the patterns in new situations and successfully apply the new behaviors. Patience is required from everyone—the client and the client's boss. The hard truth is that any change in business takes more than one fiscal quarter to see any kind of sustained results. There should therefore be no less expectation for a coaching a high-potential executive. A minimum engagement should last at least two quarters or six months and up to a year if the executive is in a mission-critical stretch assignment.

Part of the challenge to that patience—especially from the standpoint of the client's boss, who needs to see some return on the investment—is the understanding that there must be confidentiality between the coach and the high-potential client. Unfortunately, confidentiality is often misunderstood and viewed by organizations as the coach's means to avoid accountability. At the same time, ironclad promises of complete confidentiality are also unrealistic. There are many exceptions where a coach may be compelled to break confidentiality for legal reasons, safety, or a serious breach of ethics. Yet one of the reasons for outside coaches is that they ensure some degree of privacy as the client wrestles with leadership issues without fear of adverse consequences.

You can expect that a coach or coaching firm would be held under a nondisclosure agreement to protect trade secrets. Expect that a coach would encourage a client to communicate appropriately with key stakeholders their developmental objectives. However, what coaches need to avoid at all cost is to serve as an alternative communications channel between the manager, HR, or any other stakeholder. Confidentiality is not just to protect the client from inappropriate prying corporate eyes and support a trusted relationship with the coach. It also ensures that the coach does not create indirect and dysfunctional communication patterns between the coach and, for example, the manager. When the manager says to the coach, "The next time you see her, will you ask about the meeting between her and the operations management? I got some feedback that the meeting did not go well." (In this case, the effective coach will ask, "Is there a way you might best get that feedback redirected to her from the source? I would like her to have an opportunity to directly improve her working relationships.")

While trust and confidentiality are essential to a successful engagement with a coach, it's important to remember that coaches don't get the "keys to the kingdom." Behaviors and expectations must be established between the company and the coach, otherwise an unethical coach might be tempted to take advantage of soft boundaries. For example, an executive coach might inappropriately choose to do "interventions" on behalf of the client. For example, the coach may contact the manager to provide some unsolicited feedback about the manager's management style, suggesting the manager might benefit from having his or her *own* coach. Worse yet, the coach might suggest to the client that the coach be engaged on a consulting contract to do strategic planning or values clarification with the senior team. Any effort by the coach to expand his or her engagement may be highly inappropriate. Such behavior suggests that the coach has an agenda to use coaching as a means to expand his or her own consulting business. It also can suggest to the client that they do not need to be developed, but the organization or the boss needs to be fixed. This misses the point of coaching, where the coach is to help the executive be more effective in the organization they are in—warts and all. After all, truly talented and effective leaders should positively influence organizational functionality and performance. It is what a leader does. The coach is there to help improve the leader's effectiveness, not upsell their own services.

LEVERAGING THE COACHING RELATIONSHIP WITH HIGH-POTENTIAL DEVELOPMENT

Any leadership program with high potentials is built on the foundation of the one-on-one relationship between the coach and the client working the four phases of development (*awareness, analysis, action*, and *achievement*) that provides the link between self-knowledge, learning from crucible experiences, and accountability for personal development.

Today's high performers are achievement-oriented. Among this group of high potentials, create a culture of leadership development. Having a high potential program, regardless of what it may be called, is an essential business strategy to build competitive capability. It should be a program your high performers want to be a part of. Be transparent about the qualities you look for in your organization for participant selection. Heavily involve top executives in the nomination and selection of participants in the program. Make it clear to everyone that promotions, pay, and recognition as a leader in the organization are for demonstrated performance, not from participation in the program. The program should not be measured by the number of certificates of completion. Rather, the program should be evaluated on manager and participant satisfaction that the participants were able to become more effective leaders.

Build in the expectation that people invited into the program as participants will also normally rotate out of the program based on job demands, the needs of the organization, as well as the need to allow others to benefit and grow from the experience.

Finally, connect people in the program to one another as a means to expand high-performance social networks. Use coach-facilitated peer or roundtable coaching to reinforce developmental accountability and expand their exposure to other groups within the organization. Leadership development is about learning to lead in your organization. Executive coaching is a powerful tool to ensure that the potential of high potentials is realized.

When Feedback Fails
I ams what I ams!
  - Popeye the sailor man

"Joe is a bright guy. He is passionate about his work, and sets high standards for himself. He is just a little rough around the edges and rubs the CEO the wrong way sometimes," lamented the vice president of human resources. "I thought it might be good to do a 360 on him. It might give him a chance to see how others perceive him, so he might learn how to manage relationships more effectively."

It is wishful thinking that feedback alone will be sufficient to predictably drive sustained development. Assume for a moment that the 360 or "multi-rater" feedback from peers, the boss, and direct reports is of high quality. The raters were thoughtfully selected, and confidentiality of the raters is protected to assure accuracy. The data is gathered into a summary report, and a feedback session is held between the executive development coach and the client.

Experience says there will be one of three reactions:

- 1/3 of the clients will be engaged by the discussion. They will be curious about the data and if it will provide insight and ideas about what to do differently to improve their chances of getting what they need from others in the workplace.

- 1/3 will be crushed by the experience. Their reaction will be, "Don't they know I care? I want people to like me and I work hard to do my best. They do not understand what I am trying to accomplish. I feel betrayed by those I support and no longer feel I have the credibility to lead."

- 1/3 will be indifferent, or what we refer to as the "Popeye Response." "It is just the way I am. If people have a problem with me, I can't help them. I get results and that is what counts."

Multi-rater or 360 feedback is one part of an assessment to help a client piece together not only where they are most effective but also where their developmental opportunities are. It is a very important piece of the Awareness Phase of executive coaching, as it provides real information about how a client's behavioral style plays out in the workplace and how it serves as an asset and when it might get in the way.

Yet, even in the hands of a talented coach, up to two-thirds of the initial reactions to multi-rater data are counterproductive. If feedback alone could drive sustained change, managing others, executive coaching and even parenting teenagers would be easy. Self-awareness is a starting point for coaching (and most any efforts of personal growth), not the end point. The client and coach will need to sort through the implications of the feedback and form an understanding of what it means to their ability to lead others. Only then can the client and the coach form a plan with developmental goals that will be fruitful.

Some leadership development programs have intensive executive assessment with rich feedback, some leadership training sessions and even the requirement that the executive actually formulate a development plan. But even having a plan is very different from the journey to achievement. Developmental efforts, from one-off interventions to larger scale high-potential leadership development initiatives fall short of achieving real progress because they stop well before any serious work begins. This is a little like opening a store, buying the merchandise to sell and leaving it randomly on the floor in boxes for customers to pick through. You might sell something, but it takes a highly motivated buyer with time to kill.

To build leadership capability in individuals and their organizations, there must be an investment in the direct development of those who hold the most promise in their growth as a leader when facing significant leadership challenges. Development happens best when there is the prepared mind of self-awareness placed in the crucible of challenging work and supported by developmental coaching.

Chapter 11

The Five Points of Peak Performance*

Louis S. Csoka

Leadership is all about inspiring people to do what they did not think possible. It is about rising above the fray and seeing clearly what is possible and then being able to articulate that to people who need to be fully engaged with their hearts and minds. It results in exceptional or peak performance by everyone, performing at their very best when it matters the most. And it matters the most in critical situations where one action changes everything. Knowing what that is and when to do it is the key to success in work and life. Peak performance can be learned. But most leadership training today is inadequate and too narrow in focus to enable lifelong learning to be achieved for a leader to develop "on-command" peak performance behaviors.

Leadership training in today's world consists mostly of renaming, reframing, and repackaging techniques that are 20 to 30 years old. This knowledge is the *know* and the techniques are the *do* of leadership. While many of these techniques are essential to start to learn how to be an effective leader, they only provide short-term change and benefits. They do not address the core foundation of leadership.

The foundation comes from within—the ability of an individual to adapt to the circumstances, think effectively under pressure, and develop focused solutions while communicating efficiently with others. This is called the *be* of leadership.

Perhaps you are facing a critical juncture in a mergers-and-acquisitions negotiation, or a particularly challenging sales call, or even an interview with a grueling market analyst. In all these situations, there are moments that require your best performance. These moments often define success versus mediocrity or failure. How well you

---

*Copyright © 2007 by Louis S. Csoka.

perform is not a function of whether or not you know what needs to be done. It is about trusting your intuition and your heart, using adaptive thinking, and being able to bring that to bear on the right action. The *be* of leadership is the foundation and the edge that the most effective leaders have over average leaders.

It is difficult to develop the *be* of leadership using traditional methods and there is no magic pill or class that will lay the foundation. By developing people to think more effectively and to control their emotional and physiological responses, peak-performance training helps leaders achieve resilience, self-confidence, adaptability, and mental agility. Ultimately, improving these skills results in more positive and effective thinkers who can control their emotional and physiological responses to any situation. This in turn yields enhanced leadership through better personal interactions, improved decision making, and innovative problem solving. This is how you learn to be the leader you need to be. This is how to achieve full engagement.

THE PROBLEM: UNRELENTING CHALLENGES AND IMPOSSIBLE EXPECTATIONS

Business leaders daily face seemingly endless challenges brought on by external forces and events. Unlike athletes, business leaders are "in the game" all the time. There is no clearly defined time frame, no practice period, no off-season. To be successful, both individually and organizationally, they must be at their best each and every day. Consider the following summary of everyday business challenges for today's executive.

Relentless pressure to deliver. This has become especially challenging with the emphasis on cost cutting and downsizing. Inevitably, these lead to fewer people doing more and more. No matter how hard you try, at some point there just is not enough time in the day or the resources to get it done. Over time, this can lead to overload, overwhelm, and burnout.

Rapidly changing skill requirements and job assignments. In downsizing, the survivors typically are asked to engage in many tasks with which they are unfamiliar and for which they have not been trained or adequately prepared. Thrust into such situations, the chances for failing are very high, as is the anxiety. The learning curve for acquiring skills and tasks that are very different is acute. Over time this can lead to a loss of confidence.

Empowerment and emphasis on teams. Companies have come to widely adopt the use of teams as a means for increasing efficiency and productivity. However, using teams can lead to unintended consequences. Many people are very comfortable and highly productive as individual contributors, but not so when placed on teams. They find themselves very uncomfortable with the added requirement of being accountable and responsible for teammates. For them, the sense of responsibility for the team and the added accountability for others' performance can be stressful.

Transformation of work through technology. Technology has transformed the way we live, work, and play. We marvel at what technology has done to enhance our lives. However, with the good have come the bad and the ugly—the emails, the voicemails, the BlackBerries, the laptops, the PDAs, and so forth. In other words, what was supposed to be anywhere, anytime has become everywhere, all the time. Technology has intruded every aspect of our lives. Given a finite amount of time in the day, we allow demands on our time from work to creep into family time, and if our family life is important, we push that demand further into our personal time. Eventually we notice that there is little or no personal time. In the extreme, we can lose the sense of our own individuality. As a minimum, it can lead to guilt when we do choose family and personal time over work. Ultimately, technology can lead to uncertainty about work-life balance in general.

Discontinuous change. Change is constant. To be fully engaged, people need to embrace change, to see opportunities and possibilities, not to fear it. Of course, there are differences in how well we adapt. In any case, this kind of change, called *continuous change*, follows a linear path and is easier to predict and accommodate. There is another kind of change, however, that can disturb and upset the predictability we all seek in life. This is called *discontinuous change*. It is sudden, unexpected, and unanticipated and catches us by surprise. On a national level, examples include the terrorist attacks of September 11, 2001, and Hurricane Katrina. In our personal lives, it is the sudden death of a loved one or the unexpected loss of a job. Discontinuous change can create an extended period of loss of direction and purpose, a blurred vision of tomorrow. For full engagement under discontinuous change conditions, leadership must show the way.

The cumulative effect of all of the above is a tremendous amount of pressure and stress. The problem is that these are not going away. In fact, they will continue and become even more pervasive in our lives. To be able to survive and even thrive under these conditions, we realistically have only three courses of action:

1. We can always opt out of the situation, and sometimes we do.
2. We can attempt to eliminate the causes of the stress, which most of the time is out of our control or not possible.
3. We can significantly improve the way we personally respond to the pressure and stress, physiologically, mentally, and emotionally. These responses will determine our level of performance and eventually our success.

Too many firms seek motivational speakers and self-help books for answers when the real performance advantage comes from within. Ask any peak performer. Be wary of books that teach how to motivate people. You can't; real motivation is internal. It is something that individuals must develop for themselves. It is all about inspiration and passion. Leaders can influence the likelihood that their followers will find the inspiration, drive, and passion to excel, but they cannot motivate. It is certainly their job to help them. But ultimately it must come from within oneself. This is why self-awareness, self-control, and self-management are so key in achieving full engagement and ultimately exceptional performance.

LEADERS AS PEAK PERFORMERS

The first principle of leadership is the importance of knowing who *you* are. You cannot successfully lead others until you have learned to lead yourself, and leading yourself is all about self-mastery—mastery over what you think, say, and do. These are the only

Figure 11.1
U.S. Army Be-Know-Do Leader Development Model.

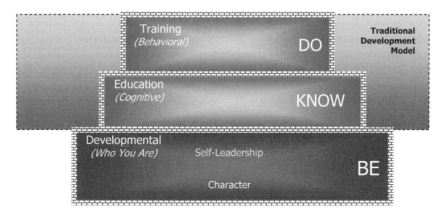

things you can directly control. Business leaders especially pride themselves in saying that they exercise control over myriad activities, events, and people. However, in truth, other than what they think, say, and do, not much else is in their direct control. That is not to say that they do not exercise influence. But influence and control are distinctively different. Once managers accept this basic tenet, real leadership can occur.

Be, Know, and Then Do

Leader-development programs need a framework to guide the education, training, and experiential activities supporting it. A useful framework has been developed at West Point and the U.S. Army. It is simple yet elegant (see Figure 11.1). Traditional corporate learning models have focused primarily on the *know* and *do* elements, that is, education programs built to increase knowledge and training programs to change behavior. But few have addressed the *be*. In many organizations, there is a reluctance to even address this element of leadership. Yet leadership is all about the *be*. It is all about knowing the essence of the individual leading—how they think, what they say, and what they do.

Using a leadership framework as depicted in Figure 11.1, organizations can focus much more on developing the *be* part of leadership, which in our framework relates to self-leadership and self-mastery. Peak performance competencies are life skills. Once mastered, they become a key part of who you are and how you function, at work, at home, in your personal life.

Self-Leadership Is about Inner Control

Elite athletes compete against each other with relatively equal skills and abilities. Yet some dominate the field and repeat as champions over and over again. The major differentiator is mental preparedness—the ability to be in "the zone," to focus on the present with no thought of the past or future, concentrating only on *what* they are doing, not on *how* they are doing. This is especially challenging for business leaders who constantly face questions from analysts and shareholders about how the company is doing. It is, of course, very important to keep an eye on the financial performance of the company for the long term. But in the day-to-day performance of a business leader, best results are obtained with total focus on the performance requirement at the moment. Elite performers are exceptionally good at this.

The key aspect of superior performance is inner control, control over mental, emotional, and physiological states that are present in every performance situation. Without mastery of these, business professionals cannot hope to gain the full engagement of their people. Trust is not present because the leader does not demonstrate the inner control that communicates calm and confidence, especially in extreme conditions.

THE SOLUTION: LEARNING TO DELIVER CONSISTENT, EXCEPTIONAL PERFORMANCE

Of course, most business leaders do learn to adapt and adjust to achieve effectiveness under trying and changing conditions. In these times of unparalleled global competition, the question has to be asked, "Is being effective good enough?" Without competition, it is. But competition changes everything. Everyone has to perform to his very best. To achieve full engagement, leaders themselves must be "fully engaged." Being effective just won't carry the day for the long haul. Besides, psychologists continually remind us that the human spirit is such that people want to excel. Taking the lead from their brothers and sisters in athletics, business leaders too can develop the mental competencies that significantly increase the chances for delivering exceptional performance. Figure 11.2 depicts a framework for training and developing the elements of peak performance that provide essential *inner* leader skills that enable them to inspire and lead people to perform beyond expectations.

As in any training and development process, quality and accurate feedback is essential for learning. Since peak performance competencies are internal, learning to master them is best achieved with advanced biofeedback and neurofeedback technologies that measure covert activities like heart rate variability, respiration, blood pressure, brain activity, and so on. Once the domain of clinicians and biofeedback therapists, these technologies now provide accurate and measurable feedback as the individual learns to master control over mental, physiological, and emotional responses to demanding and challenging events. Research in performance psychology continues to validate the importance and effectiveness of the competencies depicted in the five-point model.

HOW DOES IT WORK?

Goal Setting: If You Don't Know Where You're Going, Any Path Will Do

A journey starts with knowing where you want to end up. This is especially true for anyone who wants to become a peak performer, to reach one's full potential. Setting goals is relatively easy. Making them happen is not. A key part of any lasting goal setting process is the idea of a mission. Knowing and living a mission provides the

Figure 11.2
APEX Performance Model.

motivation and perseverance to forge ahead when the going gets tough. It is much more than having a goal.

Much has been written about goal setting and goal-setting techniques. The approach to setting the target is not so much about a technique as it is a process for identifying what one really wants to accomplish, the inclusive smaller steps needed to get there, and the positive mindset necessary for ensuring enduring determination. Stopping with a list of goals and objectives is just not enough. It does not activate the energy needed to see them through to completion. They must be deliberately connected to daily thoughts and self-talk. Transforming objectives, which in their simplest form are actions, into affirmations connects what we are doing with what we are thinking. By recording these affirmations and having people listen to them regularly, we mimic the way very young children learn language at home—hearing it repeatedly, creating new neural pathways.

Positive-Effective Thinking: Confidence

Confidence is the ultimate determinant of success. We see and hear this all the time in sports, but when it comes to business leaders, it does not appear to ring true. Yet experience has shown that confidence can very much be an issue. Confidence comes from within. No one can give it to you. It reflects how we view ourselves and our preparation for future challenges. People must absolutely have confidence in themselves and their leaders to become fully engaged, to give their all regardless of the price. So how does one go about building and maintaining confidence?

We become what we think about most. People carry around images of themselves—of who they are and how they perform. These pictures begin at birth and continue throughout the life cycle, capturing all of our experiences. These experiences reflect both the successes and failures and the manner in which they are interpreted and stored. Much of this self-image is driven by our thoughts (positive and negative) and maintained and reinforced by self-talk. Given the basic negativism surrounding our lives, being positive and having trust and confidence in one's ability is really hard work.

Martin Seligman, in his book *Learned Optimism*, writes about the power of optimism over pessimism for being successful. He explains how we all develop an explanatory style as a way to explain the cause of events. Our styles say much about how we react cognitively and emotionally in a given situation. The development of our styles comes directly from how we think and what we think about and from the repetitiveness of these patterns of thought over time and situations. Based on Seligman's work and other recent scientific research into how children learn language at home, positive-effective thinking can be systematically developed. Mastery of this competence can transform a person into an exceptional, high-performing achiever.

Stress and Energy Management: Thriving under Pressure

Stress and energy go together. Anyone can perform well when everything is going just right. But what about when conditions are unfavorable, when things are going against you, when the pressure is on, when things are not going according to plan? Who really delivers then? There are performers who actually thrive under these conditions. They welcome the pressure. It drives them. It gives them energy and desire coupled with the ultimate satisfaction of having overcome all odds while doing something exceptional. These are peak performers.

The debilitating effects of stress on the individual and the organization have been well documented in recent years. There is little debate, for example, that for business organizations, stress is a major factor that reveals itself as diminished performance and increased health care costs. One of the major stressors is relentless pressure to deliver results through higher and higher levels of performance and ever increasing productivity. Many companies offer stress management seminars in hopes of raising awareness about the effects of stress and providing simple coping mechanisms.

Research on high performance in sports and the military has shown that the ability to handle oneself in high pressure and demand situations is less about the stressors and more about the individual's response to them. The solution lies in a more systematic and integrated approach to providing the necessary tools for actually thriving under pressure, not just surviving. Exceptional performances are not about being relaxed. They are about being energized and excited and impassioned, but always very much in control. Understanding how stress works from a neurophysiological perspective, having means at your disposal for altering its effects, and receiving quality high-tech feedback on how you are doing are powerful tools for learning how to thrive in pressure situations and for living your life.

Attention Control: Concentration amid Distractions

In their insightful book *The Attention Economy*, Thomas Davenport and John Beck discuss how in today's attention economy "the new scarcest resource isn't ideas or talent, but attention itself." The demand for our attention in modern society is unparalleled in both scope and intensity.

Yet the way in which we attend has not significantly changed over time. We still primarily learn to attend to the right things at the right time through trial and error and, if fortunate, through good coaching by parents, teachers, coaches, and so on. Through this method, we learn what is useful for our attention and what is not as we encounter new situations. However, given today's stimulus-rich environment, all competing for our attention, this is not the most efficient and effective way to learn to attend. The resultant attention deficit threatens to seriously cripple the workplace. In fact, a new term has been coined by Davenport and Beck: organizational ADD, a condition wherein there is "an increased likelihood for missing key information when making decisions, diminished time for reflection . . . difficulty holding others' attention . . . and decreased ability to focus when necessary" (Davenport and Beck, 2001, p. 7).

Systematic attention control training combines a simple but robust framework for understanding how attention works, a means for navigating that framework, and new brain wave (EEG) technology that provides accurate feedback about how one is paying attention—the key to improving focus and concentration directly.

VISUALIZATION: WHAT YOU SEE IS WHAT YOU GET

Engagement without leadership at all levels is just another buzzword. Engagement means reaching the hearts and minds of employees. Once fully engaged, employees want be led. To lead, you need a true vision. You need to be able to articulate that vision through storytelling. To have a true vision, you need to learn how to truly visualize, to see the desired end state.

Achieving a really challenging goal is to see it already accomplished—to *imagine* it complete. Imagery, commonly referred to as visualization, is a powerful tool for doing exactly that. It involves using all the senses to create or re-create an experience in the mind. Everyone has the inherent capability of doing this, but how well it is developed is a function of their developmental experiences. We all use imagery in one form or another all the time. We differ, however, in its sophistication and effectiveness. Some visualize very effectively with no formal training, while most do so only after systematic training and practice of the skill. The neurological wiring, however, is in everyone. How well we do it is a function of our developmental experiences. The early and consistent use of imagination in play and work helps build the brain "muscles" for visualizing. Imagery maximizes potential for performance by helping develop greater confidence, energy, concentration, and feelings of success.

In the Five-Point Peak Performance Model, visualization and imagery are developed as a specific peak performance competency as well as an integrating mechanism. The first step is assessing how well an individual's visualization skill has developed. Through biofeedback and neurofeedback instrumentation, it has been discovered that high-quality visualization is characterized by a deep physiological and mental coherence coupled with an optimal level of alertness and concentration. The power of imagery comes from the confidence gained by seeing and feeling successful performance in the mind before it actually happens. The common description of this experience is "I have been here before."

LEADERS MUST LEARN TO BE PEAK PERFORMERS

Achieving sustained high performance as leaders and getting it from others in today's competitive and pressure-filled business environment, influenced heavily by organizational and workplace structures, policies, and processes, can be a very daunting task. Traditional emphases on organizational and workplace solutions for meeting the challenges have not produced the desired results in performance improvement and productivity increases. These methods have typically focused on the more peripheral issues and have not addressed the heart of the challenge, which is how to fundamentally change the manner by which people approach their own performance and tap into their full potential.

To have a workforce that is fully engaged, leaders must learn to be peak performers. They must develop those inner skills that make them exceptional performers, and thus by their example, pull everyone with them. The time has come for business professionals to think as peak performers and the special preparation that takes, for they, too, are expected to be elite performers. Sustaining exceptional performance levels can only be accomplished through deliberate and systematic training in those peak performance competencies that most *directly* impact what we think, say, and do in ways that unleash our capabilities and full potential in any performance situation. It requires the honesty to admit that we do not know everything, coupled with a willingness to learn and change.

Leadership at all levels starts with leading oneself, before leading others or leading organizations. Leading self means self-awareness, self-understanding, clear decision making, poise under pressure, and confidence. Self-leadership by all is a key factor that must be transferred to the workforce if full engagement is to be realized. Gaining hearts and minds can now be related to the heart–mind connection that makes self-awareness possible. To be truly effective, leaders must engage different segments of the employee population in different ways, at different times and in different situations.

REFERENCES

Davenport, Thomas H., and John C. Beck, *The Attention Economy: Understanding the New Currency of Business* (Cambridge, MA: Harvard Business School Press, 2001).

Eliot, John, *Overachievement* (New York: Penguin Group, 2004).
Gardner, Charles A., *Peak Performers: The New Heroes of American Business* (New York: Avon Books, 1986).
Gladwell, Malcolm, *Blink: The Power of Thinking without Thinking* (New York: Little, Brown, 2005).
Seligman, Martin E. P., *Learned Optimism: How to Change Your Mind and Your Life* (New York: Pocket Books, Simon & Schuster, 1998).

Chapter 12

Rebuilding Trust within Organizations*

Dennis S. Reina and Michelle L. Reina

This is a true story.

"Frank, you've got six months to improve these results, or you and your leadership team can forget your bonuses for this year," said Cheryl, the global executive vice president of HR. "Your division has the lowest employee satisfaction survey scores in the whole company—worldwide!"

These results came as a shock and embarrassment to Frank. As vice president of learning services for one of the largest and best-known financial services corporations in the world, Frank's division was responsible for helping business leaders globally carry out key strategic initiatives. In fact, the most significant initiative he was spearheading focused on increasing employee satisfaction companywide. And now his department was reporting low scores. How could they lead a global employee satisfaction initiative with credibility if the employee satisfaction scores in their own shop were suffering? Frank's leadership team's bonus was at risk along with its credibility.

An analysis of the survey results for Frank's division indicated that low levels of satisfaction were an outgrowth of employee distrust of leadership and the company overall. The people in Frank's division did not trust leadership's decisions, were unclear of the future direction of the company, and did not understand what was expected of them. They were unsure of their roles and responsibilities, who their bosses were, how they were being evaluated, and how their new jobs fit into the company's plan. Employees felt vulnerable, which caused them to be distracted, go through the motions regarding their tasks, withdraw, and avoid working to their potential. As a

---

*Copyright © 2007 by Dennis S. Reina and Michelle L. Reina.

result, in addition to satisfaction levels plummeting, deliverables were behind schedule, collaboration broke down, silos went up, in-fighting flourished, and resignations were numerous. Simply put, Frank's own people did not see a viable future with the company.

This wasn't Frank's fault. He had joined the company a year earlier and inherited a tough situation. His division had undergone two major restructurings in three years. As is common within many organizations, the changes did not yield the desired results. Frank was hired to turn the situation around. When he came on board, he knew people were frustrated. However, he viewed himself as a people person capable of developing collaborative relationships. He felt confident in his ability to build a trusting work environment that produced results.

A year later, with his confidence shaken, he wondered, "Where did I go wrong? What is it going to take to rebuild the trust? Where do I begin?"

Leaders such as Frank ask themselves these kinds of questions every day. Trust is challenged and often broken whenever there is change. However, change itself does not necessarily break trust. It is how the change is managed that erodes trust, causing uncertainty that leads people to question the intentions of their leaders and compromises working relationships and performance. While broken trust causes pain, doubt, and confusion, it may also provide an opportunity to strengthen relationships, drive performance, and motivate employees—if people choose to work through the broken trust.

This chapter is about how to help an organization heal from the pain of betrayal to rebuild trust, renew the spirit of working relationships, and energize performance. It reviews the need for trust in organizations today, explore the subtle (and not so subtle) ways trust is broken, and examine the impact of broken trust on people and performance. The chapter introduces two elements of the research-based Reina Trust and Betrayal Model: the Betrayal Continuum, to provide an understanding of the ways trust is broken, and the Seven Steps for Healing to provide a roadmap to rebuild trust. It describes how Frank used these steps to rebuild trust in his division and the results it yielded. Furthermore, we explore the answers to Frank's questions, "Where did I go wrong? What is it going to take to rebuild the trust? Where do I begin?"

Let's begin by investigating the need for trust in the first place.

THE NEED FOR TRUST

Trust has two roles within a company—to serve the human need and the business need.

The Human Need

Trust is foundational to effective relationships. People need to depend on others, and they need to be depended on in return. When trust is present, people create, innovate, and collaborate freely. They have a sense of connection and belonging; they take responsibility for results and hold themselves accountable. In trusting work environments, people want to come to work and they want to produce. They are seen for who they are, are recognized for what they bring, and feel safe to express their thoughts, ideas, needs, and concerns. Although leaders have significant responsibility to rebuild trust when it is lost, they do not have sole responsibility. Trust is everyone's responsibility.

The Business Need

Organizations that foster trust are more profitable. A Watson Wyatt Worldwide study found that organizations in which front-line employees trusted senior leadership posted a 42 percent higher return on shareholder investment over those firms in which distrust was the norm.[1]

Additionally, organizations that foster trust have higher employee satisfaction. In a recent University of British Columbia report,[2] economists found that trust in management is the most valued determinant of job satisfaction. They cite that a small increase in trust of management is like getting a 36 percent pay increase. Conversely, they found that if the same amount of trust is lost, the decline in employee job satisfaction is experienced the same as taking a 36 percent pay cut. It follows that organizations with trustworthy management do not experience the high cost of turnover. Their employees generally stay, want to come to work, and want to produce.

While trust is needed and valued, there is only one thing that builds it, breaks it, and rebuilds it—the way people behave within the context of the relationship they have with each other and their organizations. Everyone has a story of lost trust or betrayal and has experienced the impact of broken trust on them, their relationships, and performance. When trust is absent, people withdraw, abdicate responsibility, undermine each other's efforts, and question their "place" within the organization.

No relationship is perfect. In all relationships, trust will be built and broken, particularly in minor ways. The building and breaking of trust are natural elements of relationships. Therefore, to build sustainable trust, leaders at all levels of responsibility must understand this natural phenomenon of trust and learn how to rebuild it when it's broken. It is only through the capacity to rebuild trust that an organization will be successful in sustaining trust, particularly during change.

Paradoxically, while trust itself is fragile, the repairing of broken trust may actually strengthen relationships and performance rather than diminish them—provided that the breached trust is appropriately addressed. A breach of trust or betrayal can be a gift and teacher; an opportunity rather than a penalty, if we allow it to be.

A common mistake leaders make, particularly during change, is to assume that once broken, trust may be reestablished on its own over time. This view is unrealistic and irresponsible and compromises leaders' trustworthiness. It actually further breaks trust! Trust does not automatically rebuild itself. Restoring trust requires attention, intention, and thoughtful action. Rebuilding trust requires healing with courage and compassion. It takes courage to pay attention to what has caused trust to erode. It takes compassion to be sensitive to people's feelings and emotions related to broken trust or perceived betrayal.

CHANGE AS THE LOSS OF TRUST

People often experience change as a loss—the loss of relationships with those laid off or the dissolution of the "family" company environment that once existed or the loss of the way it used to be. People may resent that they are doing more work for the same pay with fewer benefits and that opportunities to earn more are limited. Further, they may perceive change as a loss of opportunity in the future. People might also perceive change as a breach of contract (and therefore trust): "This isn't what I signed up for."

People need to talk about and grieve those losses. They need to acknowledge that what they once had is no longer; the longer the employee's tenure, the greater the feelings of loss and the greater the need to grieve.

Frank discovered that the losses his people experienced regarding the changes contributed to their declining satisfaction. His people were in pain as a result of the two global restructurings within two years. They felt the loss of relationships with people with whom they had collaborated, respected, and had come to rely on for their expertise, knowledge, and skills (not to mention the comings and goings of Frank's predecessors who were supposed to lead them through these changes). There were fewer people, and so the workload for each person doubled. With the expanded workload, there were fewer resources to support meeting deadlines and getting the work done. Additionally, Frank's employees did not see potential for growth and advancement in the foreseeable future. There appeared to be fewer opportunities. In essence, they experienced loss on two levels: the loss of the way it was and the loss of what could be.

UNDERSTANDING THE LOSS OF TRUST: BETRAYAL

Most people strive to engage in relationships in a trusting manner. Yet because we are human, trust will get broken; we will let one another down, and betrayal will happen. It is part of the human condition. To rebuild and sustain trust, we need to understand what breaks it and causes people to feel betrayed.

Betrayal occurs on a continuum from major intentional betrayal to unintentional minor betrayal (see Figure 12.1). Major intentional betrayals are carried out to hurt and harm. We feel them at our deepest core. Unintentional minor betrayals are incidental to other actions. We may not pay much attention to them initially—but they do add up. When they accumulate, they may have the same impact and cost of major betrayals. Regardless of the nature of the betrayal, it erodes trust and compromises or ends relationships. It certainly impacts performance.

During change processes, trust is most pervasively betrayed unintentionally. The change may be considered a major betrayal because of the broad and deep impact on people, the culture, and ultimately performance. However, it is not the change itself that causes people to feel betrayed. It is the way change is handled that breaks down trust. During a change process, people often feel left out of key decisions, experience agreements not being kept, and information regarding the organization's future direction is not available. Communication channels become bogged down with gossip

Figure 12.1
(*Source*: Excerpted from Dennis S. Reina and Michelle L. Reina, *Trust and Betrayal in the Workplace: Building Effective Relationships in Your Organization*, 2nd ed. [San Francisco: Berrett-Koehler, 2007].)

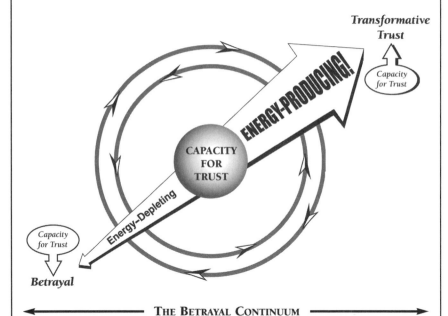

and backbiting, and there is speculation regarding expectations, roles, and responsibilities because they are unclear.

Major betrayals do happen, but most betrayals are minor. These are the more prevalent acts that happen each and every day in the workplace. People gossiping about one another behind their backs, consistently arriving late for meetings, not responding to requests made by others, blaming and finger pointing, and abdicating responsibility are examples of minor forms of betrayal. They alienate employees from their managers, peers, and subordinates. These subtle betrayals seem innocent and unimportant. They are often ignored and unaddressed with people commenting, "Oh, let's not waste time on that little stuff, let's get on with it, we have too much to do." Yet they can and do grow into more severe hurts and contribute to much of the negative feelings that employees have toward their bosses, each other, and their companies.

We may try to deny their existence, but these minor hurts do not go away on their own. Minor betrayals escalate into major ones if not addressed and resolved, particularly during change. This occurs when minor betrayals stay alive in people's minds and when the behaviors that contribute to them continue resulting in a pattern of trust-breaking behavior. Over the course of time, they become bigger than the actual event or a single act. The cumulative weight of their own thought processes makes them major.

The placement of an experience along the betrayal continuum depends on our perception of the betrayer's intent and the impact on us—in other words, the degree to which we perceive that the individual intended to cause hurt, damage, or pain to us and the degree of hurt, damage, and pain actually caused or inflicted. For instance, accepting credit for someone else's work may be a minor intentional betrayal in one circumstance, but if one person gains greatly at another's expense (for example, if someone gets promoted as a reward for something that in reality a co-worker deserved credit for), it becomes a major intentional betrayal.

The opportunity for the perception of betrayal in any relationship depends on the degree of trust we have in that individual, situation, or organization. The more an individual has invested of themselves in an organization, the greater the perceived loss they may experience during change. The more deeply they will feel hurt by the loss of relationships and the minor betrayals so pervasive during change.

THE EMOTIONAL SIDE OF THE LOSS OF TRUST

Dealing with the emotional side of change and the resulting incidences of betrayal is difficult but necessary. Many leaders are unskilled and uncomfortable in dealing with the pain their employees feel regarding change, much less able to deal with the discomfort of their own pain. They often consider this to be "touchy-feely" stuff, not the stuff of "real business." During times of change, leaders tend to retreat to the "hard side" of business for many reasons: This is where they are most comfortable, where their role is more tangibly defined, where they are skilled, where their results are most easily measured, and where they are the safest. In the retreat to the hard side, they fail to honor themselves, their relationships, and the real needs of the people they serve. They fail to honor the essence of leadership. Their search for safety puts them at risk for betraying themselves, their role, and those they serve.

Aware leaders recognize the high cost of betrayal to individuals, to relationships, and to performance. When people feel betrayed, they pull back and shut down. People's readiness to trust themselves along with their willingness to trust others is diminished. They begin to question their place within the organization, wondering, "Is this the place for me?" These thoughts make it difficult for people to concentrate, impacting their performance and contribution to their work. Morale, along with productivity, declines. People seek outside opportunities and leave the organization, they may stay and simply go through the motions, or they may choose to work through their pain to healing.

Effective leaders realize that they cannot go through the motions to rebuild trust. They realize that they must guide the healing process. They must begin by acknowledging their employees' feelings of fear and loss and work to restore their confidence. Otherwise, the betrayal continues, and people's capacity to trust in themselves, their leaders, and their organization further plummets. Survivors go into a state of resignation. They take fewer risks, blame others, go through the motions, and are not as productive as they once were. If employees have been burned before, they are less willing to give their all and come through when needed. If leaders do not deal with feelings of betrayal, they will unwittingly destroy two of the very qualities they need to be competitive: their employees' trust and their performance.

HEALING FROM BROKEN TRUST AND BETRAYAL

The Seven Steps for Healing, a part of the comprehensive Reina Trust and Betrayal Model, provides a framework that helps people work through broken trust, renew relationships, and successfully navigate change (see Figure 12.2). The Seven Steps raise awareness of the essential elements of healing that are too easily abandoned, especially during times of change. The model provides a common language and actions to support healing. Healing gives birth to renewal and reframes the losses associated with change into possibilities for the future and reengaging employees.

THE SEVEN STEPS FOR HEALING

For ease of discussion, the steps are described in a linear fashion, moving through each step one at a time. It is important to note, however, that healing is not a linear process. People may move through more than one step simultaneously and may revisit a particular step more than once.

Step 1: Observe and Acknowledge What Has Happened

The first step to healing and rebuilding trust at the organizational level requires awareness. One of the greatest mistakes leaders make in challenging times is to assume that once a major change has taken place, trust will return on its own. This view is both unrealistic and causes trust to further break down.

Figure 12.2
(*Source*: Excerpted from Dennis S. Reina and Michelle L. Reina, *Trust and Betrayal in the Workplace: Building Effective Relationships in Your Organization*, 2nd ed. [San Francisco: Berrett-Koehler, 2007].)

Assess the health of your organization. Observe and assess the climate within the organization. Notice what your people are experiencing and how they are feeling, and acknowledge it. Pay attention to what specific actions, activities, and events may be building and breaking trust. Be careful to not overlook small, subtle signs of distrust, such as people coming late to meetings, missing appointments, avoiding speaking directly to individuals, gossiping and backbiting, and so on.

Find out what is important to people. Listen to what they are saying, in the hallways and the break rooms and on the shop floor. When witnessing anger, don't just notice the anger. Listen to it. Quite often, anger represents deeper feelings of hurt and disappointment. Remember, people in pain need to be listened to. They need someone they can trust to turn to for support and understanding. They need help to understand their own feelings and experiences.

Acknowledge feelings—not only the feelings of others but also your own. Effective leaders consciously acknowledge their employees' feelings of frustration, disappointment, and betrayal. It is only after acknowledging the feelings of betrayal that leaders are able to respond to them. Leaders must work very hard not to get defensive or try to justify or rationalize what happened. It is the role of a leader to listen, observe, and acknowledge. This is the first step to healing the wounds.

You're also entitled to your own feelings. Make sure you are honoring those as well. For leaders, it may not be appropriate to express feelings to direct reports, of course. But your people can still tell if you're in denial about what's going on and how it's affecting you personally.

Step 2: Allow Feelings to Surface

Give employees permission to express their concerns, issues, and feelings in a constructive manner. Create safe forums, staffed by skilled facilitators, that support the expression of fear, anger, and frustration. Giving employees a constructive way to discuss feelings and experiences helps them let go of the negativity they are holding, freeing up that energy for rebuilding relationships and returning their focus to performance.

Frank retained outside support seasoned in rebuilding trust to conduct one-on-one interviews and focus groups with his people. Discussions were facilitated to provide people with opportunity to surface their fears and concerns in a safe, nonthreatening manner to discern the cause of distrust from the changes that occurred. In addition, a baseline trust measuring survey was administered to assess the level of trust currently in place within Frank's department, specifically, behaviors practiced by both employees and leadership that build trust. The results helped identify behaviors contributing to people's feelings of disappointment, frustration, and betrayal. Additionally, Frank drew upon the outside support to help him assess his own trustworthiness. He learned how his own actions were building and breaking trust and identified shifts he needed to make to earn his trustworthiness.

The focus groups and one-on-one interviews conducted at Frank's division helped people verbalize the pain that affected their employee satisfaction scores. Frank's role was to listen, observe, and acknowledge, not justify or rationalize. This was difficult work, but necessary for rebuilding his relationship with employees. If this expression of feelings was not supported, people's feelings would have gone further underground and caused resentment and blocked shared responsibility and accountability. Frank learned that when in pain, people do not care about the needs of the business until it is clear that the business cares and leaders about them, their needs, and their well-being.

This is the difficult work for leaders, but it is important and necessary work in facilitating healing and navigating change. People in pain need to have their feelings heard. They need to know that you are able to relate to what they are saying and feeling. When you do not acknowledge your employees' emotions, they feel unheard, resentful, and distrusting toward you. Another layer of betrayal occurs.

When Frank focused on truly hearing his people, he was able to come to understand the deep loss they experienced. They missed their former coworkers. Many doubted their own abilities to take on added responsibilities due to the restructuring, and they did not know where to turn for assistance. As a result they felt alone and isolated. They feared for their future, wondering if there would truly be a place for them. People experienced the company being performance driven at the cost of a genuine interest in people.

Step 3: Give Employees Support

Recognize employees' transitional needs that must be met before they can adapt to change. They need to know how their concerns and questions will be understood and addressed. They need to know what new direction the organization is taking, the strategies it proposes to get there, what will be expected of them, and what they can expect from their leaders. They have relationship needs associated with belonging and their role in the new organization. And they need their skills and abilities to be valued. When leaders expect people to embrace change without addressing fundamental needs, people feel betrayed.

Stand up for your employees. A leadership position allows you to be your employees' advocate. Represent your people's interests, defend them from unwarranted criticism, and lobby for resources critical to their jobs. By backing your people, you are building contractual trust and meeting the implicit expectations people have of leaders. Furthermore, you demonstrate that you can be trusted to fulfill future commitments.

Frank recognized that he and his directors needed their own support in order to provide support to their people. He engaged coaches skillful in trust building and healing for additional support. They helped him make a shift from justifying and rationalizing to taking responsibility for the situation even though he did not create it. Most important, the coaches helped Frank see the rebuilding possibilities.

Step 4: Reframe the Experience

Help your employees learn to see this experience in a larger context. This gives you an opportunity to rebuild communication trust and helps employees reframe their experience by discussing the bigger picture: the business reasons for change, for example. Honestly acknowledge the changes the organization went through and why. In doing so, you must continue to acknowledge what people have experienced. Only then will employees be in a position to accept the new direction in which the organization is headed and to see their role in it.

The process of healing from betrayal is a process of inquiry. The questions that people ask will guide their journey. Responding to their questions honestly provides employees with understanding, awareness, truth, and renewed hope for a trusting relationship with you and the organization.

Help employees realize that there are choices. Experiencing betrayal leaves employees feeling very vulnerable and at the mercy of the forces of change. They need help seeing that they have choices regarding how they react to their circumstances. The more people are aware that they can choose their actions, the more they are able to take responsibility for those actions. Employees need help examining their assumptions, breaking out of their self-limiting beliefs, and exploring options and possibilities.

Because of the multiple changes (e.g., two restructurings in two years), people in the Frank's division were feeling vulnerable to the forces of change. With support, Frank met with employees, answered questions, and openly discussed the impact that changes had on employees. He shared his own feelings of vulnerability and acknowledged mistakes that were made. In doing so, he was able to help employees shift from blaming him and the organization to realizing they had choices. He helped people see that while they may not have control over what has occurred, they did have control over how they chose to respond.

Frank also owned up to the mistakes he made. He acknowledged that in his eagerness to develop strategy and move on he neglected to hear where people were struggling. He admitted that he did not pay careful attention to people's needs and slipped into justifying and rationalizing rather than truly listening to their needs. He shared what he learned from his own mistakes about trust, healing, and renewal and most important about his peoples' needs. He then shared the possibilities and opportunities he saw for the organization in the future and the actions that would take them there.

Step 5: Take Responsibility

Take responsibility for your role in the process. It is not helpful to try to spin the truth or cover mistakes. It does not serve you or the relationship. Something quite powerful occurs when we tell the impeccable truth—without exceptions, justifications, or rationalizations. Telling the truth is the fundamental basis for trust in workplace relationships. It demonstrates one's trustworthiness. We take responsibility when we acknowledge our mistakes. Three simple words, "I am sorry," reflect taking responsibility and go a long way to rebuilding trust.

Help others take responsibility for their part. When people are in pain and fear, they tend to blame their leaders and behave in ways that contribute to betrayal. We support others in taking responsibility when we help them see their role in creating the climate of betrayal. Employees may not have control over change, but they do have control over how they choose to respond. Even though people may feel betrayed, those feelings do not make betraying in return acceptable.

Frank's employees were in pain and blaming their leaders as well, behaving in ways that further contributed to betrayal. They needed help to see the role that they had played in this time of crisis. Even though they felt betrayed, it did not justify betraying in return. The director took responsibility for the impact the changes had on his employees, even though he did not have anything to do with creating those changes. This action helped his employees take responsibility for their behavior.

Make amends and return with dividends. It is the leader's role to break the chain of betrayal and reverse the spiral of distrust. Because actions speak louder than words, it is important that you take the first step in mending fences with employees. Remember that rebuilding trust does not simply mean giving back what was taken away. It means returning something in better shape than it was originally in. If you have lost trust by taking valued responsibilities away, you can regain trust by granting people even more significant responsibilities. If this is not possible, be honest about the realities of the situation and what you can do to make amends.

Manage expectations. The level of expectations is directly correlated to the opportunity for betrayal. To safeguard yourself and your employees against future betrayals, keenly manage expectations. Employees want to know what is expected of them and what they can expect in return. Emphasize the need to negotiate with them when their expectations cannot be fulfilled. This strengthens contractual trust between you and your employees.

Keep your promises. Managing promises is important in relationships. Trust is the result of promises kept. Don't make promises that you know you can't keep; that just sets up you and everyone with whom you have a relationship for a downfall. When you realize that you cannot keep promises, renegotiate them; don't break them.

Be careful of what you promise and what you appear to promise. When you are attempting to rebuild trust, it is essential that you not try to justify past actions and that you address the perceptions of those who feel betrayed. "It is enough for an employee to have believed that a promise was broken for trust to be violated."

Step 6: Forgive

Recognize that forgiveness is freedom. Forgiveness is a gift we give ourselves. It is about freeing ourselves and others from the anger, bitterness, and resentment that can deplete our individual and collective energy and spirit and interfere with relationships and performance. When we help people forgive others, we help them free themselves. With forgiveness, they heal for their future by changing their attitude about the past. We help them see new possibilities.

Occasionally, you as a leader may need to forgive yourself. You did the best you could, and perhaps for whatever reason, it still wasn't enough. Beating yourself up mentally and emotionally is worthless and self-defeating. Acknowledge for yourself what needs to be said or done to put your mind and this issue to rest. Then just do it. Be compassionate and cut yourself some slack during the healing process.

Shift from blaming to focusing on needs. Because forgiveness is a personal matter, it is difficult for people to forgive a system. However, leaders can work to cultivate a more personal and trusting climate where healing and forgiveness can take place. They can begin to do this by helping people shift from blaming the organization or its leaders to focusing on their personal needs as they relate to business needs.

Give your people the time they need to learn to forgive as well. Don't rush them. For most people, forgiveness takes time, and it happens a little at a time. Over time, your employees may be willing to forgive, but you cannot expect them to forget. You can help them heal from the pain they felt, but you cannot erase the events of the past. Occasionally, your employees may still be a bit angry even after they forgive. It is natural that they may experience lingering feelings of anger for the perceived wrongs they experienced.

Frank helped people shift from blaming leadership and the organization to focusing on their individual needs, roles, and the needs of the business. To do so, he asked employees what they needed to resolve issues, concerns, fears, and pain. It is important to address persistent resentment and blame in an organization, as they are toxic to the individuals involved and to the whole system. They undermine trust, morale, productivity, creativity, and innovation. People continue to blame when they perceive that those who are responsible have failed to take responsibility. People in return feel that they do not have to take action and are therefore not responsible. People also blame when they are carrying experiences of the past into the present.

Help your people shift from a blaming mode to a problem-solving focus. What do your employees need to resolve issues, concerns, fears, and pain? What conversations need to take place? What still needs to be said? What needs to happen for healing to occur? What will make a difference right now?

Step 7: Let Go and Move On

Accept what can't be changed—starting with the past. Leaders can help their people accept what has happened by not condoning what was done but facing what happened without denying, disowning, or resenting it. This helps employees separate themselves from their preoccupation with the past and helps them invest their emotional energies in the present and in creating a different future.

Building trust takes time and commitment. When trust is lost, it is regained only by a sincere dedication to the key behaviors and practices that earned it in the first place. The road back is not easy. However, by listening, telling the truth, keeping promises, and backing employees, you will play an essential role in assisting your employees and the organization heal from betrayal, rebuild trust, and renew relationships.

Nine months after the rebuilding process began with Frank's department, the employee satisfaction survey was readministered company-wide. Learning Services results increased an unprecedented 25 percent—the highest single increase in the company's history. Cheryl was elated; Frank felt relieved and vindicated. Lines of communication opened up between leadership and employees, and greater collaboration was taking place between people and departments in accomplishing goals.

CONCLUSION

When trust breaks down, relationships do not have to be permanently damaged. While distrust causes pain, doubt, and confusion, it also provides opportunity for growth and renewal. If people choose to work through their pain, they can heal and renew the spirit of relationships. The hope and promise of renewing trust and the gift that it brings is possible for individuals, teams, organizations, and customers. With the loss of trust comes an invitation to heal. Through healing comes renewal and inspiration. Renewal becomes a way of life at work.

Renewal is a function of participation. For trust and relationships to be renewed, people at all levels of the organization must learn how to rebuild trust again and again.

NOTES

1. Work USA, "Weathering the Storm: A Study of Employee Attitudes and Opinions," Watson Wyatt Worldwide Research Reports (2002).

2. Jacqueline A. Gilbert and Thomas Li-Ping Tang, "An Examination of Organizational Trust Antecedents," *Public Personnel Management* (1998): 27.

Chapter 13

Fun: Essential to Creating the Culture of Engagement*

Leslie Yerkes

You and I spend more time at work than we do at any other single activity. Commonly, our co-workers see more of us during the week than our families do. Many business owners, key executives, and professionals may not even see their young children outside of weekends or looking in on them while they are sleeping. For all the time we spend in the work environment, our work experience is often not fun. Our life, it seems, suffers from a lack of integration of fun and work. That is actually detrimental to the health of our business.

But we tend to devalue the importance of fun in our working lives:

1. As a culture we believe that fun should be earned. Fun should exist only *after* the work is completed.
2. The hierarchies of many organizations send the message that fun is silly, superficial, and unprofessional.
3. The unspoken prime directive is that fun in the workplace is taboo.

The existence and continuation of these belief systems is the direct result and function of the culture of the organization. If a culture believes any of these three tenets to be true, then they are. And woe to any employee who laughs.

In 1995, I became aware that some of my clients wanted to put some fun into their workdays. Their interest in finding fun activities caused me to search for companies where people were, in fact, having fun while they worked. To my surprise,

---

*Copyright © 2007 by Leslie Yerkes.

I discovered that there were many companies and organizations like that. My research produced a book, written with co-author David Hemsath, that documented the ways in which companies were generating work experiences that had fun connected to them. That book, *301 Ways to Have Fun at Work*, became a business best-seller, with nearly 100,000 copies sold in almost a dozen languages. Though the book was highly successful, I remained unsatisfied. I knew that what we had was a collection of skits, bits, tricks, episodes, and games. Good-tasting snacks, but somewhat insubstantial eating for a main course.

In support of the book, I traveled throughout America and Europe, speaking on having fun at work. During those trips, I began to discover the universal, collective desire for fun on the job. I heard from thousands of folks who longed for a situation in which they could bring their whole selves to work, not just the serious, crank-it-out side. And while I listened to people express their wishes and desires, I found myself becoming less and less interested in learning about *doing* fun things and more and more interested in discovering what it meant to *be* fun. I was less interested in collecting tips and stories on fun things to do and more interested in finding people who were successfully integrating fun and work on a daily basis and in discovering companies whose cultures engaged their employees in fun, yet meaningful ways.

PRINCIPLES OF FUN/WORK FUSION

My research resulted in what I call the Principles of Fun/Work Fusion, 11 tenets that help generate cultures that foster good morale, promote individual effectiveness, unleash creativity, and create an enjoyable climate in which to work. Following are those principles with a brief description.

1. **Give Permission to Perform.** Allow individuals to bring the best of their whole selves to work each day. To be effective, this principle requires a superb, confident leader. Strong leadership is essential to organizational well-being. The leader creates the vision, sets the tone for the journey, and holds the value that only by integrating fun and work can the best results be achieved.
2. **Challenge Your Bias.** Remove self-imposed obstacles to the release of your full being. The bias against having fun at work prevents work from being an enjoyable experience. Our belief that "when work is done we can have some fun" is one of the strongest obstacles we face.
3. **Capitalize on the Spontaneous.** This is not a program but a philosophy. Fun doesn't necessarily happen on schedule; it grows in a culture that fosters its existence.
4. **Trust the Process.** You can't muscle energy. A laugh that is forced is not a true laugh. Americans are experts at task orientation: We thrive on to-do lists. We need help, however, with process orientation. We need to trust our people and trust the process and then stand out of the way.
5. **Value a Diversity of Fun Styles.** We don't all do it the same way. There is no right or wrong way to engage in serious fun—unless, of course, it hurts others. Be inclusive and share your fun energy with all constituents inside and outside of your organization.

6. **Expand the Boundaries.** Don't start making rules to limit the process. The ideal balance of fun and work is only achieved when all individuals involved understand the boundaries of the playing field.
7. **Be Authentic.** Where do you begin? All that is required is willingness. If you want to share this part of yourself with others, the opportunity will arise. To truly understand how work and fun integrate is to accept that it is a *being* state, not a *doing* state.
8. **Be Choiceful.** Embrace the whole person. To be choiceful means to give yourself permission. True fun is not something you choose to *do*, it is something you choose to *be*. Fun is deciding to bring the best of your whole self to work every day.
9. **Hire Good People and Get Out of the Way.** If you trust your employees with your organization's most valuable assets, why not trust them to use their judgment on bringing fun to their work? When the fun is *in* the work and results from the satisfaction of good work and working relationships, then there is little risk of "when the cat's away the mice will play."
10. **Embrace Expansive Thinking and Risk Taking.** A culture that learns how to harness and develop the full potential of its employees is a culture that is comfortable with risk taking and expansive thinking. To be successful at risk taking, we must overcome the fear of failure.
11. **Celebrate.** There is nothing more fun than the celebration of a success or a shared win. The celebration itself creates energy for ongoing efforts. What gets recognized gets repeated. What gets celebrated becomes a habit. Individual recognition and group celebration fuel high performance.

NICE TO HAVE? OR NEED TO HAVE?

The companies selected to represent the Principles of Fun/Work Fusion showed that it was possible to achieve a balance between right and responsible work and finding joy, meaning, and satisfaction. They demonstrated that work could be both fun and rewarding, satisfying and profitable. To select the 11 case companies, I looked for organizations that both performed to standard business metrics and had a reputation for a culture of fun. I wanted a representation of companies from a variety of geographical locations different in size and industry type. I scanned periodicals, reviewed the many lists of best companies, and asked consulting colleagues for their recommendations. Finally, I assembled a list of about 1,000 companies and using the criteria reduced the list to 100 and did field observations with 25 companies.

One of the inherent tests in creating a list of the best of anything is seeing how well that list weathers the test of time. Will a company, once elevated to role-model status, be able to sustain its level of validity and authenticity, much less grow? Or will it stagnate or even fail? If so, what are the causes of that decline? Creating an organization worthy to be chosen for any list of outstanding examples is difficult; staying at that level is seemingly next to impossible.

That being said, six years later, each of the 11 Fun/Work Fusion companies had prospered and grown. Not one of them was done in by having a culture of fun at work. It is *precisely* that culture of fun that allowed them to maintain their position, stay in business, and grow. In spite of national tragedy, natural disaster, and changing economic conditions over the past six years, the companies originally chosen because they had cultures that were fun and promoted engagement had prospered. It became clear that what in 2000 we had considered a *nice to have* had become a *need to have*.

This thing called fun is not merely a set of activities applied to the work situation, but rather a way of being. Fun, when it is most effective, is not *input* but *output*. Fun does not create a good work place so much as a good work place creates fun. Creating places where people love to work is about creating a culture where individuals can freely bring the best of their whole selves to work each day. It is that culture of engagement that creates an environment of fun at work.

The resiliency and sustainability that the case companies have demonstrated over the past six years can be attributed to the successful interactions of these two things: business smarts and a positive culture. Business smarts is the hard science that deals with product, good strategy, continuous improvement, service orientation, strict fiscal management, and a vision that embraces the ever-changing business environment. The positive culture, or the soft science, is about the people, their interactions, values, behavior, competency, and leadership. That is, the culture of the company.

HARD SCIENCE AND SOFT SCIENCE FORMULA

To be successful, an organization must first have powerful hard science. To be sustainable, an organization's hard science must be supported by effective soft science. Both hard and soft sciences are equal in importance—they must both exist if success is to be the result. Yet the soft science ultimately differentiates and contributes the most to long-term, sustainable success. The soft science of the culture of engagement, supporting powerful hard science, creates long-term viability.

The single most important factor in producing effective soft science is the Fun/Work Fusion. If it's not fun, the workplace simply doesn't work very well.

So how effective is the culture of engagement? How well can soft science support hard science? And how well did the case companies fare over six years? Well, with four exceptions, each company grew, expanded, and prospered. The exceptions were:

1. American Skandia, which was bought out by another case company, Prudential.
2. One Prudential Exchange, which was a program created by Prudential that was retired after it successfully fulfilled its purpose.
3. Employease, which was purchased by ADT after a two-year business partnership that convinced ADT that Employease would make ADT an even better company.
4. Will Vinton Studios, whose reach exceeded its grasp and found itself after September 11, 2001, with too many long-term projects and no short-term cash flow. Will Vinton Studios was taken over by the owner of Nike and has since split into two distinct and viable companies, each exhibiting the positive signs of powerful soft science supporting strong hard science.

Pike Place Fish, Southwest Airlines, Harvard University Dining Services, Process Creative Studios, Blackboard, Lee Hecht Harrison, and Isle of Capri round out the 11 successful companies.

Each of these organizations has stories replete with people being given permission, expanding the boundaries, celebrating, and in short, having fun at work. Each follow-up analysis of these organizations has shown increases in revenue, awards, employee satisfaction, and size. While some of the employees may have changed over the course of the six years, the tone and culture have not. Each has exhibited a strong correlation between fun at work and financial success, between having a culture of engagement and the trappings of success.

ISLE OF CAPRI CASINOS: BE AUTHENTIC

There is one company, however, whose story fairly shines and bears a more detailed retelling. Like the other organizations representing one of the 11 Principles of the Fun/Work Fusion, Isle of Capri showed itself to be a great place to work, a company whose employees loved it and loved working there. Yet none of the other companies had to face and overcome as much adversity as Isle of Capri–Biloxi, a gaming resort that represented the Fun/Work Fusion principle of "be authentic."

Being authentic says that for individuals to be engaged in their work life, they must *be* fun, not simply *do* fun things. Fun isn't something we can apply like a coat of paint or a suit of clothes we choose to put on because it's appropriate for the occasion. Fun is the way we really are; it's who we are at the very core of our being.

To be successful and to have fun at work, we need to be authentic. For a company to be successful, its employees need to be authentic. When we are under stress and duress, our real selves will out. If we are projecting a facade, it will crack under strain. If we are authentic, we will make the right decisions at the right time for the right reasons.

Authenticity cannot be learned, and it cannot be faked. Being authentic requires us to be and act ourselves; it requires us to trust that who we are is the right person to be at the time. When we are authentic, we can trust our response to any situation. We don't smile because we *should*, we smile because we *can't help ourselves*. When we are authentic, we are our best selves at all times. When we are authentic, fun naturally integrates itself into our work.

That principle represents perfectly the attitude of the people who work at Isle of Capri. It's something they call Isle Style. And it's an internal being, not a learned set of behaviors. The goal of Isle of Capri is to anticipate their customers' every need and supply them before they are asked, and for employees to enjoy themselves every moment of working. When I first visited Isle of Capri–Biloxi, I was overwhelmed by the outstandingly positive attitudes of everyone I encountered. They truly did anticipate my needs, and I was left with nothing to do but have fun during my stay.

That authentic way of being was tested in 2005. On August 29, at 6:10 a.m. Hurricane Katrina hit Buras-Triumph on the southern coast of Louisiana as a category 3 storm with sustained winds of 125 mph. Katrina maintained hurricane strength well into Mississippi, 150 miles inland. At Meridian, Mississippi, Katrina officially ceased to be a hurricane. Near Clarksdale, Tennessee, it was downgraded to a tropical depression. In its rampage across Florida, Louisiana, and Mississippi, Katrina claimed at least 1,836 lives, making it the deadliest hurricane in the United States in nearly

80 years. The current estimates of damages exceed $81.2 billion (US$2005), the costliest natural disaster in U.S. history.

Katrina passed directly over Biloxi, Mississippi, home to the Isle of Capri–Biloxi.

As we all know, good behavior has a much easier chance to exist when conditions are good. The question that was answered was how would the Isle Style of Isle of Capri–Biloxi hold up under the battering winds, rain, and flooding of Hurricane Katrina?

Like most of America, I watched the television as this massive hurricane ravaged the Gulf Coast of Mississippi, leaving behind results comparable to the aftermath of war. In Biloxi alone, more than 45,000 homes were destroyed. The downtowns of many south Mississippi cities, towns, and communities were decimated—some flattened level with their concrete slab foundations. Commerce in this historic tourist region was brought to a standstill in the best cases and obliterated in the worst.

Because of my journey to Biloxi and meeting the people of the Isle of Capri casino, I had a personal interest in what was happening. I had friends who lived in the path of Katrina, and I wanted to know if they were alive and well. A week after the storm passed, while much of America was still focused on the drama unfolding in New Orleans, I sent an email to Robert Boone, vice president of HR at the Isle of Capri–Biloxi asking how he, the employees, and the casino were holding up. His response was immediate and positive: "In general, we're doing okay."

What did *okay* mean?

Consider that the Isle of Capri–Biloxi casino was a floating barge, per Mississippi law. Consider that it was a total loss. Consider that all 1,200 of its employees were instantly out of work, most of their homes destroyed, all of their homes damaged by the storm. Consider the story of Rex Yeisley, Isle of Capri senior VP of finance.

We had ridden out Hurricane George with no problems. This would be easy, we thought. As the morning wore on, the rain and wind intensified. We watched from a protected alcove on the west side of our house. When the darker clouds passed over, the winds began to circulate like a tornado. As each burst occurred, we could hear shingles tearing off the roof and see them flying with other things that should have been securely attached to someone's house. We also heard a pounding up in the attic. By the early afternoon, the pounding in the attic had grown louder. My son called me upstairs to his room and we discovered the pounding was the side of the house flapping like a sail against the studs it had pulled away from. I was in the attic trying to find a solution when a wall blew away and exposed the open attic to the wind and the rain. At that moment, it was no longer fun. We all knew the house would suffer a fair amount of damage. We also knew that it was better to stay safe than try to save the house. Being there allowed instant mourning of our loss and at the same time created a bond to keep each other safe.

Yeisley and his family weathered the storm, their home is now rebuilt, and things truly are okay for them. The same cannot be said for Doug DeSilvey, a 14-year Isle of Capri employee. He and his in-laws, as they had done for previous hurricanes, decided to ride out the storm in his in-laws' home. At one point, water started to enter the living room, 18 feet above the ground. Within hours, Doug, his daughter Donna (also an Isle employee), his ex-wife, and her parents found themselves in an upstairs bedroom looking out at 30-foot palm trees covered in raging water. With a loud crack, the roof suddenly blew off and came crashing back down at an angle into the bedroom. Water immediately rolled in and rolled everyone out. Doug was separated from the others and wound up in a magnolia tree. Hours later, when the waters began to recede, he was safe. Not so for his daughter, ex-wife, and in-laws whose bodies he saw floating in the receding water.

DeSilvey credits Isle of Capri and its employees for getting him through the aftermath of that experience. Because the company moved so quickly to help its employees and to rebuild the casino, Doug said he was able to focus on others and their problems instead of his grief. He is back at work, wearing his daughter's ID card under his own and telling everyone he meets, "When you get up in the morning, tell your loved ones how much you love them."

Bill Kessler agreed with DeSilvey on how well Isle of Capri took care of its employees during the immediate recovery period. "The Isle did more for my family than FEMA or SBA. I have worked here for 10 years and am very proud to be part of the Isle family. After losing everything, the Isle kept me sane and still keeps me that way. The Isle was the only thing normal left in my life. Thank you for the last 10 years and hopefully, at least 10 more."

Now consider that the Isle of Capri hotel, built on land, came through in good shape and was open and in use within a week, housing workers, utility people, and employees. It even hosted the state's reconstruction planning meeting.

The first press release issued by the Isle of Capri indicated that while the extent of the damage was not yet known, the company announced they would pay *all* employees for at least 90 days and salaried employees for 6 months.

Consider that Isle of Capri Corporate started a Katrina Relief Fund that distributed $2.1 million to employees to help with recovery costs.

After such considerations, it was apparent that to Robert Boone and the entire staff of Isle of Capri that "okay" meant they were going to make it. When all was said and done, Isle of Capri–Biloxi would be bigger and better than before. Isle Style had survived.

Certainly, I thought, they *sounded* positive. I wondered if they would be able to pull it off.

I knew Katrina would be the ultimate test of the Isle of Capri's Isle Style philosophy. Teamwork, authenticity, and fun are a *nice-to-have* when things are going well. The question was how well would those soft sciences hold up under the stress of catastrophic natural disaster? Would they be there when they were a *need-to-have*?

The answer was that the soft sciences of Isle of Capri not only held up well, they were the most important part of ensuring that the casino would not only be rebuilt and be the first to reopen, but also that the company would grow and improve.

To be successful, good companies need their hard sciences to be in good working order. They need a good vision, a good mission, a good action plan, and a good product. Great companies need not only great hard science but also great soft science. That is, they must also have in place a *culture of engagement* that makes work fun. Isle of Capri's Isle Style is more than a set of rules about what employees should say and do in certain situations. Isle Style is a philosophy and a set of behaviors that define and influence how employees think, act, and behave at all times under all situations.

For example, one of the first things Robert Boone and his team did after Katrina was over was to hold a payday pizza party in the parking lot the Monday after the storm. Not only did the company pay their employees on time, they also told them they would be paid for the next 90 days, whether or not they were able to work. (When it took 120 days to rebuild, they continued to pay them until there were jobs for them.) The party also provided food during a time of stress and allowed team members to connect, share stories, and offer support for each other and for the company as they all began the process of rebuilding.

By December 2005, Isle of Capri–Biloxi casino was the first of the dozen or so casinos destroyed to be rebuilt and reopened to the public. Isle of Capri president and chief operating officer Tim Hinkley said,

Reopening the Isle–Biloxi marks a major milestone for the state of Mississippi, as well as for our company. This casino was originally the first to open in the market back in 1992 and we are the first land-based Gulf Coast casino to open following the devastation of Hurricane Katrina. Our goal was to put our team members back to work as quickly as possible and I am happy to say that we have succeeded. Our team members are excited to get back to the business of welcoming guests in Isle Style.

Of the 1,200 people employed before the storm, 900 chose to remain in Biloxi to rebuild and to grow with Isle–Biloxi. More than 100 chose to move and work for another Isle of Capri casino. By fall 2006, Isle–Biloxi had grown to 1,700 employees, with the vast majority of the new employees coming from the ranks of those who once worked for other casinos that were not yet reopened. Isle Style scored another win when 90 percent of those new employees chose to remain with Isle of Capri even after their original casinos reopened and offered them back their jobs.

One such employee was Melanie Pankonin.

I worked at [another casino] for six years before Katrina. After the storm, [my casino] wasn't open but I was able to get a job as a Guest Service Representative at Isle–Biloxi. When the [first casino] reopened, I decided to stay on at Isle. I love this job and the people I work with. Management treats me like a team member and not a number and that's important to me. They care about me and they value my opinion.

Brian Casey agrees with Melanie. "Everyone in Biloxi knows that the Isle stood by its people during and after the storm. I was able to get on with Isle–Biloxi as a manager and they've given me the opportunity to demonstrate my abilities. I hope to stay here for a long time."

There were four external factors that allowed Isle–Biloxi to reopen quickly.

1. Isle of Capri's insurance was so good that payments covered their damages within 2 percent.
2. Because Isle–Biloxi was in the midst of an expansion project when Katrina hit, they had already ordered all new slot machines that had yet to be delivered. This allowed Isle–Biloxi

to have nearly instant access to the mechanical heart of their gaming operation—slot machines—once the new structure was completed.

3. It was clear to everyone, including the Mississippi legislature, that the state law requiring casinos to be built floating on water was the cause of huge amounts of unnecessary damage and expense. The Grand Casino, for example, which had also essentially been built on a barge, was ripped from its moorings and pushed 1,000 yards inland. (The structure had to be cut into quarters and hauled away for demolition.) Seeing the result of their original well-intentioned but impractical regulations, the legislature quickly passed a new law that allowed for the construction of on-land casinos. Without this, it is unlikely that many casinos, if any, would have been rebuilt. Since casinos supply the second-highest level of income, taxes, and financial return to the area, gaming's wishes were seriously and speedily considered.

4. Mississippi came to a political action plan faster than did neighboring Louisiana. Within days of the storm's first impact, Mississippi governor Haley Barbour put together a commission to jump-start rebuilding and asked Netscape founder Jim Barksdale to be chairman. Barksdale funded the commission with $1 million of his own money and encouraged the Knight Foundation to match it. As of fall 2006, New Orleans had *no* plan for demolition, clean-up, or reconstruction.

While their hard sciences were excellent, their planning was top-notch, and they were fortunate in having instant access to replacement slot machines; there is no question that it was the strength of their soft sciences that allowed Isle–Biloxi to recover as quickly as it did from the ravages of Katrina. Not only were they the first casino to reopen, but when they rebuilt they expanded. Now, Isle of Capri–Biloxi plans to build a second casino on the Mississippi Gulf Coast.

Hurricane Katrina was a natural disaster on a scale that had not been seen in this country in our lifetime. While it may take decades for the entire region to recover fully from the effects of the storm, the culture of engagement of Isle Style has allowed Isle–Biloxi to withstand the worst possible outcome: closing up shop, moving away, and taking 1,700 jobs with them.

Katrina was also a test of the authenticity of the members of the Isle–Biloxi team. It is not unusual to get good performance from companies and individuals in good times. It's what happens in hard times that matters. If relationships are strong and people truly authentic, it will be obvious in both good times and bad.

When a company's culture does not support or invest in its employees, what those employees do in hard times will be uncertain. If, however, a company has a robust foundation of trust, respect, and loyalty, and has learned to laugh and love together, that company will be able to weather any storm. Even a storm called Katrina.

CONCLUSION

Success is no longer determined simply by the ability to be smart and strategic. To be successful, we need to create environments that resonate with the workforce, places that are fun to work, situations that fuel deep relationships. Well-being used to be a *nice to have*. Six years ago it was hard for some organizations to buy into the need to be as proficient in soft science as well as hard science. But in a world filled with terrorists, school shootings, missing children, and a changing world economy, organizations have begun to realize that well-being at work is now a *need to have*.

If companies are going to be healthy, viable, and robust; if they are going to be sustainable; if they are going to be able to compete, survive, and thrive, then our work experience must be fun. If organizations, and the people who make them up, are ultimately to be successful, we must balance our environments with strong hard science and effective soft science.

No longer is employee engagement a *nice to have*, today it is a *need to have*. To survive, organizations need to place equal emphasis on hard and soft sciences. Then, they need to generate and maintain a culture of engagement. And that includes a healthy respect for fun.

Chapter 14

Ten Things You Should Know about Executive Search Now*

Gordon Thomas

It's all about the talent, right? We've heard this for years, and the War for Talent has been a battle cry for almost a decade. Back in 2000, we even declared talent to have won the war. Corporations gave in to the talented (and untalented) during the dot-com boom. Have a résumé? Here is your job and new Razor scooter. MBA? Here's a million bucks worth of stock options, a business to run, and a private espresso bar. Six months of experience at a much-hyped online version of a bricks-and-mortar business? You get all of the above and two years of runway to sort of prove a business model.

During this time, corporate recruiting organizations had no leverage. Zip, zero, nada. They were told: "Give candidates what the market says to give them." This was essentially the strategy. It had to be because the pickings were slim. The best-qualified candidate for a job was simply the best candidate *available* for the job. As far as strategic hiring, bench building, top grading, and so on were concerned, sadly this was mostly window dressing. When it came to hiring, there simply was not enough time to really take the steps required to even do a passable job at being strategic.

When the dot-com bubble burst, the top-talent bubble burst right with it. Companies finally had the time to assess who the real top talent was. And the rest were laid off. Have a résumé? Put it in the outplacement folder. MBA? Your options are now "individual contributor" or "consultant." All of that plus six months of experience at the much-hyped online version of a bricks-and-mortar business? You might want to just leave that experience off your résumé.

---

*Copyright © 2007 by Gordon Thomas.

We are now in the midst of an upturn in the demand for talent again. Hopefully, by following the 10 guidelines discussed in this chapter, you will be able to better utilize the executive search industry to build a top-flight organization. Leave the Razor scooters in the garage.

SELECTING THE RIGHT FIRM OR CONSULTANT WILL HELP YOU BUILD AND ENHANCE A HIGH-PERFORMING BUSINESS

When I arrived at America Online (AOL) as the director of staffing in fall 1999, the boom was booming. Still, we used to force-rank our employees from a performance standpoint. Those in the top 10 percent of performers were designated top talent. These people tended to be easy to identify. They simply delivered results. As I work with high-performing organizations today, I find that most have a similar dynamic and are actively trying to increase the numbers of this class of employee.

A players have a broad network of A player contacts. Leveraging this network of top talent for clients is the single most valuable service an executive search firm can offer—assuming, of course, that the firm itself is staffed with A players. The firm you choose to help you with an executive search should be able to rapidly and specifically cite the successes that their search work has produced. This is not in the number of hires per year but in the reference-able *results* that the executives they have delivered to their clients have produced.

Insist on talking to a search firm's previous clients and ask for the specific successes the candidates they delivered have produced.

Take the time and talk to at least two or three of the search firm's clients—making certain you are talking with the direct supervisor of the hired executive. The question is a simple one. "Has the executive you hired from the search firm delivered on the specific goals and objectives you had for them?" Listen for the specific quantifiable results rather than the general subjective comments. "He's a great guy," "We're happy with our hire," or "We'll use the search firm again" are generally positive comments that tell you next to nothing about the net result on the purpose of using a search firm.

Make hiring a search firm that focuses and executes on delivering talent your top priority. It is more important than specialization, geography, size of firm, or any other quantifier. Big and fancy executive recruitment firms aren't necessarily your best bet. When one company needed to hire a CFO, they called in the "usual suspects"—two of the four largest search firms in America. One of their board members was also a board member of one of these firms. Both of these firms came in prepared with their mastheads, scale, and laundry lists of other representative searches to establish their worthiness for conducting this search. But they were unable (or unwilling) to provide the name of the individuals who would actually be working on this critical project, let alone specific contacts who could attest to the results.

So they called a very small search firm that had delivered winners for the CEO in the past. Despite the fact that this search firm had not "worked on" hundreds of Fortune 500 CFO searches as the larger firms had, they had done the one thing that should matter most. They had already delivered top talent for the CEO. And they were willing to meet the client's requests from the outset. They performed on the foundation of their well-developed networks and customer service philosophy, rather than resting on their laurels.

SEARCH SUCCESS DEPENDS ON THE PEOPLE DOING THE SEARCH, NOT THE TECHNOLOGY

How do specialists in executive recruitment do what you, as part of a corporation, cannot? You actually could do the job yourself if you were willing and able to put forth the dedicated, focused effort that is required. There is no mystery, no secret sauce, or patented intellectual property that I am aware of that sets executive recruiters apart when it comes to finding talent. The real secret is that executive search firms simply have invested more of their resources toward finding great talent on a consistent basis. They don't look at the search consultants who work for them as overhead but as profit centers. This makes all the difference in the world.

Over the years, one metric I have seen established is that a great recruiter can do a thorough and high-quality job of executing on no more than three search assignments at a time. In contrast, I work with a corporate executive recruiter at one of our Fortune 100 clients who regularly has over 40 open director-level and higher searches on his plate. He demonstrates the rule, rather than the exception, at most corporations. Are our employees better than he is? Maybe not. I suggest that my employees are just better set up to succeed by having realistic performance expectations and are invested in as a profit center rather than an overhead department.

Today, performing an executive search is a function of the amount of focused and dedicated manpower applied to the search as opposed to a unique type of expertise.

This statement was not as true when I started in the search business in the mid-1980s. At that time, the recruiter's Rolodex really was all that mattered. Back then, it was very difficult, time-consuming, and expensive to find qualified candidates. The best recruiters in the business were the ones with the most time invested in the business. Over time, they simply had developed large networks of trusted and helpful people who they could contact on a regular basis to find out who they should talk to in regard to a search assignment. Executive recruiters had to be specialists. It was too inefficient to try and build effective candidate networks and databases in more than one industry or functional expertise.

The sources that search firms used to find people to contact were primitive compared with today—professional association directories, corporate phone books, alumni lists, and so on. We had to rely on the U.S. Postal Service to deliver résumés! Only the largest firms could afford to pay for FedEx or purchase fax machines. We contacted candidates only one way—calling them on their land line and hoping they answered. It took a tremendous amount of man-hours to conduct the most basic research on an assignment. On top of this, we had to explain to a large percentage of the candidates exactly who we were and what we were doing. Most candidates had no idea what an executive search firm did or why they should bother returning a call. Nobody could talk about such a sensitive thing at work, so we had to have most of the conversations in the evenings and on weekends. Perhaps one in 10 would be willing to recommend an appropriate person by name.

The research and candidate development portions of a search easily took 75 percent of the total time to conduct a search. We shorted the most important aspects of recruitment: evaluating, vetting, and preparing a candidate for a new role.

Today, that research and candidate development typically takes less than 20 percent of the total time to conduct a search. This is ultimately a very good thing, as it enables us to spend much more time on the evaluation and vetting of candidates, rather than spending such a disproportionate amount of time just trying to find people to talk to.

I truly can't remember the last time I had to explain to a candidate what I did for a living and why I was calling, and I get an incredible amount of candidates who seek me out to help them move forward in their careers. I can use any number of inexpensive and efficient databases to find not only names of people to call but also a good portion of their bio (think LinkedIn). Everyone has a cell phone and can take time to talk any time, or IM, or text with me without a need for secrecy. Nine out of 10 people understand the value of networking, and I now have to manage those referrals down to only the most applicable.

For a period of time in the 1990s, technology advances, especially the development of candidate databases, required a significant up-front investment, and large annual budget for maintenance that only the largest executive search firms could afford. These technologies provided a competitive advantage that small firms and individuals had a very tough time competing with. It was very logical to make the case that the price paid by clients for access to the efficiencies was well worth it. They could simply get to more people faster.

Today, the advent of widespread, inexpensive, self-administrating data sources has dramatically leveled the playing field when comparing executive search firms of any size. For the cost of one executive search, a small company can buy access to the highest-end information services, candidate networks, and databases.

The objective of the executive recruiter has been consistent over the decades, while the means of executing on that objective has changed dramatically. This has brought the emphasis to where it really should be for the client company: evaluating and selecting a search firm or executive recruiter. Instead of a major portion of the cost of a search going to the underlying mechanisms (other than the salary) of enabling the search process, today the vast majority is invested where it should be—in the professional expertise and ability of the individual actually doing the work.

Insist on knowing which individual is doing every aspect of every search.

If you are evaluating an executive search partner, and can't get a straight, immediate answer to the question of who is actually going to conduct this particular search, move on. Since most of the underlying mechanics of a search are relatively equal among search firms, you deserve to know exactly what differentiating factor (person) you are paying for. Today, that person will be actually conducting most of the research, prioritizing whom to contact according to the insight they have personally received from you, making the initial calls to candidates, conducting the interviews, doing the comparative assessments, negotiating the salary, checking the references, and closing the deal.

At one point in time, these responsibilities may have been spread across as many as five or six different people. Today, other than the administrative tasks of scheduling and coordinating travel and interview logistics, the executive recruiters will be doing the rest themselves.

The focus of your evaluation needs to be entirely on these individuals. They will be the people analyzing your requirement, digesting your corporate culture, and serving as the initial point of contact between your company and the candidate marketplace. They will be the people who handle most of the communication during the process and portray your mission, values, and potential. Their intuition and evaluation skills will have a tremendous impact on which candidate you end up hiring.

SEARCH FIRMS ARE STRUCTURED IN DIFFERENT WAYS

Historically, there have been two types of executive search firms: *retained* search firms and *contingency* search firms. Today we can add two more, the first being search firms that operate under a hybrid model and refer to themselves as either *con-tainer* or *re-tingency* firms. The other type of search service is the individual or firm that provides executive search services under a fixed hourly or monthly rate.

Retained Search Firms

These firms typically work on a fee structure that is based on a negotiated percentage of salary of the hired candidate (more on this shortly) and bill their fees either entirely up front or in monthly installments. This is how most of the big firms (Korn-Ferry International, Heidrick and Struggles, Spencer Stuart, Russell Reynolds) operate. Many liken themselves to management consultants that focus on the best practices of recruitment. The larger firms will have global reach via their own offices or international partnerships.

Most retained search firms will also have staff with relevant domain expertise to assess candidates' functional strengths and witnesses. This is why CPA firms or law firms will sometimes add search practices to their service offerings. These firms also usually ensure some degree of exclusivity to you regarding the candidates they present. They won't present the same candidate to multiple client companies at the same time.

In addition to the fee calculation and structure issues, there are a number of flaws in the traditional retained model. The largest of these is the fact that these firms aren't financially tied to their performance. They get paid whether or not they deliver.

Also, in addition to the fee, there is almost always a provision for additional costs, such as allocated expenses. This catch-all category covers the monthly fees for phone bills, utilities, office space, and other overhead expenses of the business, essentially guaranteeing that the fee itself is net profit.

Contingency Search Firms

These firms will also work on a fee structure that is based on a negotiated percentage of salary of the hired candidate. However, they don't bill the client until there is an actual hire.

Again, the fee calculation and structures are problematic, but more important there is absolutely no assurance that even "best efforts" will be used. About the only time I recommend using a contingency firm would be to provide résumé examples for a proposal. However, today you can probably get a better value by purchasing a short-term access to a résumé database.

Hybrid Search Firms

These firms combine various aspects of the above two models, as the name implies. As the purchasers of executive search services have become more sophisticated, these models have been developed to try to overcome the obvious shortcomings of the pure retained or contingency models.

For example, a *re-tingency* firm may leave a small part of the fee contingent on an actual hire. Or, a *con-tainer* firm will promise some degree of exclusivity of candidate exposure or level of effort.

Some of these efforts are simply negotiation tactics dressed up as business models. In the past five years I have seen executed contracts from the largest retained search firms in the world that fix a set fee or leave a portion of a fee contingent on a hire. The bright spot in this is that it signals that the industry is finally recognizing, albeit slowly, that there needs to be dramatic change in how we structure agreements and respond to client needs.

Contract Recruiters

These individuals (or firms that provide them) will take on a search and simply bill a fixed hourly or monthly rate for the amount of time spent conducting a search. The plus side of this type of agreement is the simplicity. The sometimes not-so-obvious problem is once again there is no connection between cost and results.

I have worked with and employed some amazing recruiters in my career. I have also been completely shocked by the utter ineptitude of others. During the dot-com boom, the amazing recruiters billed clients at $200 per hour, and the inept billed $100 per hour. I have never seen the marketplace bear, under an hourly concept, billing rates that would pay the amazing recruiter commensurate with their comparative degree of expertise over the inept. You are buying results, not someone's time. So don't structure your agreement based on hourly or monthly rates.

YOUR EXECUTIVE SEARCH FIRM WORKS FOR YOU, SO MANAGE IT

At AOL, we once conducted a search for a key vice president role that appeared to have difficulty getting traction. It took a week of calling the executive search firm, one of the world's largest, to find out who was in charge of the search on their end, and get a status report on where they were in the process. I dug up the one-page contract that was dated over four months before, and found out the six-figure fee had already been paid in full. Clearly AOL did not have the power in this relationship.

I was finally sent a report with over 40 names the firm reported as candidates who had been contacted and were interested in pursuing this opportunity. To jump-start the search, I decided to call the 10 or so names that looked especially interesting. The second name I called had been deceased for over a year.

Fast forward to today. Lessons haven't been learned. I was recently called to conduct a search for a Fortune 100 client. The boom is beginning to boom again. The company has virtually unlimited resources, a premium brand name, and recruiters everywhere. The search I was asked to take on is described as the most important search in the company. Still, the position has already been open for seven months. A six-figure fee has been paid in full to one of the world's largest executive search firms. Three candidates have been interviewed. Nobody has been hired, and the search firm is not interested in doing any more work on the assignment. No deceased candidates this time, but there was not much more on the results front. My estimate is that they have spent at least a million dollars in the last year for searches that have not yielded a hire. That's actually probably low.

Different decade. Same results. Basically the same issue.

The key in keeping these types of things from happening to your organization are relatively simple and most revolve around managing the search process.

You can control the success of a search by how you manage it.

The entire search process should be a partnership effort between you and the executive search firm from the very beginning. The search firm is simply supplying the dedicated, focused manpower to complete this process in an efficient manner. You are still providing the need, the standards, and the expectations.

Ideally, the search firm will provide you with a step-by-step process that they can demonstrate to have worked for numerous clients. Use the following basic process outline as a sanity check against what they propose. Hopefully, you will never find yourself expecting a long-deceased candidate to come in and interview for your high-profile executive role.

RECRUITING PROCESS OUTLINE

Days 1–30

- Perform in-depth analysis of the requirement, position description, and hiring team.
  - This will include interviews by the search consultant with all key stakeholders for the hire.
  - Provide immediate access to these stakeholders, and the meetings should be done in person so the search consultant can assess team chemistry and culture.
  - The result of this effort will be a very descriptive and accurate position description that you will sign off on.

- Search firm conducts initial research to develop a target candidate pool, and begins sourcing candidates in parallel.
  - The initial feedback from the sourcing conversations should be built into the analysis of the position description, as well as any obstacles encountered in the search.
  - Starting this on day one allows time for the referral-based networking to pick up momentum.
- Search firm conducts exploratory candidate conversations.
  - It is not uncommon that the candidate who is ultimately hired is actually identified in the first weeks of a search.
  - Expertise of the search consultant in managing expectations of the candidates they speak with at this point is at a premium.
- Search firm gathers marketplace feedback for client.
  - This involves compensation surveys, assessments of marketplace reaction to the company and the opportunity.
  - This information will also help refine and finalize the position description and direction of the candidate sourcing.
- Focus weekly client meetings on pros and cons of target candidates.
  - Weekly means weekly. Make this the meeting you do not miss every week until the employee has started working for you.
  - The discussion of target candidates always helps the search consultant understand the preferences of the hiring manager. Better to do this early in the process with "potential" candidates than "actual" candidates.

Days 30–60

- Search firm performs candidate development and evaluation.
  - The target candidate pool will develop into an actual candidate pool.
  - Interviews and reference checks are conducted with candidates of mutual interest.
  - Desire a goal of twice the number of candidates shown needed by historical hire-to-interview ratio.
- Focus weekly status meetings on pros and cons of candidate bios.
  - Try to screen in rather than screen out.
- Refine position description as needed.
- Schedule candidates for initial meetings with the hiring team.
  - Make this your top priority—reschedule other conflicts.
  - Candidate availability drives the interview scheduling, not hiring team availability.
- Search firm should be providing real world, firsthand marketplace feedback from candidates.

Days 60–Hire Date (90–120)

- Evaluate and select candidates.
- Vet candidate backgrounds via references.
  - This is key and arguably more important than the actual interviews.
- Focus weekly client meetings on client interview processes.
  - You control whether this process goes on for an extra month or two, or three.
- Manage the feedback cycle.
  - 24 hours to collect feedback, 48 hours to distribute feedback. Every time.
- Compare finalists and verify candidate credentials.
- Hire.

Time kills deals—especially those involving highly talented and sought-after people. If you are going to build a high-performance organization with top talent and high-passion employees, make certain this process is a high priority. Don't fall into the trap of rescheduling or delaying interviews. Most searches bog down just when the actual interview process begins. The urgency that pressed the decision to go to an outside search firm diminishes because there is a comfort level in knowing that candidates are on the way.

YOU HAVE MORE CONTROL OVER THE FEES THAN YOU MAY THINK YOU DO

The executive search industry is no different than any other when it comes to trying to identify the drivers and motivators for business. Take a look at the contract and fees, and you will probably get a very good idea of the primary business drivers.

Although there are a couple of different types of executive search business models, the fees among the vast majority of the companies in the industry are remarkably similar. This fee is usually based on a negotiated percentage of the hired employees' first-year expected compensation. It seems simple, but it's not.

Over the past three decades, the percentage that the fee was based on has swung from 15 percent in the down times, to upwards of 33 1/3 percent in the boom times—with a guaranteed minimum. When I was AOL's director of staffing at the height of the boom, the blue chip search firms would caveat that this fee had to equal at least $100,000 (and 1 percent of the stock if the client was a startup) or they wouldn't even take a look at the search. The number that the fee was calculated on included base compensation, highest potential annual bonus, and sign-on bonus combined. If the candidate was hired in at base salary of $200,000, was eligible for a 100 percent performance bonus, and was given $50,000 as a sign-on bonus, the fee was calculated as one third of $450,000 or $150,000.

On the contrary, in late 2001 and early 2002, the fee might have still been quoted as 33 1/3 percent, but it was calculated only using the base salary—in the example above this would have equaled only $66,666.66. As a percentage of the total components above this fee is actually only about 15 percent. What a difference a year makes.

Over my career, I have tried to get a philosophically sound explanation for how our industry continues to use percentage of compensation as its standard fee. The most logical explanation I can report to you is "it's simple."

Historically, there seem to be a couple of different rationales, such as the legal industry once offering placement services to their clients, and just continuing to use their established fee mechanism, or "clients don't understand what we really do, so we offer this easy-to-understand system." The rest of the explanations involve variations of "that's how it's always been done."

There are basic flaws with this "simple" system. The first and most blatant problem with this is the inherent conflict of interest it creates. You, the client, are hiring an executive search firm to go out and find an executive. We, the search firm, are working for you, and you will ultimately write us a check. However, the amount of that check is directly proportionate to the amount of annual compensation the hired candidate gets. The worse job we do for you in terms of working out compensation, the better our fee is.

If you ask us to work on two absolutely identical searches with the only differentiator being compensation, we will most likely have an easier time getting a candidate to accept the position with the higher compensation. However, you will pay us a higher fee on this "easier" assignment.

What can you do as the client with regard to fees? *You can insist on a flat and fixed fee.*

If a search firm (or any business for that matter) truly knows and understands its business as well as it should, it should absolutely be able to determine what it costs to complete an assignment. A great search firm, whether large, small, or an independent consultant, will do the appropriate amount of due diligence on your assignment *before* it quotes you a fee. It should completely understand you, your culture, and the good, bad, and ugly about the requirement. It should have a feel for your reputation in the marketplace, the demand for the type and quality of candidate you want to hire, and the compensation requirements and expectations. It must know how long it will take and the associated costs of their part of the recruiting, interviewing, and selection process. It should take the time to find out in advance the amount of time it will take, and the effectiveness of your parts of the selection process as well.

How does a flat, fixed fee translate into building and running a high-performance organization with top talent/high-passion employees? Primarily, by making certain that the person or company responsible for the search truly understands your business, and the unique challenges and benefits of working with you before you engage on an assignment.

It takes time and slows down the process in the beginning. It may feel frustrating. But it's worth it. The up-front due diligence will often uncover what is truly needed versus what is thought to be needed in a new employee. Your selection team will all be on the same page regarding priorities, and the communication to the candidates will be clear and consistent.

You will also be able to work with an accurate budget—knowing exactly what the cost of the assignment is going to be—and avoiding the temptation to balance search fees with candidate compensation. If you end up raising your compensation for the hire, you do not raise your search fee.

THE FEE STRUCTURE ON THE SEARCH ASSIGNMENT SHOULD MIRROR YOUR DELIVERABLE NEEDS

The other major component of executive search finances is how the fees are structured. In the traditional retained search model, the client essentially guarantees that the executive search firm will be paid their fee on a search assignment, regardless of the outcome, with the total fee billed in predetermined increments.

The standard fee structure for most retained search firms is "a third, and a third, and a third." A third of the fee is due when the contract is signed. The second third of the fee is due after 30 days. The final third of the fee is due after 60 days. If the compensation ends up exceeding the initial estimate that established the fee, a final "up-tick" fee will be charged as well. Ironically, if the compensation ends up being less than the initial estimate, there is no "down-tick" refund.

The main problem with these traditional fee structures is that the contractual and financial motivation for the search firm is not aligned with the clients' interests. The search firm is motivated to have 60 days on the calendar transpire so they can collect the full fee, as opposed to efficiently and effectively using the time to actually complete a successful search. However, you are most likely trying to get a top-notch new hire on board as quickly as possible. That's why you engaged a specialist devoted to doing this one thing, rather than have it be lumped in with a handful of other pressing needs on the desk of the corporate recruiter. Your motivation is to get the best person hired as quickly and efficiently as possible. So set the search firm up to have their motivation in alignment with yours.

You can insist on a deliverable-based fee structure. First of all, make certain that the due diligence is done by the executive search firm prior to agreeing to engage. If needed, agree to have this analysis done under a completely different contract. For the search itself, set appropriate milestones that trigger payment for real value received, not just for passing time. For example, have the first portion of the fee due upon delivery of a satisfactory list of target candidates. Fifty target candidates complete with names, current titles, and appropriate experience (and preferably alive) could be your goal. The second portion could be due after you have agreed to have two or three candidates, qualified in your opinion, entered into your interviewing process. The final portion should be due upon hire or start date.

The payment installments should be proportioned to make sure they are relative to the amount of work and value of each segment of the process. The bulk of the actual work and costs associated on an executive search are done well before the actual hire. The first fee installment should reflect the time and effort required in pulling together and finalizing the position description, surveying the marketplace for compensation, conducting research to generate a large enough candidate pool to ensure results, breaking down target companies for targets, and so on.

The second installment should be the largest of the three. This will cover the heavy lifting of a search—contacting, recruiting, evaluating, and preparing for hire of target candidates. This is by far the highest value and most critical part of a search assignment, so let the fee for this reflect it. Even if the search does not result in a hire for some reason, the amount of value you have received and the amount of real work that has been done by the search firm should be well worth the amount of money you have paid out to this point.

The final installment should also be the smallest installment. Although many people believe that the "high value" work of selecting and closing the finalist candidate is the most valuable part of a search, it should be largely performed in the earlier portions of the project. Most important, the search firm simply does not control this aspect of the search—remember only you, the client, can actually make a hire and control this payment.

EVERY DETAIL OF YOUR CONTRACT MATTERS

One thing I have been amazed at over my career is many of the "standard" terms and conditions included and omitted from business contracts. At AOL, I was told by the head of human resources that in the year before I arrived, we had paid over $1 million for executive search assignments for which we had zero hires. I work with a number of other similar clients who report as bad or worse statistics from previous encounters with executive search firms.

I believe one of the main reasons for this is the actual contractual terms (or lack of them) in the search firm agreement itself. Top-tier, well-respected, Fortune 100 companies will sign agreements that essentially commit to paying hundreds of thousands of dollars with little to no performance guidelines, deliverables, or even expectations. You have agreed, essentially, to pay these firms for depositing your check into their accounts.

You can insist on a search agreement with deliverables and common-sense details.

Tie the fee structure to specific deliverables that the search firm should be happy to commit to. While no search firm can ever guarantee that you hire a candidate (you are the only party with that legal authority to do so), they can and should commit to performance of some kind other than "we will try our best to compete this search."

If your internal statistics show that you hire one out of five candidates that interview, then ask the search firm to deliver at least five qualified candidates as part of the agreement. Other deliverables you can and should require are:

1. A clearly defined and well-written position description that reflects both the responsibilities of the role and prior experience that demonstrates a candidate can perform those responsibilities.
2. A comprehensive, quality assured, and proven search process that shows it is reasonable to expect the firm can and will generate enough candidates to ensure success on the project.

3. Feedback from the candidates and marketplace regarding availability of candidates, comparative assessments of candidates, how your company is perceived in the marketplace (even if the news is bad), and what your competitors are doing.
4. A clear understanding of your corporate culture, goals, and what success looks like in your organization.
5. Regular, detailed status reports that address candidate development pipelines, the market response to the search, and any obstacles that could impede the success of the search.
6. Complete and detailed reference checks and verification of candidate credentials.

You should also expect a fair and common-sense agreement that includes clear definitions of items such as:

1. Which individuals at the search firm will actually be conducting the work.
2. A guarantee on confidentiality with regard to sensitive information the search firm will need to be given.
3. A guarantee to replace any candidate that is hired if the search firm misrepresents or does not properly verify credentials, prior employment, or any other aspects about the candidate that you have asked them to verify.
4. A guarantee to provide follow-up in the months after the candidate is hired.
5. A guarantee to not solicit for recruitment any employees that the search firm has developed a relationship with during the search assignment for a reasonable period of time, typically six months to a year.
6. A commitment to work at that highest degree of business ethics.
7. A commitment to the adherence of equal opportunity, affirmative action, and any other relevant legal requirements.

The contract details do not guarantee the search will succeed, but they can help ensure that your partnership with the search firm is aligned and motivated consistently with your needs.

THE WAY AN EXECUTIVE SEARCH FIRM EVALUATES CANDIDATES IS EXTREMELY IMPORTANT

There have literally been hundreds of attempts at bottling the ability to predict the future success of a newly hired executive. From interviewing techniques, to psychological profiling and testing, HR consultants have developed a cottage industry by capitalizing on the next best way to guarantee the success of a new hire. I have been exposed to many methods firsthand, and certainly have my preferences. However one tool that I have noticed over the years that has consistently outperformed the diagnostic tool du jour is the application of well-executed reference checks.

There are two distinct aspects to the reference check process. One is the obvious demonstration of firsthand witness to examples of desired skills and personal attributes. Almost more important, though, is the search consultant understanding and being able to communicate what is really needed in the target role.

I am often surprised by the lack of consistency among hiring teams in the message of what skills are required for a candidate to be successful in target role. This confusion of priorities among interviewers sends a mixed (and poor) message to the candidate, as well as complicating the actual evaluation of the candidate.

One of the first search assignments I was asked to conduct after I started my current firm in 2001 was for a chief operating officer for a successful startup company that was on the verge of making it to the next level of success. Their feeling was that if they improved their operations, the increased efficiency would help them move up to the next level. They had already been presented a proposal from another large search firm. I was brought in as the reliable second opinion. I insisted on meeting with the entire executive team and a couple of the company's outside directors before I would even submit a proposal.

After these interviews (which only took three days), it was quite apparent that the last thing the company needed was yet a new operations executive. There were at least three highly capable operations executives on the staff already. What they needed was a person who could bring in powerful partnerships that would accelerate the rise of the company. They needed a president. I shared my findings with the founder and board members, and they had an "a ha!" moment. I was given the search assignment, and we found the executive who brought the needed partnerships to the table. Two years later, this company was acquired for cash by one of the remaining blue chip Internet and Fortune 500 companies.

What does this have to do with references? Well, if we had taken the search as presented and evaluated candidates based on the reference-able examples of operations expertise, we would have helped build an exceedingly well-run operation that did not capitalize on its potential. Instead, we built the reference targets on the demonstrated ability to bring premium partnerships to the table and a track record of capitalizing on those opportunities.

You can insist that executive search firm validate the supposed experience that will indicate success in the role you are trying to fill.

The actual process of evaluating candidates' chances of being successful in the now accurately defined role is relatively straightforward. Ask candidates to outline specific examples of things they have done in their careers that are relevant to the new position. This should be easy for the right candidate to do if he or she has actually done the needed things. Look for specific names, dates, and results in what they present. If they don't offer it—ask for it pointedly.

The next step is to talk with as many people as possible to get substantiation and confirmation of what has been spoken to by the candidate. Let the reference know what skills you are looking for. Ask them to walk you through, again via specific examples, situations in which the candidate has demonstrated the desired skill. Then, ask that reference (not the candidate) for another person that you can speak with who can add to the picture.

These are not 15-minute conversations. Let the reference know that you would like to spend 30 minutes to an hour with them talking about the candidate. At face value this may sound like a huge imposition. However, my experience is that when it comes to great talent, people want to be part of their success. The best hires I have been involved with in my career have one thing in common—an almost never-ending line of people with a number of specific examples of real accomplishments by that candidate that they are more than happy to talk about.

THERE ARE SPECIFIC THINGS TO DO TO MAKE THE MOST OF A NEW HIRE

You have just spent over $100,000 in just the search fee to hire a new executive. You have interviewed eight wonderfully qualified candidates that required over 100 man-hours by your hiring team to conduct. Over 20 man-hours have been spent just on conducting references. Over 400 external candidates have been touched by the process. You have spent well over $200,000 in relocation expenses.

The candidate shows up at his new job, and doesn't have a working phone, except his personal cell phone for two days. He has to wait more than a week to get his laptop configured. He's frustrated and doesn't know whom to talk to. He doesn't want to be perceived as a whiner, but he wants to be up and running on day one. These little frustrations eat at him over the next couple of weeks and start to foster feelings of buyer's remorse. He resigns a month later to go to your competitor who had started recruiting him during the three weeks between the time he resigned from his previous job and his start date with yours. How could this have happened?

You should insist that the search firm provide a follow-up program for the new hire.

A great search firm will verify that your on-boarding process is what it needs to be, and it will help you address it if it is lacking. They will also hold up their end of the process by making certain that a candidate is transitioned smoothly to the new role. This includes guiding a candidate through the resignation process. I recommend that the search firm maintain two to three contacts per week with candidates between the time they officially resign and the time they physically start the new job. The hiring executive should maintain at least weekly contact during the same interim.

Continue to have weekly status reports with the search firm during this period as well. The meetings will be short, hopefully, but focused on any issues that arise so they can be handled efficiently.

After the new hire's start date, the search firm should maintain at least weekly contact for the first month to make certain those little annoyances don't fester into larger issues. It gives the new employee the vehicle to vent any frustration, which there is bound to be, without having to feel that he or she is complaining to the new boss.

From the end of the first month to the end of the first year, I recommend at least a monthly status update by the search firm with the candidate. This level of contact is not meant to position the search consultant to meddle, but again to hopefully lock in the positive results of the search and do what they can to proactively address any issues that arise.

YOU CAN DO IT YOURSELF (IF YOU HAVE THE NERVE)

Executive search is not rocket science or even bottle rocket science for that matter. Today, with all of the technology available, the candidate marketplace awareness of what executive search is, the lack of stigma associated with multiple job changes during a career, and so on, the number of barriers to building a world-class executive search capability of your own are significantly lower than they have ever been.

I believe that 90 percent of world-class executive search practices are based on the "blocking and tackling" aspects of search and can be reproduced rather simply. We are not cracking DNA sequences here. What we are talking about is dedicated, focused manpower being applied to a problem.

Copy the search firms who are thriving today—small- and medium-sized firms that have no problem attaching costs with delivered results. Combine this with a philosophy of investment rather than overhead. Hire great recruiters.

There is one caveat to this. Over the past 20 years I have hired and trained a very large number of recruiters. To me there is only one aspect of executive search that I gave up trying to teach about a decade ago. That "it" factor that separates great recruiters from good recruiters is an uncanny, intuitive ability to match the intangible chemistry between a high-performing business and a high-performing candidate.

The fact is that hiring managers will not hire the most qualified candidate for a position. They will hire the most qualified candidate who fits the intangible, interpersonal chemistry of the hiring manager, stakeholders, and company culture. Great recruiters get this intrinsically. Don't waste your time trying to train it, just go out and hire the executive recruiter who has demonstrated this over the course of a career.

You might want to consider using an executive search firm for this project.

Chapter 15

Compensation Strategy: A Guide for Senior Managers*

Sibson Consulting

Most senior managers wish, at least sometimes, that they could ignore compensation. No other organizational system is so weighted with values and emotions, so visible to employees, or so much the subject of internal dissent. Nearly everyone has opinions—usually strong ones—about rewards. And any change in compensation usually attracts loud complaints from employees who feel disadvantaged by the change. In view of these difficulties, can busy senior managers safely take the easy way out and leave compensation decisions to their compensation specialists? Or should they devote significant personal attention to compensation?

In fact, senior managers should be heavily involved in setting the strategic direction for compensation, and there are some fundamental choices they need to make during this process.

In the past, compensation systems demanded less senior management attention than it does now. Senior managers generally left the design of employee compensation systems to technical specialists. This was possible partly because professionally managed compensation systems looked very much alike from one company to another. For most firms, the goal of compensation design was simply to avoid a competitive disadvantage by keeping labor costs in line with those of competitors, and the goal of compensation administration was to keep employee noise down.

---

*Copyright © 2007 by Segal Co. Reprinted from the *WorldatWork Journal* (First Quarter 2000). Original authors (Gerald E. Ledford Jr. and Elizabeth J. Hawk) from Sibson Consulting, a Division of Segal. For more information about the Sibson Rewards of Work model, please contact Jim Kochanski, senior vice president, Sibson Consulting, the strategic HR consulting division of Segal, at (919) 233-6656 or jkochanski@sibson.com.

The picture changed greatly in the 1990s, as companies throughout the economy began rethinking their compensation systems in the search for competitive advantage. Base pay, incentives, benefits, and pay for corporate performance all changed dramatically. The strategic demands of new competitive forces, new organizational forms, an increase in knowledge work, and recognition of the importance of compensation to organizational effectiveness largely drove these changes. Top managers could no longer afford to leave compensation solely in the hands of compensation professionals.

There are some basic principles of compensation strategy that senior managers need to understand. The alignment of compensation with business needs, the goals of the compensation system, reward system levers, and basic choices managers need to make are among these principles. A foundation of knowledge will help senior managers use compensation as an important tool for managing the business.

ALIGNING COMPENSATION AND BUSINESS NEEDS

How does one decide among compensation alternatives? The easy way is to imitate other companies. Indeed, imitation is a fine art in compensation practice. Compensation specialists learn how to create standard base pay plans, benefit plans, and incentives that look like those of labor market competitors and use compensation surveys to keep pay rates in line with labor market competitors as well. Even innovations in compensation tend to be imitative. Organizational leaders "want one of those plans" because of an article they read or contacts they made with industry colleagues, even though "one of those" might be the wrong idea for their specific company. There must be a better way.

To be effective, a compensation system needs to be aligned with business needs as well as with other human resources systems. Figure 15.1 shows an alignment model. It makes the point that compensation is just one oar in the water moving the organization forward. The compensation system is effective to the extent that it pulls in the same direction as other forces propelling the organization. This need for alignment suggests why organizations should not simply imitate the compensation designs of other companies. Because different organizations have different business needs, pay practices should be tailored to the particulars of the organization. Specifically, pay practices need to reinforce the organization's business strategy, organizational structure, and desired organizational culture if they are to be effective.

As Figure 15.1 indicates, the starting point for compensation design is the business strategy. Key elements of this strategy are

- The business conditions facing the organization.
- How the firm plans to gain competitive advantage in its environment.
- The metrics and targets by which management will judge performance.

Compensation is important in supporting the business strategy because it conveys loud messages and can reinforce patterns of behavior that are necessary to realize the

Figure 15.1
A Compensation Alignment Model.

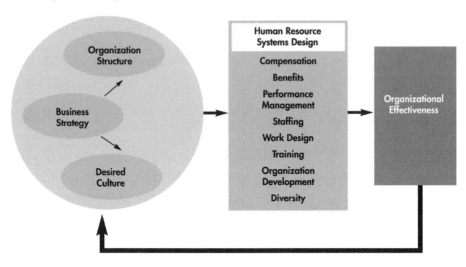

business strategy. In the 1990s and early 2000s, high-tech firms often created risky but incentive-rich compensation packages that relied heavily on stock options. This type of pay system wed employees to the success of their business. Conversely, organizations that value stability and long-term effort have tended to emphasize job security in their compensation approaches.

Organizational structure is important in channeling employee behavior. Compensation sends powerful and subtle signals about what units and what levels of the organization are most important. For example, reliance on a traditional merit pay system sends a message that individual accomplishment is more valued, not team and organizational performance. Conversely, if individuals are paid partly on the performance of their team or unit, the pay system signals the importance of team or unit performance.

It is important to know how compensation focuses attention in an organization. Emphasizing the wrong level can *lower* total performance. For example, rewarding performance only at the individual level when employees are members of interdependent teams (such as product design teams) can reduce overall performance by impeding teamwork. Also, it may be necessary to reward performance at a higher organizational level than is preferred if there are no good metrics at the desired organizational level. For example, team-based organizations often want to pay for team performance but pay for unit performance because they lack good metrics at the team level or because people tend to be members of multiple teams.

Additionally, the right compensation strategy can create (or at least support) the desired corporate culture. And the wrong strategy can compromise the desired culture. The organization's *desired culture* expresses its most deeply rooted values, beliefs, and assumptions. The culture helps define for employees what is good, proper, and sensible. Compensation helps shape organizational culture through its influence on communication, motivation, satisfaction, and a sense of belonging. For example, if management wants a culture of high employee involvement, it should consider the following:

- Involve employees in the design and administration of compensation.
- Lean toward a base pay system that rewards valued skills, knowledge, and competencies.
- Teamwork should be reinforced by a group incentive system.

Indeed, such practices are more likely to be found in and are more successful in organizations with a high-involvement culture.

Finally, Figure 15.1 emphasizes the importance of aligning rewards with other human resource systems, such as training, selection, communication, and work design. Any specific pay plan affects these systems. For example, successful group incentive plans may require business training so employees know what to do differently to receive an award. Such plans also typically require considerable communication about business performance, may require job design changes to increase employee involvement, and may require the selection of employees who work well in teams. In fact, aligning pay systems with other HR systems is probably a more important determinant of success than the design of the pay system itself.

CHOOSING COMPENSATION GOALS

One reason that designing compensation systems is so difficult is that these systems can have many different and conflicting goals. Because the selection of goals indicates how the pay system will be used to help manage the business, senior managers (rather than the HR department) need to determine pay system goals. Potential goals of compensation include

- *Control compensation* costs by paying no more than is needed to attract competent employees from the labor market.
- *Maintain internal equity* by paying employees fairly compared with others in the organization.
- *Attract and retain talented employees* by providing a level of compensation that is competitive in the labor market.
- *Motivate high performance* by paying greater than market compensation for high performance at the individual, team, unit, or corporate levels.
- *Make compensation costs vary with ability to pay*, increasing pay when the company performs well and decreasing it when the company performs poorly.
- *Reinforce the desired company culture.*
- *Help define the organization's structure for employees.*
- *Support the organization's business strategy.*

The first three goals (cost control, internal equity, and attraction and retention) are conventional goals of compensation systems and are important business goals in many organizations. Motivating individual performance has been a traditional goal of compensation systems, but more recently companies also have used pay systems to motivate team, unit, and corporate performance. Making costs variable is a newer goal. In good times, labor costs vary with the organization's ability to pay increases in employee compensation above levels that would be prudent every year. Conversely, in hard times the company can cut compensation costs rather than jobs, increasing employment stability.

The biggest problem in selecting goals for the compensation system is that all of these goals are desirable and potentially important, yet they cannot all be realized simultaneously. There are trade-offs to consider, but what are the important trade-offs that need to be made?

CONTROL OF COSTS VERSUS EQUITY VERSUS ATTRACTION AND RETENTION

Consider the first three goals of compensation systems. The surest way to increase attraction and retention rates—at least temporarily—is to pay everyone more. But this conflicts with the goal of controlling compensation costs. Perhaps then, management decides to overpay only for critical "hot" skills for which there is extreme labor market competition. Such a step, of course, conflicts with the goal of preserving internal equity, because it means paying some employees highly compared with the value of other positions within the firm that may have equivalent education, experience, and other requirements. Most organizations attempt a compromise. A typical stance is to pay market rates and communicate to employees that the internal slotting of jobs, and therefore internal equity, is based on the market value of jobs. This permits high pay for positions that are paid highly in the market and attempts to define internal equity and equity in the labor market as equivalent.

MOTIVATING EMPLOYEES VERSUS OTHER GOALS

Who would argue against motivating high performance as a high-priority goal of the compensation system? Managers can motivate employees by tying higher compensation to performance. A pay system linking pay to individual or team performance often is highly motivating because employees have a large degree of control over such performance. That is, there is a strong line of sight between employee behavior, performance, and pay. (Assuming, of course, that the organization can measure individual/team performance effectively—a big assumption in many companies.) So what's the problem with this type of pay for performance?

First, unless the definition of internal equity that management espouses and employees embrace allows for strong differentiation based on performance, many employees may reject the system as inequitable. Pay systems like sales commission plans and individual piece rates can provide two to three times as much pay for high performers as low performers who are doing the same job. This is seen as fair in some organizations but not in others. Moreover, employees may leave if they see the compensation system as unfair, which would work against the attraction and retention goal.

Second, such a system may be seen as undermining collaboration among employees who need to work together in the interests of larger unit or total organizational performance. If the business strategy of the organization requires such collaboration, too much pay for individual or small team performance can be a problem.

Third, paying for individual or team performance may work at cross-purposes with the goal of varying labor costs with the organization's ability to pay. That is, individual and team performance (for example, productivity and quality) may be high even if corporate performance (such as profitability) is poor and vice versa. Firm profitability is tied to market conditions, competitor behavior, and the general state of the economy, which are beyond local control.

RESOLVING GOAL CONFLICTS

Goal conflict is inherent to pay system design. Because the goals of the pay system reflect fundamental choices about the business, senior management cannot escape responsibility for making hard choices. Three points may help in exercising managerial choice among goals.

- Compensation communicates above all what performance levels, behaviors, and values management thinks are important. The reward system puts money where management's mouth really is. Therefore, it is helpful to ask what management most wants employees to know, do, and care about. That is what the pay system should reinforce. For example, many entrepreneurial firms offer below-market base wages, few benefits, and extremely lucrative incentives (such as stock options and bonuses) for individual and corporate performance. Such highly leveraged packages send clear messages about what counts, vary pay with performance, and support an entrepreneurial culture while accepting risks of high turnover and continual battles over internal equity.
- It is helpful to articulate the goals of the compensation system in a formal statement of compensation philosophy. This document becomes a touchstone for the design and evaluation of all compensation programs. It can help ensure that the designers of each new compensation program have a clear understanding of management's goals and that existing programs are meeting their intended objectives.
- Finally, different parts of the compensation system can address different goals. For example, management may limit fixed pay costs by setting base pay to market levels; support cultural values of caring for employees and their families through a generous benefits package, motivate high performance through individual or group incentives, and make pay costs variable through profit sharing. Most companies meet their various goals through different parts of the compensation package, and this is appropriate. However, there are dangers in this approach. Unless the overall design is managed carefully, the total compensation package may become too expensive. Also, employees may receive so many different messages through the system that they hear no message clearly. Trade-offs, then, cannot be avoided.

DELIVERING REWARDS THAT EMPLOYEES WANT

If the organization is to motivate employees, the rewards it links to performance must be rewards that employees value. What do employees value?

Compensation clearly is neither the only reward that employees value, nor the only meaningful incentive for better performance. A fuller picture of the types of rewards that employees value is shown in Figure 15.2 in the Sibson and Company Rewards of Work model. A total reward system pays attention to all five types of rewards and ensures the alignment of all five types with business needs.

DIRECT FINANCIAL REWARDS: QUESTIONS SENIOR EXECUTIVES FACE

Once the decision is made to focus on direct financial rewards, senior managers face many questions as their organizations develop compensation strategies and the programs that embody those strategies. Executives need to recognize

- Situation-specific judgment is always required. There is no single, silver bullet–style answer to these questions.
- Management must be prepared to shift its position on these issues as business demands change. Managers need to give themselves a process—and permission—to reexamine these questions regularly, and evolve the pay system as the organization evolves.

HOW MUCH DO I RELY ON PAY TO DRIVE MY BUSINESS?

How much attention should managers devote to pay when creating business changes? Of course, management must use all the tools at its disposal in motivating change. For example, a compelling vision, clear goals and accountability for meeting them, and communication about the business and its needs all help motivate change. Using pay without using such levers is a recipe for ineffectiveness or a very expensive pay program. If management has decided to use pay as a driver, in concert with other tools, pay could be

- *Highly prominent:* The centerpiece of communication about the business. Many companies focus on the implications for people, their performance, and the pay plan in every business discussion.
- *Less prominent:* Playing a supportive role only. In these companies, people understand how their pay works and know that pay supports the same things called for in the company's vision and goals, but that's about it. These companies make much more use of the other choices as clear drivers of results.

Managers in companies with highly prominent pay need to be open and comfortable in pay discussions with employees. They need to be willing to live with the inevitable conflict over pay. They tend to be comfortable in holding employees accountable

Figure 15.2
Sibson Consulting's Rewards of Work Model. (*Source*: Reprinted by permission of The Segal Group, Inc., parent of The Segal Company © 2007. All rights reserved.)

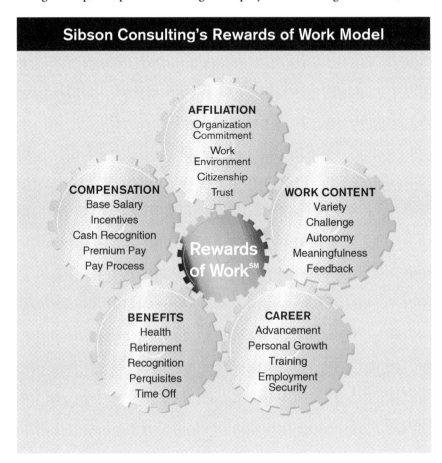

for poor performance by withholding rewards. If management does not have these characteristics, it is safer to give less prominence to pay in creating change.

HOW MUCH SHOULD PAY PLANS VARY ACROSS THE COMPANY?

This question is like asking, "Should we centralize or decentralize our organization?" It depends—on the needs of the business and market, the capabilities and history of the organization, and the inclination of leadership. Moreover, the answer is likely to change over time as the conditions change.

A forest products firm is a good example. During an era of decentralization in the firm's management, the company adopted a decentralized plant incentive strategy that made sense at the time. Over a number of years, plant managers and their employees built numerous site-level incentive plans. The plans had the benefit of local ownership because they were developed locally. However, a new top management team began centralizing management of the firm for business reasons and began centralizing the design of the incentive plans as well. This was the result of some pointed questioning by the new executives about whether the many different plans supported new corporate priorities, how they could evaluate plans with so many different goals and metrics, and whether there was adequate stretch in the goals of the plans. The pendulum swung back toward common plan design elements across locations. Local ownership and adaptation to local conditions decreased, but corporate priorities were better supported. Which approach was right?

Many organizations face this issue by using a "mass customization" approach.[1] In the *mass* part of the equation, a common direction on pay is established and communicated across the company. This provides a framework for program development. For example, the company might define how it wishes to pay versus its marketplace for talent, its philosophy on variable versus fixed pay versus ownership, and its performance priorities—say, cycle time, quality, or achievement of a global perspective.

Then company units are free to develop their own pay programs, as long as they stay within the framework. That's the *customization* part. The company gains the benefits of common direction while still allowing a level of local ownership.

The framework can be broad in some areas and restrictive in others, depending on the amount of variation the company believes it can stand. The degree of direction provided may change over time. Indeed, management should set the expectation that it will conduct regular strategy reviews and that changes will occur in response to changing business conditions.

SHOULD WE CARE MORE ABOUT INTERNAL OR EXTERNAL EQUITY?

What leader hasn't felt tied in knots over the perpetual argument over external versus internal equity? The problem is that managers must be concerned with both. No organization can afford to be governed completely by one or the other. However, most companies have a history of practices and beliefs that clearly emphasize one or the other.

Today, most companies are focused more on internal equity, attending to their own pay structures, their own method of valuing jobs, and pay levels that provide for smooth comparisons across different kinds of work. However, there has recently been an explosion of interest in pay systems that put greater focus on the external market and help companies take off their internal blinders. Companies need to pay greater attention to external market factors when

- *Their workforce has many employment choices.* This could be because of a low unemployment rate, a more mobile and informed generation of employees or less "cradle-to-grave" loyalty from both employees and companies.

- *A rising tide has lifted all boats.* Companies that are very internally focused tend to pay all functions similarly—accountants, engineers, and marketing types are on the same pay structure. That may well mean that management pays more than it needs to for some jobs. Allowing the tide to float all the boats diverts resources that could be better spent. At the same time, under this situation, management is doubtless paying too little to some functions.
- *The company needs more emphasis on pay differentiation.* Some companies tend to pay everyone about the same, regardless of factors like performance or contribution. One way to move toward a more refined pay differentiation is to develop a clear business case around external market pay practices.

Of course, the definition of "the market" is something of an art form in itself. Most companies consider the market to be their competitors for talent; some add their business competitors. Even the talent market is likely to have multiple definitions. For example, companies attract nonexempt employees locally but managers nationally. The source of software engineers or lawyers may be very different from the source of production or service supervisors. It is important to define these sources clearly, spelling out specific companies or comparison groups (for example, the industry used for corporate performance comparisons in a proxy). Comparing wages to the Fortune 100 may feel good but will usually force higher overall labor costs.

HOW DO I MAKE IT FAIR?

Management needs to be concerned with the question of fairness, if only because employees will be. However, fairness, like beauty, is in the eye of the beholder.

Unfortunately, this is an arena in which human nature reigns supreme. There is probably no standard of fairness on which everyone agrees. Inevitably, the standards selected favor the selector. Longer service employees tend to select seniority or continuity or knowledge of the organization as key factors that should help define "fair" pay. Newer people stress current skills and the application of new ideas. A manager's perspective on the importance of profit growth versus the absolute level of profit contribution depends on whether the manager is in a start-up business unit or a cash cow. This is where management comes in. Managers should begin with the question, "What does the business need?" An understanding of the answer is needed to maneuver on the rocky road ahead. The standards of fairness a company uses will inevitably make some people angry, and they will blame management.

Some employees inevitably will consider any pay programs to be unfair. The most important thing is to make sure that the right people feel that way (for example, the lower performers in a pay-for-performance company).

WHO MAKES PAY DECISIONS?

Of course, it depends. Obviously, there are some decisions that have to be made high in the organization. For example, the board of directors must make the calls about CEO and top executive pay. But for the most part, pay decisions should be treated the same as other decisions about running the business. As companies move decision making down, they should move decisions about pay down in the organization as well.

Administrative systems have tended to centralize meaningful decision making about pay in many companies. The ubiquitous "merit matrix" is an example. All one needs to do is plug in a performance rating and a current position in range, and the matrix spits out a salary increase amount, perhaps offering a range of a few tenths of a percent. This is a "system says" approach (e.g., the "system says" how large the increase will be), and no one except the matrix developer has to think about it.

Managers are expected to make all kinds of difficult business decisions every day. Why exclude decisions about pay, which are so critical to the business, from their area of responsibility—however difficult they may be? Managers may need sound information, tools, and perspectives to make good decisions, but the same is true of many other areas for which they are accountable.

Further, the organization can involve employees in the design and administration of pay systems. Research on incentives provides clear evidence about the positive effects of involving employees in plan development and operation. Plans that have greater employee involvement up front achieve greater buy-in and more success. That means the companies that use the involvement approach obtain a greater return on their incentive investment.

None of this, of course, relieves executives of the responsibility for making strategic decisions about pay and other rewards. These decisions must be based on the broadest view of the business needs, now and future, so top management needs to make the calls. However, once the strategy is set and communicated, pay decisions can be made much closer to the action.

CONCLUSION

Some topics that senior managers must understand if they are to guide the strategic design of reward systems have been addressed. These include the alignment of business needs with compensation, the compensation system goals, types of rewards that employees value, and key choices that managers need to make in managing direct financial rewards.

The focus here did not include many specific compensation innovations that managers might adopt because the emphasis on specific pay programs is misplaced. The choices among alternatives will not be made in a way that meets business needs unless managers understand the issues discussed here. If managers understand these issues, they are able to ask much sharper and more informed questions about specific design alternatives. They may well avoid the temptation to go after the latest pay fad, applying instead a business-based decision process.

Compensation has become a highly specialized area, and senior managers need to work closely with functional specialists in human resources. Compensation specialists can provide data, alternatives, and strengths and weaknesses of different options, but it is the responsibility of senior management to set the strategic direction that gives such technical information context and meaning.

NOTE

1. P. V. LeBlanc, "Mass Customization: A Rewards Mosaic for the Future," *ACA Journal* 6, no. 1 (1997).

Chapter 16

Engagement Journey: Caterpillar*

Brian Gareau, Kate Parker, Sarah Zigler, and Tom Doolittle

At Caterpillar, employee engagement isn't just an ideal; it's a way of life. In Caterpillar facilities around the world, employees continually strive to consistently live Caterpillar's values, form relationships with colleagues, and make and provide quality products and services—and engagement is a constant factor.

According to Jim Owens, Caterpillar's president and CEO, engagement is key to achieving the company's aggressive goals. "Our goals for the future require a coordinated, unified effort across our entire company. The only way we'll achieve these goals is with the enthusiastic, passionate commitment of every employee. You can instruct employees to reach certain goals, but you'll only get to the highest levels if you engage your people—their hearts and minds—in achieving them together. That's what it takes to become a great company."

Every organization has assets, but only one can appreciate with time . . . provided you appreciate it. And that is people. In more than 82 years of operation, Caterpillar has always been aware of the close connection among employees, profitability, and long-term marketplace potential. But historically, that key business fact didn't always hold our full focus and attention the way it should have. It does now.

In 2004, our chairman issued a challenge to the company worldwide to create a 15-year plan of action. The plan, Vision 2020, brought people forward as one of three

---

* Copyright © 2007 by Caterpillar, Inc. Special thanks to Marv Rosser, Jim Blass, Tom Bluth, Suely Agostinho, Keith Butterfield, Claire Putman, Joanne Miller, and Carol Villeneuve for agreeing to share their engagement success stories, and the more than 94,000 members of Team Caterpillar.

critical success factors—the three pillars of success we would build our entire future upon. In turn, the people critical success factor would be created by only two components: safety and engagement. Our mandate was simple and unmistakably clear.

Since the inception of Vision 2020, we are working to create a core culture of engagement, integrated throughout every business decision we make. Part of this vision is to create a unified Team Caterpillar of over 94,000 worldwide employees who are nurtured, challenged, motivated, and rewarded for the great work we do. In this way, we connect the hearts, hands, and heads of talented and dedicated people around the world. And we pull together, passionately doing the right thing at the right time, the right way, for the right reason. This is what engagement means to us inside Caterpillar (Cat).

Everything we do is integrally tied to our principles of engagement. Likewise, everything our engagement principles represent is tied to everything we do—from the safety practices we follow and the quality of our products, to our manufacturing processes, leadership development strategies, and the way we uphold accountability. It's all inside our culture of engagement. And in our culture, the accepted or perceived way we do things, engagement is integrated into every aspect of the company.

Many people pulling together in so many ways requires us to "connect the dots" for our employees, partners, and customers. When we say, "connect the dots," we're not just referring to a two-dimensional child's game in which one simple line pulls together an equally simple drawing. We're talking about a three-dimensional structure in which multiple connections are made to each other in multiple ways—critical in a global matrix organization like Caterpillar.

It's impossible to track comprehensively in a single chapter every point of contact between our engagement philosophy and the daily operations of a company with so many employees—over 94,000 in 300 locations and 40 countries across the world. This chapter, rather, tells the story of how we are building our global company—creating a rewarding, values-based culture. This chapter will focus on our most significant initiatives:

- **Relentless execution of leadership basics,** in which leaders provide timely feedback, ask for input, take action, and empower and recognize their employees.
- **Integrated engagement,** which ties to our strategy and values, business processes, and learning, recognition, and succession planning initiatives.
- **Employee Opinion Survey,** in which we used a respected methodology—Six Sigma—to transform this into a deeply important, significant, and essential process.
- **Caterpillar Production System**, in which we use our engagement values and practices to create and sustain a manufacturing process and culture that will drive us toward 2020.

Of course, no story of how a company has rededicated itself to its people can be told without stories of the people themselves. So this chapter also includes short examples of how the concepts and values we developed are actually experienced on a daily basis by Cat employees. As we have gathered these stories from around the globe, we are reminded yet again of a simple fact: People are the same all over the world. We may have to deliver engagement to them in slightly different ways, but the need to meet both their rational and emotional requirements through their work is universal. Beyond the needs for fair and competitive compensation, safe working conditions, and a chance to build a better future for themselves, their families, and their communities, we have also made sure Caterpillar responds to their needs for what we call the three I's: identity, importance, impact.

Identity refers to the gratifying sense of self and belonging the employee experiences by being a member of Team Caterpillar. *Importance* refers to why it's important to do things the Caterpillar way, following our policies, procedures, and processes and living our values in action. *Impact* refers to employees' understanding of how their individual role affects the bigger picture—affecting not only Caterpillar's potential as a company but also the world at large.

We are still a story in progress, by no means anywhere near arriving at a complete understanding of engagement's full potential within a single company—especially a company as large, diverse, and complex as Caterpillar. But after three years of full commitment to this effort, we have some very interesting results to report.

BACKGROUND

When Caterpillar began its current engagement journey in 2004, the company was made up of 28 business units throughout the world. We absolutely knew that people were very important to the success of the organization, and we had already been promoting and measuring engagement for several years. But we did not have executive office sponsorship that could have unified all our efforts. Everyone was working on their own individual set of priorities, with each business unit approaching its people initiatives from a variety of different angles. If they wanted to work on engagement, that was fine. If they didn't, that was also fine, as long as their business results were acceptable. If a unit didn't have any attrition problems, if safety was good, and if productivity was good, we assumed the unit probably had an effective approach to the way it addressed its people and culture issues. Thus, we didn't hold each business unit specifically accountable for the people side of its individual culture.

Before 2004, we knew engagement was important but, as a company, we weren't willing to put the necessary discipline in place to make it happen in a cohesive, comprehensive approach that would leverage the best of what we stood for companywide. Not surprisingly, our numbers reflected our distracted approach to engagement: 20 of the 28 units had lower than 60 percent engagement. Only three units scored 70 percent or higher.

But *now*, due to the significant change in focus that we have undertaken over the last three years, 17 business units now carry scores of 70 percent and higher; an additional eight units score above 80 percent. Three years ago, 20 units came in at below 60 percent engagement, whereas today only 5 units are in that category. The difference between then and now? We started to pay specific attention to engagement; we started getting purposeful; and we started connecting the dots.

RELENTLESS EXECUTION

A critical element of any engagement journey is leadership accountability. Leaders must relentlessly execute the basic elements of their jobs—asking for feedback, taking action on that feedback, and recognizing their employees' contributions and successes. A leader must be engaged to engage the hearts and minds of his/her employees.

The same was true for Caterpillar's journey. Our transformation began in 2004, when our newly appointed chairman, Jim Owens, announced that he wanted to create a sustainable, simplified growth plan that would take Caterpillar into the future. Unlike most incoming corporate leaders who might aspire to establish a five-year plan as a way of creating a legacy, Owens put the company to work on developing Vision 2020, with a strategic review committee specially tasked with identifying the essential building blocks for achieving our vision. A bold goal of 90 percent engagement was set as an initial target for 2010, with a focus on achieving world-class engagement. Jim's commitment to this goal and our vision is a prime example of relentlessly executing leadership basics. Jim would hold himself and all 94,000 Team Caterpillar employees accountable for achieving this goal and knew that if he was engaged in the process, his employees would also be engaged.

Ultimately, we knew if we didn't do a better job of attracting, retaining and engaging our workforce, we were going to fall short of realizing our potential and achieving Vision 2020. Consequently, in the name of simplification, the strategic review process took us from 14 strategic objectives to only three critical success factors today: people, product and process excellence, and profitable growth. As mentioned earlier, there are only two key metrics under the people objective: Safety is one; engagement is the other.

As we took on this challenge and realized the importance of having the right leadership team in place to relentlessly execute the basics, we began to see a turnaround in many of our facilities. Three global success stories follow.

CATERPILLAR XUZHOU

Location: Xuzhou, China
Function: Manufacturing
Number of employees: 1,250

As companies become increasingly global, one question remains: Just how different are people from country to country, really? Through Caterpillar's knowledge and experience in engaging employees around the world, an answer has emerged: People are basically the same, no matter who they are or where they come from. Local customs may be different. Traditions may be different. Languages are almost certainly different. And a country may be going through an entirely different phase in its social and economic history than its neighbor. People are still the same in what they desire and what inspires them. Around the world, people want to have their basic needs met. They want to be able to take care of their families and feel good about the work they do and the company they do it for. And they want to be recognized and appreciated, not only for who they are today but also for the potential they offer the future.

In 2004, Marv Rosser capped off his 30-plus-year career at Caterpillar with one last assignment—general manager of the Caterpillar plant in Xuzhou, China. During his nearly three-year tenure there, he used Caterpillar's engagement process to awaken the true potential that was waiting to be noticed and appreciated, opening up a new set of possibilities for Xuzhou employees. His story follows.

The plant had been here about 10 years when I got there and had a fairly stable product line. It was very good at process and manufacturing and planning. The operational side of the house was very strong and well done. But I would also say there were opportunities on the people side. The engagement level from the corporate opinion survey was only 40 percent. But when I had my first meeting with the leaders, you could just look at them and tell that there was so much potential. There was so much optimism.

The average age in the plant is 25 years old. So almost all of the employees, certainly the new ones, are single-child people—kids themselves, really—and throughout their whole semi-adult life all they have seen is growth and prosperity. There's just so much enthusiasm for the future in China!

These were people who were bursting to take their game to a higher level, take on more responsibility without being told, make more decisions on their own, and look beyond their own job responsibilities to anticipate problems or notice where else they could contribute. But the way the plant had been run, people were still very isolated in their own work and thinking. The production employees, especially, had been looked at only in terms of process, but they certainly had never been invited to consider their own career growth and how to apply their personal skills and energy to a higher level. They just hadn't been challenged to do more and actually enjoy it. Here was the chance to help them understand their role as a member of a *global* company and how they, too, could grow with the company through their own efforts.

One of the first things we did was conduct an extensive, three-week Caterpillar Cultural Assessment Process (CAP)—which is patent-pending—at our facility. This was their first big chance to for everyone to share their opinions, let us know their problems, and express their hopes and expectations.

Fourteen action items came out of that process, and we took them all very seriously. One issue was that everyone wanted opportunities to grow their careers with Caterpillar. We were more than willing to give them information about these opportunities, but proceeded with a note of caution: To become a salaried employee at Xuzhou, they had to be able to speak English. We took this back to our employees, who said, "Great, give us the opportunity to learn."

Business had been picking up during that time and we needed everyone at work. So we told them we would find the classroom and pay for the instructors. But the classes would have to be on their own time. Of the 1,250 employees at the Xuzhou plant, 900 are taking English courses, twice a week, on their own time, no pay, all in the dream of bettering themselves and their prospects. And that's exactly what has happened: Last year one-third of all our people were promoted. This is a fabulous testament to the people of Xuzhou and their willingness to take their own time to realize their dreams.

One of the other biggest concerns was an example of what can happen when people aren't paying attention to changing environments. Somewhere in the past, someone had laid down a law requiring hard hats in all manufacturing areas. Everyone, no matter what his or her job was, had to wear a hard hat. Obviously, in some areas it's still essential for safety. But if you're on a fork truck or light assembly area, you don't need a hard hat. And they're very cumbersome and extraordinarily hot in the summertime. So we changed the rule right then and there. Basic human need. It was so simple, but it had such a deep impact.

When I first arrived in Xuzhou, I kept hearing concerns about the buses. Everyone takes buses to work; they're company buses and we pay the costs. But I kept hearing about how bad they were. So one afternoon I checked them out. They were horrible. They were dirty and they leaked water. We changed them immediately. I saw them on a Wednesday or a Thursday, and by Monday we had all new buses.

There was important symbolism attached to the general manager personally going out there and checking them out. It was meaningful to our people on several levels.

The longer I was here, the more I appreciated how big the smaller, basic human needs really are. The cafeteria, for instance, was horrendous. So we came in during the May holiday in 2005 and completely renovated it—even gutting it. Now it's beautiful and colorful. Everything about it is better now. The service. The menu. And it cost virtually nothing compared to the pleasure it gives our people who eat there now.

And we've kept up the communication. The HR department came up with a program called "We Are Listening," and every week, during every shift, a small group from the HR team goes to bus stops and the lunchroom to provide a forum where people can bring up any issue that's on their minds. And on Monday afternoons, without fail, they post a list of the issues, what will be done about it (or not, at times), and who is responsible for each concern.

We also have a lot of visitors and customers come to the factory. And we use those visits as opportunities to talk to the people, so the employees can see how what they do is connected to what goes on outside the walls of the factory. It's a huge boost to their self-esteem!

You have to take care of all the basic human needs. Having started as an hourly employee myself, I fully appreciate that production employees have dreams and hopes. And they may want to be the chairman of Caterpillar, too, one day. But it all starts with the basics—the basics in quality, in compensation, in safety, in just some of the smallest creature needs you can think of. When you address those, you instill in your people a hope for even greater opportunities. Hope feeds upon itself. When you do things right, success follows success.

PONTIAC FACILITY

Location: Pontiac, Illinois
Function: Manufacturing
Number of employees: 1,100

Increasing engagement in Pontiac involved changing the culture of the entire facility—a change that began with one man taking the time to meet and engage nearly 750 employees. When Operations Manager Jim Blass arrived in Pontiac in January 2004, there was an obvious lack of engagement among his production workforce. Everyone in the facility seemed to be simply going through the motions, and Jim made it one of his first priorities to change the culture by motivating the workforce. Here's his inspiring story.

When I first got to the facility, it was intuitively obvious to me and anybody who would walk through that the workforce was really down—down on themselves and down on Caterpillar. When you walked on the factory floor, people looked at the floor or at the ceiling—anywhere but at you. The negativism just radiated. So I started digging through all the rationale as to why that could be, and it quickly came down to three main reasons. The first was the loss of a major client. Our employees assumed that the loss of this business would result in a loss of their jobs. The second was management turnover—in four years, there had been three different plant managers, me being the fourth. The last was their physical work environment, which was desperately in need of renovations.

It became obvious to me that I had to work on understanding this workforce and how I could reach them—figuring out how I could regain their trust and confidence. So we immediately got to work cleaning up the place—moving out 4 million pounds of machines, steam-cleaning the building, putting up 25,000 gallons of white paint, cleaning up the restrooms, installing ice machines, improving the cafeteria food, sprucing up the locker rooms. Most of the ideas for improvements came from the employees after they saw we were serious about cleaning up the plant—not to sell it but to stay in it—and I responded to just about all the suggestions. And this restored a sense of ownership among the employees to the entire plant and our prospects.

We also had to revitalize the management team, who had a lot of skepticism about what I was up to. I was saying all the right words, but they had heard all of these many times before. Some of them got it, some of them had given up. We had many good folks who just needed hope and were very receptive to change. Others just couldn't put their heart into this one more go-around. So I spent some time moving the managers around. Unless the leadership team gets engaged, employees won't see that modeling, that coaching, that teaching, and that day-to-day behavior that is at the heart of an engaged culture.

Part of our new culture involved celebrations and recognitions. Every time something good happened in the plant, we'd celebrate it—even if we had to look for things to celebrate. But pretty soon we found plenty of things to celebrate: six months without an injury, new production records, and improved quality ratings. The underlying emphasis of every celebration was to build a connection between the management team and our employees. During these celebrations, we served the employees the food or treats, which gave us a personal chance to say thanks. I even started having breakfast with employees who were retiring or celebrating service anniversaries. I wanted a forum to personally thank the people that had dedicated themselves to Caterpillar and were going above and beyond.

No one was left out. We have 11 shifts, running 24/7. All shifts had something to celebrate, so we'd be there to celebrate with them. And we made the commitment to have one-on-one conversations with each person for 5 to 10 minutes each. When you work Saturday and Sunday nights, it's hard to feel like you're a part of the operation because the bulk of what happens in the business happens on the day shift, Monday through Friday. So you just have to be there. Maybe not *every* weekend, but you have to show up on a regular basis. And when you do celebrations, you have to celebrate those folks, too.

Another thing we wanted to do was to strengthen our employees' identity with Team Caterpillar. To do this, we made sure all new hires were given Caterpillar T-shirts and that other employees had easy access to affordable, Caterpillar apparel. We *wanted* to give our employees access to this apparel, and to increase their loyalty to and identity with the company.

We had payoffs almost right away. Cleaning up the plant, for instance, ignited a renewed interest in cleanliness and housekeeping. And that turned our safety record around drastically. We went for as long as two years without anybody getting hurt. We also hit some pretty unbelievable efficiency improvements. On one of the lines, we improved efficiency by 13 percent. On another, we saw a 54 percent improvement.

One of the biggest "ah has" that I experienced at Pontiac was watching how the attitudes and behaviors on the floor changed from a "we/they" to an "us." The animosity that was once there is gone. And people know each other again. New business is coming in. We're set for future EPA emissions regulations. And because we are taking care of issues as they come up, they don't automatically become grievances. Employees now know they can go directly to their bosses with issues.

When I walked in, I saw that I had to change just about everything: the culture; the manufacturing process; the way we shared information; the way we interacted with the workforce; the way we showed recognition. Everything had to change. This is when the people who want to do the right thing begin to emerge. They've been there all along. Either they haven't been given the opportunity or the leadership to do it.

When you see them start to turn back on again, that's when it really gets fun.

Since Blass arrived at Pontiac, engagement scores have more than doubled.

CAT FRANCE S.A.S.

Location: Grenoble, France
Function: Manufacturing
Number of employees: 2,325

Every Caterpillar location, business unit, division, regional center, and department joins our current engagement journey from its own level of cultural, managerial, and process excellence. While we do have target numbers identified for 2010 and do celebrate movement in the right direction, our goal is continuous improvement. At Cat France, although there had some been ups and downs, the former engagement index reported stagnant numbers in the low 50s for several years. But in the space of just one year, Cat France's engagement scores jumped nearly 20 percent.

Caterpillar France Managing Director Tom Bluth says Cat France's engagement story has only just begun (as compared with other facilities such as Cat Brasil) and that the real story would be better told two or three years from now. But from the standpoint of taking a snapshot in time of what can be accomplished with focus and determination, the Cat France story even now is an example of what a difference a year makes. This is the Cat France story as of now.

It's possible to track engagement-type initiatives being done in the past, but if we were being really honest with ourselves, we'd have to ask, "Were people really number one or not?" And the answer would have to be no.

As a leadership team, we began to honestly ask the team, "What are your priorities?" "What's most important here?" And the response here was normally that making shipment plans was the top priority. Rarely would we hear that people were the priority—or even safety, or even quality, for that matter.

We tried to make it very clear to people, starting with our managers, that people were our number one priority. A significant part of this people priority also included safety. The second priority was quality. Everything else comes after those two things. We reminded the employees of this every chance we got; every single speech and every written communication. After a couple of months, the team began to say it and believe it.

We are beginning to see the results by placing people and safety first. In 2005, we had over five accidents per 1 million hours worked. Last year, we were able to drop this figure over 20 percent. And so far this year, things are really clicking, dropping another 30 percent. Over the last year and a half, the same time we began to see safety improving, we could also see engagement improving. By following through on our safety strategy and demonstrating by action the priority of "people" we improved the overall employee engagement.

Next came accountability. If people are the most important thing, how do we measure the ways we show that? We were generating reports down to the greatest detail on what the shipment plans were, whether the suppliers were on time or not, that sort of thing. But when it came to employee engagement, we didn't break down reports by sections and individual supervisor levels. It was just a broad-stroke treatment.

We had to be very clear with our managers, but in a supportive way, not a punitive way. When in the plant, we always try to ask, "Tell me about the survey results for your section—What are the issues? What are you doing about it as a team? What's your individual action plan? How can we help you with this?" It sounds like a very simple approach, but people determine what's important to you by the questions you ask.

Cat France had also had a number of focus groups set up to tackle issues across the organization. In the past, the group would select problems that were easier to solve but not take on some of the more difficult people issues. This year, though, we conducted a focus group, which we used to discover and rank the top 10 most pressing people issues. And we committed ourselves to taking those issues on, even though they might not be simple or quick to resolve.

In the past, subteams would go off and do the work of resolving the issues that focus groups uncovered. But in this case, as a leadership team, we decided to take personal leadership responsibility for each of the subteams. So it became the very top leadership taking responsibility in a very visible way.

Then we communicated on our progress. We would create a two-page update every four weeks and put the report in the employees' paycheck envelopes. We also give updates in our person-to-person meetings, as well as in our monthly magazine. It was very important for everyone inside Cat France to see that the leadership was personally responsible for making the necessary changes and improvements.

In addition to hearing what the leaders were reporting, it was also important that the employees knew they were being listened to and had opportunities to develop themselves and grow in their jobs. See? The basics are still the basics, no matter where you are in the world.

We're in the early stages of our engagement journey, so it feels like we're rushing things to be talking about them now. But in a couple of years I hope to see the evidence that all our efforts have paid off. I'll know we've arrived when we have empowered team leaders in the Cat Production System, individuals who will act as leaders and drive ideas from the rest of team. I'll know we've arrived when we see ideas for improvements and driving change coming up from the bottom rather than only top down. I'll know we've arrived when anyone I talk to on the floor brings me ideas and knows exactly where our business is against our goals and where it isn't. I want to hear, "Here's what I think we should do!" or "Here's what we're doing!" That's what I'll look for to know that those things we're doing today will have lasting effect.

INTEGRATING ENGAGEMENT INTO ALL WE DO

Every company has its own definition of engagement and how it is reflected in its people. At Caterpillar, we distilled the concept into three major components: The extent to which our people are committed to their work, the extent of their effort, and their desire to stay. We knew embedded in those three components were three broad objectives that moment by moment secure the relationship between our employees and the organization.

- **Caring.** We need to demonstrate to all our employees that we *care* about them, not just by what management says but by what the individual leaders do on a daily, person-to-person, moment-by-moment basis.
- **Credibility.** Leadership must be a *credible* source of information.

- **Trust.** The foundation of all good relationships is *trust*. Our culture must be one in which people trust that leadership will look out for their best interests as well as those of the company.

With this foundation, the dots that required connection began to emerge. From strategic to tactical to practical, we realized all the dots were inextricably connected when our business processes, values, and behaviors were in place and working at optimal levels.

When it comes to providing a workplace in which our people are inspired to return every day and give their utmost, it's impossible to remove any one of these elements without deteriorating the fabric of engagement to which we've committed ourselves.

At Caterpillar, we take a rigorous process approach to everything we do. So we knew that if we were going to increase awareness and understanding of engagement in action, we needed to put it in some type of structure. To ensure engagement became integrated into the Caterpillar culture, we devised a set of principles to sum up the major points we needed to remain focused on—especially as we took on the immense challenge of embracing engagement as not just merely nice to do but as an essential element in our culture. To make these principles all the more compelling, we frame them as imperatives—as *must-dos*.

- **Actively integrate engagement into key business processes.** Engagement must be integral to the entire culture and community inside Caterpillar. It cannot be a simple add-on that can be easily extracted when another approach might be more tempting. We have integrated it into everything we do: our Performance Management Process, Cat Production System, Talent Management System, leadership accountability, rewards and recognition practices, and the entire business strategy throughout the world, internally and externally.
- **Institutionalize the language.** If we do not share the same vocabulary company-wide, we cannot share information effectively, learn from each other, or measure the same things the same ways. Building a common vocabulary and common measures has become increasingly essential as we continue to welcome more and more new people from all over the world.
- **Balance the rational and emotional side of engagement.** When people are passionately engaged, they're doing the right thing at the right time, the right way, for the right reason. That's when we get sustained behavior and the results we're looking for. If it's not sustained, we'll go back to the old way. Passionate engagement *begins* with making sure that we meet employees' basic needs for competitive wages, safe work environments, and proper tools and training—the *rational* side. But we know that immense value comes from making sure employees' emotional needs are also being met. According to the Corporate Leadership Council, employers could provide anywhere between three-to-one or four-to-one return on their investment if they move their focus from the rational to the emotional side of engagement. At Caterpillar, we separate the emotional side of engagement in three categories—identity, importance, and impact, which were discussed earlier.

- **Reinforce sustained behaviors versus beliefs.** From a management perspective, it's more effective to impact behaviors rather than try to change personal beliefs. One of the major challenges on our engagement journey is to provide clarity as to what the specific, expected behaviors are and then reinforce them. Here we turn to Our Values in Action, which were rolled out with our strategy in 2005, as well as an additional set of 15 guiding principles, which have been introduced along with the Cat Production System.
- **Synchronize all 10 cultural support systems.** As we moved forward with engagement initiatives, we discovered that even if we did all the prescribed communications, told people what we were looking for, and provided training, people still didn't absorb the engagement message or change their behaviors as we had expected them to. Using Six Sigma, we found that there are a total of 10 systems that support culture; however, we were too often focused on just a couple of the systems, not all 10. These are the 10:

    1. **Communications:** Share information to generate understanding, which in turn reinforces or introduces behavioral change.
    2. **Learning opportunities:** This is not just a matter of giving employees the chance to acquire new knowledge. A company moves from "good" to "great" when it gives employees the chance to actively apply that new knowledge in the workplace.
    3. **Performance management:** Our performance management process must set clear expectations for both results and behaviors. Too often, people ask "What was your engagement score?" We need to spend an equal amount of time asking, "How did you get it?" When we roll out this process to salaried/management employees, in conjunction with our Values Based Competencies, employees will realize even more that values play an integral role in all we do.
    4. **Leadership reinforcing the behaviors:** Leaders throughout the entire organization must model, coach, and teach the behaviors we ask employees to demonstrate.
    5. **Measurement:** Caterpillar values the discipline of measuring anything we can: processes, output (of course), even behaviors—especially those of managers and leaders. Measurement is an integral part of the entire engagement initiative.
    6. **Recognition:** Recognition, specifically nonfinancial forms, reinforces desired behaviors and drives essential change. We consider recognition to be a 360-degree process, something we can all do for each other. Peers can recognize each other, bosses can recognize employees, and employees can recognize their bosses. Recognition is the most powerful form of appreciation and helps reinforce behavior—existing or new.
    7. **Policies and procedures:** We must be consistent with policies and procedures. If we're inconsistent among supervisors, shifts and lines, people will perceive favoritism. Then we will have lost the emotional side of the engagement equation.
    8. **Selection:** When filling positions, we must be consistent in reinforcing desired leadership behaviors.
    9. **Decision-making processes and procedures:** Decision making drives a greater degree of empowerment. The more we equip all employees to make independent decisions essential to their work, the more we reinforce a culture of accountability, responsibility, and authority.
    10. **Clear lines of sight:** Employees need to be able to see how the choices they make and the job they do have a direct impact on the company's performance.

- **Remember that leadership can't be a spectator sport.** According to the Hay Group, as much as 35 percent of the variability in discretionary performance is a result of *managerial styles and behaviors*. Superior leaders deliver two times more "productivity" than average leaders. If you can take a process and isolate one element that can have a 35 percent impact on the end results, you're going to work on it. We make this a responsibility for each and every leader.

  In our employee opinion survey (which we'll describe in greater detail later), we ask survey participants to respond to two statements that specifically point to this particular concern: "The person I directly report to demonstrates genuine interest and concern," and another, similar question for the senior management with whom they interact. When we correlate those questions to the engagement of our people, if people say, "No, there's no genuine interest or concern being exhibited by my immediate boss or the other management that I interact with," we discover that the engagement score is also very, very low. If the answer is "sometimes yes, sometimes no," then the scores correlate at around the 50 percent engagement. But we have seen that when employees and their leaders both report high experience of caring, the engagement scores also increase dramatically.

- **Use the right metrics to enhance accountability.** According to a study by the Gallup Organization, about 80 percent of Fortune 500 companies perform some sort of employee opinion gathering activity. But surprisingly, according to the findings, 60 percent of these companies reported morale and effectiveness *went down* the year after the survey was conducted. There are two reasons why. First, the companies that report these declines are also the companies that don't provide timely feedback postsurvey. Second, the managers don't take action or make changes based on the results of the survey.

  Using Six Sigma methodology, we have the right metrics in place, not only for the engagement index that we measure in our employee opinion survey, but also for the other strategic initiatives that are important to us, such as safety, leadership, change management, and so on.

- **Focus on correlation versus causation.** Many companies around the world feel the need to find a way to discover what kind of return on investment employee engagement offers business. But in a culture like Caterpillar's where engagement is being integrated into all the systems, processes, and philosophies of the way we do business, we cannot assign a value to something that is a contributor—but not the *sole* contributor—to the improvement we see. We will address correlation versus causation at the end of this chapter, but for now it's important to simply say that we have noticed that where other important measures are high (such as safety), engagement is also high. Conversely, where these important attributes are down, so is engagement. Because of our fundamental premise that engagement is intertwined with every other value and principle that drives Caterpillar's success, the correlation of engagement with these other essential measures is sufficient for us to know that engagement is an indispensable aspect of Team Caterpillar's culture.

While each of these principles is important, the recognition element of the integration efforts became a more intense focus in 2006, which marked the distribution of the first annual Chairman's Recognition for Engagement Awards. Over the years, we have had two Chairman's Awards, one for quality and one for safety. With our new emphasis on people as a critical success factor, it became pretty obvious we needed to acknowledge engagement activities and improvements through a similarly high-level award program. When Chairman Jim Owens approved this idea, we conducted a Six Sigma project and asked ourselves, "What should it look like? What are the other awards that we give? What behaviors are we trying to drive through the awards program?"

To determine award recipients, we first took the 30 business units and divided them into three categories—operations, marketing, and service. We determined we would have a Best in Class and a Most Improved year on year. But sustainability is also important to us. We decided to have an Honor Roll, which required the business units to reach best-in-class levels of both participation and engagement. First-year Honor Roll recipients receive a Bronze Award. Awards continue to progress to year five, which is marked with a Diamond Award.

When we presented this plan and the list of the first winners to our 36-member administrative council, which is made up of our chairman, group presidents, and vice presidents, they requested an additional award for facilities—Distinguished Operations Facility. Twenty-two individual facilities received the special honor.

All award recipients were given a trophy and specially designed banners and posters they could display in their facilities. They were also given a special identifier for use on letterhead and presentations, denoting them as 2006 award winners.

One of the 2006 Distinguished Operations Facility winners was Cat Brasil. Their story reflects at 10-plus-year journey, relentless execution, and a holistic approach to engagement.

CATERPILLAR BRASIL

Number of employees: 4,718
Engagement score for 2006: 96 percent
Chairman's Engagement Award: Best in Class
Turnover: 0.3 percent

In Brazil, Caterpillar's engagement story is about standing on the shoulders of giants. Since its inception in 1954, the Cat Brasil spirit has historically been something special, staffed by several generations of talented and dedicated people. That special Cat Brasil (CBL) spirit was called into action in 1996, when it was selected to undergo a complete change and modernization to produce the full range of state-of-the-art, world-class products. Chris Schena, president of CBL at the time, recognized that the transformation strategy had to include the total engagement of CBL's people as full partners in the change journey. Today, with extremely low turnover, CBL has been on Brazil's Great Places to Work list three years in a row, achieving first place in HR Best Practices last year in another important HR survey conducted by Hay Group in the category of 4,000—10,000 employees.

This is what Suely Agostinho, human resources and corporate affairs director at CBL, says about the company—then and now.

Our story is the result of many years of respect and care, qualities that go all the way back to our beginnings. In 1996, it was up to us to prove that we could accomplish the change that headquarters had planned for us. Because of the sense of pride and responsibility instilled in our culture, we decided that we would meet this challenge head on.

One of the first things we did was establish a slogan: "Our future today." We then envisioned what the future would be like and how we would make that future happen now. We knew it was impossible for leadership to do this alone, so we developed a business and communications strategy that involved *everyone* in the plant.

In relation to people, though, the strategy then is the same strategy that we have today: thinking, caring, and sharing.

We knew from the very beginning that our employees had to understand exactly where we were going, what we were doing, and how we were going to do it. We need everyone's hands, hearts, and heads. So we implemented an intense and dynamic communications plan to make everyone well aware of the whole strategy. We utilized videos, strategy action meetings, forums, and an electronic bulletin updated daily to tell everyone what was going on that specific day.

We're committed to everyone having the same opportunity to receive the same information. But not everyone has access to a computer. So every morning the secretaries print and distribute hard copies of the bulletins to all supervisors to discuss with their employees in the meeting at the beginning of each shift.

We also know that a team's engagement is never higher than the engagement of its leader. So we produce an extra bulletin every other week, called *Something More for You*, in which we give extra information to help our leaders model our values and communicate our strategy using the right emphasis, focus, and voice.

Our employees are very proud—not only of what we do, but also of what we represent. We take a holistic approach for our employees. It's not just about who they are and what they do at work. It's about their children, health, the community, the environment—all those things that really drive the triple I—identity, importance, and impact. We invest a great deal of resources, time, and energy in education both for our employees and their families at home and in the schools. When their children are out of school, we invite them to come here for a series of fun activities designed to teach them about safety and other strategic subjects. We know that if they learn about safety and other things here, they'll take those lessons back home and teach them to their parents.

Our caring approach also includes a consistent social responsibility philosophy that has both internal and external components. Inside the plant, we have a very safe operation with some of the lowest incident numbers. We also operate a very clean facility with a recycling program that involves all the employees. Since 2000, our shop floor employees work in TAGs (self-direct teams), in which they assume team production responsibilities and where the responsibility is pushed to the lowest level possible in the organization. In this participative environment, the supervisors act as facilitators and consultants. The environment created is one of total commitment to excellence and teamwork.

Externally, we work very closely with the community on sustainability. It's our mission to help the country take care of its environment. We've helped create several essential pieces of legislation to protect the environment, as well as participating in the effort to sustain clean water in the world helping to manage the Brazilian portion of the US$12 million investment made by the corporation to the Nature Conservancy. Again, we're involving the children in this, too. We've got several educational programs that teach children about their roles in saving water, waste in urban areas, and sustainable logging. We always bring the programs here first so the children of the employees can participate in them before they are distributed throughout the country.

Starting with Chris Schena, Caterpillar has helped us envision all the possibilities we had and gave us the opportunity to prove that we were capable of becoming a winning team. Bill Rohner taught us the importance of values to Caterpillar. That was very important to us Brazilians because we put a lot of emotion in everything we do. And now, of course, we're especially proud of Natal Garcia. He was one of our employees and a son of Brazil. For the first time, we have a Brazilian as the president, and we're very proud to have him as a leader. Natal led us in the development of the Strategy 50+ that will help CBL maintain its competitiveness and guarantee a bright future for all of us.

We don't have a job. We have a mission. With a mission in our hands, it's important that we have a passion for what we do. We're not perfect—every organization has problems. But people have the solutions. Our job is to facilitate the process of putting the problems and solutions together with passion.

OUR CULTURE AND VALUES IN ACTION

It's commonly believed that a defined, unifying corporate culture can have a strong, positive impact on a firm's long-term economic performance. But with over 94,000 people around the world in 300 Caterpillar locations—everyone independently working in business units within the context of different national customs and laws—we needed to define the unifying parameters of all those things that make up a culture: how we approached business decisions, treated each other, what we tolerated, and what we encouraged.

As we continued to develop Vision 2020, we determined we would have one Team Caterpillar with one strategy and one set of corporate values. We already had a code of worldwide business conduct dating back to 1974, which, in general terms, outlined a set of behaviors expected to reflect Caterpillar's values. After a major Six Sigma study on the value of business values and how they impact business results, we updated and refined the values that set forth the ideal (but very realistic) picture of how we treat our customers, communities, and environment. We managed to make that ideal set of characteristics both simple and comprehensive. There are four core values:

- Integrity—which embodies the "power of honesty."
- Excellence—which embodies the "power of quality."
- Teamwork—which embodies the "power of working together."
- Commitment—which embodies the "power of responsibility."

While the code tended to reflect the baseline behaviors employees *shouldn't* do, setting a bottom line, our values in action have no upper limit and inspire our employees to be their best. It wasn't sufficient for us, however, to design a series of posters or a wallet-sized reminder card printed with these values. Keeping in mind that we cannot see beliefs, but we can see behaviors, we wrote 31 different behaviors that illustrate precisely what we mean by these values and describe how the values in action can create, in the words of engagement as we have defined it, the type of environment where you get the most commitment, work effort, and desire to stay.

In keeping with the Caterpillar culture of inclusion and learning, we rolled out this clearly articulated and unified values set to all our employees worldwide over a six- to eight-week period, using leaders as teachers to conduct classes and ensure everyone understood these values equally. As follow-up, a code of conduct awareness and understanding assessment is distributed annually to employees.

We also dedicated ourselves to supporting employees in living these values everyday. That commitment, in and of itself, embodies all four values. We know that working within a myriad national laws and customs—not to mention moment-by-moment hard choices—can make living these values difficult at times. But we also know these values foster a trusted reputation around the world, and everyone—internally and externally—can expect a consistent standard of behavior and the decision-making process.

GLOBAL HR SERVICES CENTER

Location: Peoria, Illinois, and Panama City, Panama
Function: Service
Number of employees: 110 (from the combined offices)

Pick any moment, any day, any Caterpillar facility around the world, and you will witness Caterpillar's people demonstrating our values in action. That's the way it's supposed to be. With 31 specific behaviors attached to those values, the way Caterpillar employees do their work, treat each other, make decisions, and keep their commitments all point to integrity, excellence, teamwork, and commitment. But there are few stories that have demonstrated all Caterpillar's values all at once—like the transition of the HR Services Center from Peoria to Panama. Ninety people in Peoria have been dedicated to helping their Panamanian counterparts become successful doing the jobs that were once theirs, all the while facing a future of their own filled with uncertainties, losses, gains, discoveries, and ultimately, new growth and new opportunities.

Keith Butterfield, director of the Global Human Resources Shared Services, and Claire Putman, manager of the Americas Human Resources Services Center, have been running this transition. This is what they have to say about, as Keith says, the miracles that happen every day.

Keith: The team in Peoria had been formed in January 2003 and by the time I got there, I felt like I had landed in an engagement paradise. Housed in a building separate from headquarters, they had become a family, doing things together outside of work. They kept talking about Leo Night. And so I had to ask, "What's Leo Night?" It was "Let's Eat Out Night" when they would all go out to a restaurant together—the whole group, even their kids.

This was a phenomenal team of people who were completely passionate about their work and loyal to the entire Cat team. When you looked at what they did and how they did it—with the complexity of all the processes and a tremendous amount of variability—I knew they were making miracles every day for Cat employees. The knowledge these folks carried around in their heads was amazing. But it wasn't thoroughly documented. So we needed them to go to Panama and do this knowledge transfer one-on-one with the very people who were going to take their jobs. We knew that they deserved to be cared for with the same values and dedication they had shown Caterpillar over the years.

Announcing that we were closing the Peoria Service Center was one of the hardest things I've ever had to do. We started by taking over 2.5 hours to make the announcement and answer their initial questions. Our main message to them was that this was the beginning of another journey. They were going to have a fantastic opportunity to leave a legacy for Caterpillar by helping create a great service center in Panama. This was a chance to leave their mark on the future. My request to them was "Please champion this initiative with us and become part of the solution."

But I also had to tell them, "Life as you know it is going to change. Every job is going to be impacted through this process." We told them we needed their help in making the transition, and this would be an opportunity for them to build new skills and gain new experiences.

Claire: There was a lot of shock and tears in the room. Then Jamie Irven, Peoria HR Service Center operations manager, stood up and said, "Let's embrace this change, learn a lot, meet some new people." We have all come to learn so much from Jamie. The team trusts her, and she's been so effective in quietly helping everyone work through the anxiety that comes with this process.

One of the first things we did was show the Peoria team how much they had in common with their Panama counterparts. We brought their counterparts up from Panama and both teams got to know each other very well—just by doing ordinary things like going out to dinner and going shopping. Then we started sending Peoria people down to Panama. They'd come back with pictures from their trips and stories of how they worked with the new team. When you see that people think like you, talk like you, and value the same things you do, you really can connect with them—even when they are from entirely different cultures and countries.

In the meantime, while our Peoria team was preparing the Panama team to take over the work they had been doing, we wanted to prepare the Peoria team for the next phase of their lives. The Peoria-based service center will very soon be completely dismantled, and these people deserved all the help Caterpillar can give them to help them find other jobs.

A significant majority of our people have already been placed in new positions, but are still hanging in there with us because we still need them to continue the knowledge transfer of the most complex processes. So far, some have gotten promotions, and most have gotten lateral moves. But no one has gotten a lower-level job.

Keith: Caterpillar has fantastic tools to help our employees manage their careers. We engaged corporate experts to help them update their résumés and brush up on their interview skills. Volunteers from other parts of the country held mock interview sessions. And even some of our team themselves became certified in giving mock interviews so they could understand what happens on both sides of the interview desk.

The whole company got involved. There was an internal job fair in the cafeteria where representatives from all the big departments came and talked about career pathing in their particular areas of expertise. A big challenge was working with the hiring managers to wait until we could release them. These employees had already established such a strong network and name recognition because of the care they put into the work they did, they'd already been known for their fundamental commitment, loyalty, work ethic, and values they would be bringing to their new jobs.

Claire: It was well past time for many of these people to go on to their next challenge. I can think of one employee who is now an administrative assistant on a special project Caterpillar is starting in the health care arena. He's like a teenager again—so excited, so engaged. He just wrote me a note saying how he feels as though he's starting a whole new career within the same company.

When they first leave the team, they usually send long, tearful emails about how they miss everyone. It makes you feel good to know that they care enough to say goodbye. But you also know that a week later you're going to hear from them again reporting how happy they are in their new job, learning new things, and meeting new people.

As much as we hold people accountable for their own actions, we also provide them with the support they need when weighing a difficult set of choices. We expect them to report code violations when they occur, secure in the trust that we will support them. We provide five different help lines, email addresses, or faxes they can use to seek the support from our Office of Business Practices, which is an independent staff function with worldwide responsibilities for keeping the code a living part of the employees' lives. In addition to monitoring compliance issues, they also continue developing corporate policies and procedures to uphold the values, as well as develop ongoing training.

The Office of Business Practices also produces a Web site that provides Caterpillar employees with detailed discussions of behaviors that support the values of integrity, excellence, teamwork, and commitment. Every month, the office posts a "scenario of the month" as an exercise to help employees freshen their understanding of how they can make ethical choices.

THE CATERPILLAR EMPLOYEE OPINION SURVEY

Measurement is critical in our engagement journey. However, the employee opinion survey that existed at the time did not align with Vision 2020 and was too long, too general, too cumbersome, and too difficult to turn into specific, actionable initiatives. In fact, it actually played a part in *disengaging* our employees. With this rededication to our people as a critical success factor, we reengineered the employee opinion survey process—not only the survey itself but what happened with the results.

In 2003, each unit was still very much self-directed and had at least one customized version of the survey. When we inventoried the full scope of the survey, we discovered that there was far too much individual division customization. Altogether, the survey—in its many iterations—contained 486 different question configurations.

These configurations presented a few significant challenges. First, few of the core questions or the supplemental business unit questions were engineered to hold leaders accountable for making improvements. Furthermore, the individual customization made it very challenging to leverage and compare results. In addition, the total process time (from identifying targets to collecting data to generating reports) took 426 days. In fact, it took more than 10 weeks to generate reports after data collection was completed, which made it difficult to take action and generate tangible improvements by the next survey period. Consequently, the employees often pointed to the survey itself as a *dis*engaging factor.

Consistent with our drive to integrate employee engagement in all our processes—and integrate our best processes in employee engagement—we used Six Sigma methodologies to analyze the many parts that went into the current process and how we could transform the survey into a deeply meaningful tool for our culture. Our goals were the following:

- Streamline the collection of employee opinions;
- Improve the velocity with which the results were reported to the managers and reported back to the employees;

- Give leaders the ability to take timely and effective action on the results, and;
- Find a way to save $400,000 from of the annual expense of the survey.

Consistent with our culture, which celebrates diversity and inclusion, we convened a team of members representing Caterpillar's worldwide presence (with individuals from North America, Europe, and South America) to make sure all global needs were addressed and that the words and phrases we used would be understandable throughout the world. Then we got to work—analyzing what was already in place, benchmarking with other companies, and working with survey vendors to understand the critical issues surrounding survey administration, cycle time, content, and of course, accountability.

The result was one annual enterprise employee opinion survey that is administered globally. Questions are divided into 13 indices, with each directly tied to Caterpillar business strategy. Some indices have 1 to 3 questions; other indices have 9 to 11. Each of these dimensions is owned by an internal content expert, who is responsible not only for question design (each must be clear, consistent, and tested for relevance and effectiveness), but also the follow-up support for the manager (more on this below). These indices are:

1. Engagement
2. Diversity
3. Change
4. Learning and development
5. Workgroup effectiveness
6. Six Sigma
7. Values
8. Safety
9. Executive management
10. Compensation
11. Strategy
12. Quality
13. Leadership

These survey changes have dramatically improved employee participation rates. In 2002, just 50,000 employees completed the survey. In contrast, over 82,000 employees participated in the 2006 survey, a 60-plus percent increase. The last five years have seen a continuous improvement in participation rates, which are currently at 90 percent. The number of questions has been reduced by 40 percent, and only one version—translated in 15 languages—is now available, in both online and paper formats. Furthermore, 25,000 employees have chosen to complete the open comment section. Our cycle time has been reduced 64 percent. Most important, managers and their employees alike are able to track changes and improvements that directly result from the survey responses—quickly.

As an example of significant velocity improvement, the 2007 Enterprise survey will close on a Friday. Enterprise results will be available within one week. Then, over the next three weeks, we will cascade over 5,000 individual leader reports. Managers are completely supported in this process—which can be emotional as we encourage employees to give us candid feedback. Via a specially dedicated Web-based tool containing prepopulated PowerPoint presentations, leaders have a selection of discussion questions at their fingertips, which can be used to facilitate group discussions with their employees to get more work-group-level communication about specific troubling issues. No manager has to venture into potentially difficult and emotional conversations about the survey without expert support.

Once that feedback and dialogue session is completed, managers can return to their online report. With the click of the mouse, managers can generate an agenda of all the action items they (and their work group, when appropriate) can take to address the particular concerns that have come up in the survey results. An online monitoring system continues to support the manager's progress.

Tapping into the emotional side of engagement, we are seeing that the enhanced timeliness and accountability built into the entire survey process serves to boost the individual employee's sense of engagement overall. The employees who were disappointed by the lack of feedback and visible actions resulting from early survey versions are now reporting that the mere fact they see results from their efforts is an engagement factor in and of itself. Over the last two years, we have seen that leaders who use their action planning tools received a seven-point higher engagement score the following year than their peers who did not.

Based on Caterpillar's global 2006 Employee Opinion Survey, employees who reported they received timely feedback on the survey they filled out the previous year showed a 17-point difference in their engagement scores from those who did not report timely feedback. Those employees who saw the survey process result in actual action from their managers showed an engagement increase of 31 points versus their peers who did not.

There was also the challenge of saving $400,000 from the annual survey budget. We were able to meet that objective by streamlining the process, making every component essential and significant, and providing the reporting system and support materials online with preprepared PowerPoint presentations for managers to use. Additionally, external partners are noticing the effectiveness of the new survey process and are requesting this system for their own companies. Consequently, offering this integrated employee opinion survey process to our distribution partners (independently owned dealers) is helping us leverage external best practices and lessons learned.

FINNING (CANADA)

Location: Edmonton, Alberta, Canada
Function: Caterpillar Dealer
Number of employees: 3,700

As with most companies that integrate a formal set of values into the way they do business, Caterpillar's values were developed as internal tools to help drive the way their people treated each other and their external partners and customers. But the value of teamwork took on a new meaning in 2005 when Finning (Canada)—a Western Canadian Caterpillar dealer—asked Caterpillar to help them improve their own employee engagement process. Finning had used various outside vendors' survey tools in the past, but felt that they just captured snapshot of opinions without giving Finning the tools it needed to actually advance employee engagement in a meaningful way. Having developed a people strategy, the company needed a tool that provided relevant benchmarking data and a process for taking action based on the great ideas of its people.

With 3,700 employees in 2006, Finning was facing the challenge of doubling its employee population by the end of the decade in order to achieve its 2010 strategic plan. By then, it had already begun to feel stiff competition for skilled employees, given the unprecedented growth of the local economy. As Senior Vice President Dave Parker recalled, "It became clear to us that in order to achieve our desired business results and promote the success of all key stakeholders we needed to put more focus on our people and working together to improve their level of engagement."

In that instant, employee engagement moved beyond being a nice-to-do item and took a more powerful place as a must-do. Finning believed that Caterpillar's engagement process offered tremendous potential—not only by measuring engagement in a way that was relevant to their industry, but by creating a culture of ownership and accountability for action planning throughout the organization. So the two companies entered into a multiyear partnership to customize Caterpillar's survey tool to Finning's needs, and roll it out across the entire organization.

Joanne Miller, manager of Corporate Communications, and Carol Villeneuve, general manager of Organizational Effectiveness, reflect on how the project unfolded.

Joanne: Over the years, Finning used a number of tools to capture employees' opinions, but we weren't able to achieve much traction with them. These tools didn't provide us with the data we needed or a process by which we could take employees' ideas for making improvements and turn them into action. And there wasn't the accountability at either the employee level or throughout the organization to actually create change and sustain the change process.

We regularly look to Caterpillar for best-in-class practices. And the way Caterpillar measures and implements employee engagement is the best we've seen. Caterpillar had already identified and developed a set of customized survey questions. We were invited to participate in a Six Sigma process to further refine them to make sure that they would work for our culture and business environment.

Carol: Our employees are very proud to be associated with the Cat brand. They had confidence in Cat's engagement tools and told us "if they work at Caterpillar, then they have a great chance of working for us." We also knew that by partnering with Caterpillar, their team would be there to support us along the way.

One thing that we did differently from Caterpillar was to conduct the survey completely online—there were no paper-based surveys. Within a three-week period, all participants had taken the survey. A key benefit of the online approach was the quick turnaround of our survey results. Within 10 days after the survey closed, the results were presented to our executive team—including our union leadership.

Joanne: Within days of the executive presentation, our senior leaders were dispatched across our branch network to deliver the survey results to our employees. Our expectation was that within 60 days after having received the survey results, employees had to do two things: create an action plan around learning and development and choose one other action item to work on—something that was within their control that's a priority within the work group.

We also expected that all employees would be involved in developing action plans—not just the managers. We wanted to create a sense of ownership starting at the grassroots level. This was relatively easy to do because the employee opinion survey was simple. The questions were easy to understand, the process was easy to execute, we were able to do it in a short time frame and everyone was clear about what they had to do.

Carol: To demonstrate senior leadership commitment to the action planning process and create accountability for action planning, we initiated weekly calls to selected branches during which our senior management team ask our employees about progress made with their action plans. We encourage managers and supervisors to invite their employees to participate in the call. Then we encourage them to go back to their work groups and report back so that everyone knows we're dedicated and committed to this process.

One of the keys to our success is having a robust communications strategy in place to sustain the momentum throughout the annual survey cycle. We also created accountability for action planning at all levels. For salaried and management staff, accountability is reinforced by tying action plans directly to their performance reviews.

We'll launch our second employee opinion survey in September 2007. There are two really important questions that we'll add: "Did you receive feedback on the results of last year's survey?" and "Have you seen tangible actions as a result of last year's survey?" We're hoping that the responses will illustrate a strong correlation between engagement, timely feedback, and the action planning process.

As a result of the success of the Finning/Caterpillar collaboration, other dealers are stepping forward to be part of the process to move their own engagement journey forward. Ultimately, it is hoped that the entire dealership network will benefit from the shared gains in knowledge and experience.

THE CATERPILLAR PRODUCTION SYSTEM

When people speak about employee engagement—especially in the context of U.S.-headquartered enterprises—it's easy to assume they are talking about a knowledge- or service-sector environment in which the business trades on ideas, data, or behaviors. While Caterpillar does support a variety of marketing and service functions, we are also a manufacturing company. "We make most of our revenue by making things like backhoe loaders, hydraulic excavators, soil stabilizers, pipe-layers, and diesel and gas generator sets," said Jim Waters, vice president of the Caterpillar Production System Division. "Consequently, most of the action is on the Cat production floor. And, most production processes in most manufacturing companies—which predictably focus on precision, efficiency and quality—don't usually include employee engagement considerations."

At Caterpillar, our production process does include engagement. As we stated at the beginning of the chapter, we are committed to integrating employee engagement into every aspect of Caterpillar. So this commitment of integration by necessity must include the actual manufacturing process that drives what we do on the plant floors around the world. If people are truly one of only three strategic goals, the way we treat people through manufacturing activities has to be one of the critical ways we achieve success in building products.

Over the past 25 years, we've stayed current with all the latest manufacturing theories and techniques: Deming, Juran, Kaizen, Six Sigma, ISO and QS9000, lean manufacturing, Class A certification, and so on. Like peers in other manufacturing companies, our strengths were in the rational side of manufacturing, focusing on factory layout, flow of material, the placement of tools—all those tangible, traditional, operations concerns. But we never received full return on the dedication of our people because we never spent enough time on the behavioral/emotional side of the way they experienced their work. We would make a wide variety of up-to-date physical changes, but never took full advantage of those changes—we didn't spend enough time on the leadership or employee perspective of the work. "We didn't commit to changing our behaviors along with the processes," said Jim. "So, whatever behaviors we did temporarily change would slip back to our old habits, resulting in wasted efforts."

In 2006, under the mandate to improve the safety, quality, velocity, and cost of our production processes, we launched the Caterpillar Production System (CPS), which integrates people, culture, and values into the actual manufacturing process. We divided it into three components: the operating system (the tangible aspects of building our products), the culture system (the way we think and behave), and the management system (the way we lead). The engagement philosophy touches all three of these components and pervades every aspect of the way we approach production.

For instance, we developed an assessment process based on 15 CPS guiding principles every plant must follow, which are presented below. Nine out of the 15 principles are clearly cultural and management system principles. Every plant is scored against how well it adheres to these principles. Of the 75 total points a location can earn, 45 must come from these people-oriented principles.

Borrowing from the Toyota Production System, we also identified eight wastes, which we are consistently trying to identify and eliminate. Seven of those come from Toyota's system: overproduction, waiting, transportation, inventory, motion, overprocessing, and defects. The eighth is ours: unused capability and creativity. "We have waste when we don't use the capabilities of our employees—when we don't use their ideas, when they're injured and can't be at work or when they lack the Team Caterpillar spirit and don't invest their efforts with us," explained Jim. "And we're glad to see it, because our new attitude toward waste says that every piece of waste is a found opportunity."

"No matter what the nature of the waste is, we are training our people to spot it and identify it as a source of opportunity, not something to hide," said Jim. "In one exercise, for example, we give digital cameras to all the participants of a training program and assign them with the challenge of spotting examples of all eight wastes and coming back to class with pictures documenting what they saw. Every time these classes complete their assignment, they bring pictures of things we have walked by every day and never noticed. We just never see it. When we finally do recognize the waste, we see it as an opportunity to manage cost, quality, and velocity of our products to market."

CPS is absolutely critical to our company's engagement and its future. Jim Owens said it best at the 2007 Engagement Conference, commenting, "If we get to $55 billion in 2010, and we don't materially improve our quality and velocity numbers by nailing CPS the right way, it will be the hollowest victory we've ever seen."

INITIAL RETURNS

An ongoing challenge for almost everyone in the employee engagement conversation is how to connect their engagement initiatives to real, measurable financial advantages for the company—the return on investment (ROI) of their people practices. We at Caterpillar have debated and researched this return issue for some time. Bottom line, we have agreed to focus on causation versus correlation.

We speak of causation versus correlation when we speak of the value of employee engagement inside our company. Engagement is integrated into every aspect of Caterpillar, so it would be impossible—and certainly inappropriate—to try to tease out a single incidence of cause and effect to prove engagement's value to the company.

However, we have seen plenty of results on the correlation side of the conversation. Many studies have shown correlation between business metrics and engagement. For example, Towers Perrin shows a positive correlation between engagement and quality, customer service, cost, and retention. Additionally, DDI shows that engagement positively impacts absenteeism, turnover, and quality. A study done by Gallup revealed that as engagement scores increase within a company, so do earnings per share.

At Caterpillar, we have seen a positive correlation between engagement and business results. A engagement increases,

- attrition and absenteeism decrease.
- the number of new products released increases, as do our quality and reliability numbers.
- the number of union grievances decreases.
- the number of recordable injuries decreases.

In our 2006 annual report, you'll find another internal example of the correlation between engagement and better business results. In the report, you'll find the success story of a manufacturing facility that accomplished nearly a 50-point increase in engagement, while also boasting seven months of injury-free work, a 70 percent decrease in lead times, and as much as an 80 percent improvement in productivity.

Seeing these results, it's impossible not to realize the impact of engagement on our business. Knowing the impact, it's impossible not to take our engagement challenges seriously. "The profitability of your business depends on the business you're in," said Caterpillar Vice President Sid Banwart. "Engagement helps make you more efficient and effective in competing in your business."

CONCLUSION

If you go back to the fundamentals of engagement, you see it's really just about connecting the employees' heads, hearts, and hands to the mission of the organization. We need their heads because that's where the great ideas come from. Who knows better about a function than the people actually doing the work? We need their hands because we still need that physical capability, whether employees are working at a computer keyboard or welding or assembling a machine or engine. And we need their hearts because their passion for their work helps the employees truly buy into what Caterpillar stands for. They see how they are making a difference in the company, in their families, and in the world—making progress possible through the work they do.

The defining moment of a culture is when an unsupervised act is done, but not necessarily rewarded. It's the ultimate proof that the individual has done the right thing, the right way, at the right time, for the right reason—and it's powerful. We will know we have reached the next pinnacle in our history when all our employees consistently behave according to our values, look for waste, look for ways to improve the quality and velocity of production processes, and do all these things because they believe in what Caterpillar stands for and what it does for the world. When everyone across all Cat locations around the world fully embraces the identity, importance, and the impact of their roles within Caterpillar, we will know we have accomplished one of the most significant achievements in Caterpillar history.

Caterpillar's history can be told as an ongoing journey from good to great, built up of the many positive ways Caterpillar has reinvented itself over time. The success Caterpillar enjoys today is due to multiple generations of leaders, each one bringing a new iteration of understanding, invention, and innovation to their roles.

Solving problems is no harder today than it was in the past. Problems change, but the world moves on and competition moves on, making its own progress. It's our turn to leave a legacy for the next generation of Cat people. For our generation, the legacy is the people themselves—or, should we say, ourselves.

Index

Abstractions, 45–46
"Accomplished contributors," 102–3
Accountability, 227; ensuring, 40; shared, 31; using the right metrics to enhance, 231
Action planning, 78
Adaptation, capacity for, 146–47
Aging workforce, 125
Aligning business practices, 42–44
Aligning employees, 42; with diverse interests around shared goals, 32
Alignment of the total employee experience, 108
Allison, Mike, 52
APEX performance model, 163
Army, U.S., 36, 161
Aspiration of leaders, 147–49
Attention control, 165
Authenticity, 4–5, 34, 184, 186–90

"Bait and switch," sense of, 108
Balance, 126
Banwart, Sid, 243
Beck, John, 165
Be-know-do leader development model, 161

Bell, Mike, 93
Bennis, Warren, 54–55
Best practices, approaches to engagement based on, 95–97
Betrayal, 171–73; Seven Steps for Healing, 174–80. *See also* Trust
Blogs, workplace, 19
Branson, Richard, 10
Buddhism, 83
Burud, Sandy, 136–37
Business needs, 113
Business practices (and behavior): misaligned, 46; preventing bad, 32
Business strategy, and compensation, 209–10
Buy-in, 36

Career decisions made for wrong reasons, 59–60
Caterpillar, 220–22, 244; Cat Franc S.A.S., 227–28; Cultural Assessment Process (CAP), 224; Employee Opinion Survey, 237–39; Finning (Canada), 239–41; global HR services center, 235–36; Pontiac facility, 235–37; Vision 2020 (15-year plan of action), 220–21, 223

Caterpillar Brasil, 232–34
Caterpillar engagement journey, 220–22, 243–44; background, 222; culture and values in action, 234–35; initial returns, 243; integrating engagement into all they do, 228–32; relentless execution, 223; success stories, 223–28, 232–36, 239–41
Caterpillar Production System (CPS), 241–42
Caterpillar Xuzhou, 233–35
Celebration of success, 184, 226
Change: discontinuous, 160; as loss of trust, 171
Children, caring for, 129–30
Coach: picking one who will make a performance difference, 150–52; role of, and shifts in expectations and performance, 150, 151; who should have a, 148–50
Coaching, 56–57; business-driven executive, 152–55; the high performers/high potential-driven, 148; the high performers with low potential, 149–50; the high performers with moderate potential, 148–49; the high potential-driver/mid-performer, 149; vs. mentoring, 56–57
Coaching process, contracting and managing the, 152, 153
Coaching relationship, 154; leveraging it with high-potential development, 155–57
Cognitive overload, 60
Collaboration, 13; telework and, 24–25
Collaborative leadership, 8–9
Command-and-control environment, 65
Commitment, workplace flexibility and, 134
Communication, 9–10, 38–39, 230; breakdowns in, 45. *See also* Electronic communication
Community, sense of, 32
Companies, characteristics of the best, 97–98
Compensation, 218–19; aligning it with business needs, 209–11; control of costs vs. equity vs. attraction and retention, 212; emphasis on pay differentiation, 217; fairness, 212–13, 217; internal vs. external equity, 216–17; motivating employees vs. other goals, 212–13; prominence, 214; relying on pay to drive business, 214–15; resolving goal conflicts, 213; variation in pay plans, 215–16; who makes pay decisions, 217–18
Compensation goals, choosing, 211–12
Competence and connection, blending, 41
Concentration and distractions, 165
Concours Group, 97
Confidence, 163–64
Container Store, The, 99
Control, inner: and self-leadership, 161–62
Costello, Carol, 85
Cultural Assessment Process (CAP), 224
Cultural challenges, managing, 135–37
Cultural support systems, 230
Culture, organizational, 30, 210–11; copycat cultures, 45–46; defining moment of, 244; and engagement, 31–33, 188; nature of, 31; taken too far, 46; telework and, 25
Culture creation, as continuous effort, 33
Customer needs, 113
Customer relations, employee engagement and, 2
Customer satisfaction, characteristics of companies with highest, 97

Danforth, William H., 48–49, 63
Davenport, Thomas, 165
Decision-making processes and procedures, 230
Demanding disconnects, 104–5
Denton, Elizabeth, 81
Development activities, measuring and rewarding, 61–62
Development opportunities, 13
Disengagement, cost of, 3
Drago, Bob, 136, 137
"Dual-focus"/"dual-centric" workers, 125–26

Electronic communication: advantages, 16–18; disadvantages, 17–20. *See also* Technology

Emotional connection, providing, 32
Emotional engagement, 12–13, 229, 239
Emotional/relationship skills, 147
Employee-career fit, 59–60
Employee decisions, guiding and inspiring, 32
Employee-job role fit, 58–59
Employee needs, 113
Employee-organization fit, 59–60, 100; supporting, 32
Employee orientation, use of technology for, 21–23
Employee performance: actions and results, 113–14; organization results require, 113. See also Lost 20 percent
Employees: why they choose to stay or leave, 114–16. See also specific topics
Empowerment, 159
Engagement, employee, ix, 146, 243–44; the case for, ix–x; characteristics of companies with highest, 97; components, 111, 228–29; definitions and meanings, 111, 228; and desire to stay, 114–16; drivers of, 12–13; emotional and rational, 12–13, 229, 239; employees' choice of disengagement or, 114–16; integrating it into key business processes, 229; is not about best practices, 95–98; must start at the top, 3; nature of, 4; nice-to-do vs. must-do aspects, 2–10, 191, 229, 240; "talking" vs. "doing," x; variation in practices, based on each company, 97. See also Caterpillar engagement journey; specific topics
Engagement index, 72
Engagement levels, 111–13, 118
Executive search(es), 192–93; control over fees, 200–202; details of contract, 203–4; doing it yourself, 206–7; fee structure should mirror your deliverable needs, 202–3; insisting on search agreement with deliverables and common-sense details, 203–4; knowing who is doing each aspect of, 195–96; making the most of a new hire, 206; managing, 198; recruiting process outline, 198–200; success depends on manpower/people doing search, not expertise/technology, 194–96; ways of evaluating candidates, 204–6
Executive search firms/consultants: asking their previous clients for their candidates' successes, 193–94; con-tainer, 196, 197; contingency, 196, 197; hybrid, 197; insisting they provide follow-up program for the new hire, 206; insisting they validate the criteria for success, 205–6; managing your, 197–98; retained, 196; re-tingency, 196, 197; selecting the right, 193–94; structured in different ways, 196–97
Expectations, managing, 119, 179
Expressive legacy (work value), 101

"Fair and square traditionalists," 102
Family, work and, 129–30, 132–33
Family systems theory, 130
Feedback: 360-degree, 55, 56, 62, 152, 156–57; on surveys, 239
Financial rewards: direct, 214. See also Compensation
Fisher, Bruce, 54
FIT model, 115
Flaherty, Patty, 79–80
Flexibility: of leaders, 7–8; workplace, 133–35
Flexible support (work value), 103–4
Focus groups, 228
Forgiveness, 179–80
Foundation talent practices, 116–19
Fun/Work Fusion: culture of engagement and, 188; importance, 182–83; as luxury vs. necessity, 184–85, 190–91; principles, 183–84, 186

General Electric (GE), 35–36
George, William, 80
Gwilliam, Gary, 88–89

Haughey, John C., 82
Hemsath, David, 183
High-performance culture: characteristics, 31; how it can enhance engagement, 32; practices for building and sustaining, 32–46. See also specific topics
High performance selection grid, 146

High potentials, 145
Hinduism, 83
Hire orientations, new, 43
Human resources (HR), 21, 108
Hurricane Katrina, 186–90

Identity, 222
Imagery, 165–66
Inclusivity, 7–8
Individual expertise and team victory (work value), 102–3
Innovation, encouraging, 32
Inspiring employees, 40–42
Islam, 84
Isle of Capri casinos, 186–90
Isle Style, 186, 188–89

Job assignments, rapidly changing, 159
Job autonomy, 132
Judaism, 83

Kelleher, Herb, 10
Kraack, Tom, 57–58

Leader development model, be-know-do, 161
Leaders, 141–42; buying *vs.* growing, 142–43; characteristics of high-potential, 145–48; investment of personal time, 55–56; knowing your employees, 41; leading from the heart and soul, 85; making yourself known, 41; must be authentic, 4–5; must be communicative, 9–10; must be consistent, 5–6; must be flexible, 7–8; must be imaginative, 7; must be service-oriented, 8–9; as peak performers, 160–62; relentless pressure to deliver, 159; self-awareness, 4, 5, 41; unrelenting challenges and impossible expectations, 159–60. *See also specific topics*
Leadership, 158; the "be" of, 158–59; can't be a spectator sport, 231; discontinuous change and, 160. *See also specific topics*
Leadership development: business demands and, 152, 153; key ingredients linked to, 144
Leadership mentoring, measuring and rewarding, 61–62

Leadership skills, developing: *vs.* other skill development, 143–45
Leading self. *See* Self-leadership
Learning, capacity for, 146–47
Learning opportunities, 230
Limited obligations (work value), 104–5
Lost 20 percent, 49–50; common themes in tapping into the power of the, 54–57; identifying and helping the, 57–62; stories of helping the, 50–54

Manager actions/behavior, 13, 115–16, 231; as key to engaged workplace, 110–23; make a difference, 119–21; telework and, 25
Manager capabilities, developing your, 121–22
Managers: development questions for, 121–22; in the middle, 40. *See also* Leaders
Maslow, Abraham, 60
Mass customization approach to pay, 216
Massih, Paul, 50–51, 58–59
"Maverick morphers," 103
Meaning, providing, 32
Mental preparedness, 161–62
Mentoring: *vs.* coaching, 56–57; that makes a business impact, 52–54
"Merit matrix," 218
Middle managers, 40
Miller, David, 86
Miller, Joanne, 240–41
Mission (statement), corporate, 31, 37; authenticity, 34–35; clarifying, 33–34; communicating and translating, 37, 38; examples, 34
Mitroff, Ian I., 81
Modeling values, 39–40
Moore, Kenny, 84, 87–88

Neal, Judi, 81
Needs, 113; hierarchy of, 60; most critical, 116, 117

One-to-one dialogue: before, 118; during, 118; level of engagement and, 118
One-to-one dialogue framework, 116–18

Optimism, 164
Orecchia, Joyce, 89
Organizational ADD, 165
Organizational culture. *See* Culture
Organizational structure and hierarchy, 210; designed to help people succeed, 60–61
Owens, Jim, 220, 242

Paid time off (PTO), 130
Parents, caring for aging, 129–30
Pascale, Richard, 54
Peak performance, 158; learning to deliver consistent, 162
Peak performers, leaders as, 160–62
People, as the secret to success, ix
Performance: lagging (*see* Lost 20 percent); startling an employee into better, 50–51. *See also specific topics*
Performance management, 43, 230
Performers, star: attracting and retaining, 32
Positive-effective thinking, 163–64
Potential: drivers of, 145–46. *See also under* Coaching
Pressure: to deliver, 159; thriving under, 164–65
Process fairness, 49
Productivity, characteristics of companies with highest, 97

Rational engagement, 12–13, 229
Recognition, 226, 230
Recruiters, contract, 197
Reina Trust and Betrayal Model, 174–80
Relationships: power of, 62–63; trust in, 170 (*see also* Trust)
Relationship skills, 147
Religions, 83–84. *See also* Spirit/spirituality
Remote work. *See* Telework
Respect, 6
Responsibility, taking, 178–79
Responsiveness, 7, 8
Retention, 212; workplace flexibility and, 134
Rewarding: development activities, 61–62; leadership mentoring, 61–62
Rewards, 103; direct financial, 214; that employees want, 214

Rewards of Work model, 214, 215
Risk taking, 103, 184; encouraging, 32
Risk with reward (work value), 103
Role clarity, technology and, 15–16

Salaries. *See* Compensation
Secure progress (work value), 102
Self-actualization, 60
Self-awareness, 4, 5, 41
Self-efficacy, technology and, 14, 15
"Self-empowered innovators," 101
Self-leadership, 166; inner control and, 161–62
Seligman, Martin, 164
Service-oriented leaders, 9
Signature experiences, designing innovative new, 106–7
Signature processes, 98–100, 107; finding your unique signature, 105–7. *See also* Work, roles/values it plays in our lives
Six Degrees of Preparation, 1
Skill requirements, rapidly changing, 159
Social responsibility, corporate, 132, 233
Spirit and work movement (and related movements), 82
Spirit/spirituality (at work), 79–80; defined, 80–82; implementing, 89–93; and the law, 88–89; need for, 84; practices found at work, 86–87; understanding, 80–88
Spiritual Audit of Corporate America, A (Mitroff and Denton), 81
"Stalled survivors," 103–4
Starbucks, 35
Sternberg, Robert, 59–60
Storytelling, 39
Stress, workplace flexibility and, 134–35
Stress and energy management, 164–65
Suarez, Raquel, 52–54
Survey programs, engagement, 64–65; branding, marketing, and communicating the value of survey participation, 73–76; communications and activities that increase response rates, 73–76; confidentiality of data, 75; languages offered to employees, 76; postsurvey activities, 77–78; stakeholder analysis, 65–66; survey administration, 75–76; survey

Survey programs (*continued*)
administration timing, 66–68; survey development, 71–73; survey partner selection, 68–71; survey partner services, 69, 70. *See also under* Caterpillar

"System says" approach to pay, 218

Talent, 119–21; engaging and retaining, 119–20. *See also* Foundation talent practices
Talent variables, 115
Taoism (the Way), 83
Team member talent plan, 119–21
Teams and teamwork, 32, 102–3, 234; emphasis on, 159
Technologies, new: involvement exercised by affected workers during introduction of, 14–15
Technology, 11–12; effect on work tasks, 14; and engagement, 12–14, 27–28; implications for managers and companies, 26–28; for managing work life, 20–23; reinforcing managers' efforts, 26; role clarity before it came on the scene, 15–16; that affects how work gets done, 14–16; that enables communication, 16–20; that enables workforce flexibility, 23–26; transformation of work through, 159–60; uses, 20. *See also* Electronic communication
Technology-enabled self-service, 20; advantages, 21; disadvantages, 21
Telework, technology-supported, 23–26; factors influencing the engagement effects of, 25–26; flexibility, 23–24; and productivity, 24
Thinking: embracing expansive, 184; positive-effective, 163–64
Thomas, Bob, 54–55
300 Ways to Have Fun at Work (Yerkes and Hemsath), 183
Transformational life events, 54–55
Trilogy, 98–99
Trust, 32, 168–69, 180–81, 229; business need for, 170; change as loss of, 171; emotional side of the loss of, 173–74; human need for, 169–70. *See also* Betrayal
Tyson Foods, 92

United States Army, 36, 161

Value proposition, 106; identifying your current, 105
Values, 37, 234–35; assessing your employees' preferences and, 106; authenticity, 34–35; clarifying, 33–34; communicating and translating, 38; examples of core organizational, 35–36; modeling, 39–40; shared organizational, 31; that work plays in our lives, 100–5
Villeneuve, Carol, 240, 241
Visualization, 165–66

Wagner, Mary, 91
Wells, H. G., 63
Women in workforce, 125
Woods, Henry, 49
Work: context of, 20; roles/values it plays in our lives, 100–5
Work environment, 115
Workforce, greater selectivity for a tighter, 108–9
Work-life balance, 126
Work-life effectiveness: defined, 126–28; organizational support for, 128–29
Work-life portfolio, 129; caring for dependents, 129–30; community involvement, 132; creative use of paid and unpaid time off, 130–31; financial support, 132–33; proactive approaches to health and well-being, 131–32
Work-life professional, role of, 137–38
Wright, Kim, 85

Xilinx, 35

Ziegler, Reinhard, 55–56, 58, 62
"Zone," ability to be in the, 161–62

About the Editor and Contributors

Martha I. Finney is a writer and consultant specializing in employee engagement and leadership communications. A business journalist for 20 years before entering the consulting field full-time, she brings the qualitative perspective to the conversation of employee engagement. With a special passion for the voice of the employee, she helps companies and leaders tell the story of what it means to love working at companies where employee engagement is paramount. Her interviewees and clients have come from such organizations as the U.S. Central Intelligence Agency, Intuit, Hewlett-Packard, Newell Rubbermaid, Caterpillar, Starwood Hotels and Resorts, Marriott, America Online, Yahoo!, and the New York Philharmonic. The author or coauthor of more than 13 books, her original research into joy in the American workplace was featured on CNN, NPR's *Morning Edition*, and in major newspapers throughout the United States. Learn more at www.marthafinney.com.

Derrick R. Barton is the founder of the Center for Talent Solutions, focusing on helping companies understand the practical implementation of talent practices and what it takes to engage and retain global talent. He has worked with leaders and managers from virtually every part of the world, including India, Russia, Europe, and all across North America. Derrick is a member of the National Advisory Board for the Human Capital Institute, and he heads up the Thought Leadership Panel charged with outlining cutting-edge practices around engaging and retaining global talent.

Louis S. Csoka, Ph.D., founder of APEX Performance, has designed, developed, and implemented leadership development programs with a primary focus on sustained peak performance. He has successfully delivered targeted results as a performance consultant with various organizations across a multitude of disciplines and industries. He has worked with business, military, and sports organizations in applying peak performance concepts and technologies as primary levers for achieving extraordinary results. Louis's engagements have focused on the following areas: creating peak performance centers and providing peak performance mental skills training; designing and implementing performance-based leadership frameworks and programs; providing executive performance coaching; developing high-performance executive teams; and training and developing athletes in mental skills for sustained peak performance. Louis served as Professor of Psychology and Leadership at West Point as a career army officer, Director of Research at the Conference Board, and Senior Vice President for Human Resources at New Holland.

Thomas O. Davenport is a principal in the Change Implementation line of business in Towers Perrin's San Francisco office. Tom focuses much of his attention on helping clients improve the people-focused elements of business strategy implementation. He is the author of *Human Capital: What It Is and Why People Invest It* (Jossey-Bass, 1999). In his book, he discusses why companies should treat their employees not as assets but as owners and investors of human capital. Tom has also contributed chapters to *Making Mergers Work: The Strategic Importance of People* (SHRM Foundation, 2002) and *Knowledge Capital: How Knowledge-Based Enterprises Really Get Built* (Oxford University Press, 2003). Tom's comments on human capital management have been quoted in such publications as *Fortune, Harvard Management Update,* and *Human Capital Strategies and News.* His articles have appeared in *Across the Board, Management Review, Journal of Organizational Excellence, WorldatWork Journal,* and *Employment Relations Today* and in various general management and strategy publications. He holds a master's degree from the Haas School of Business (University of California, Berkeley), a master's degree in journalism from the University of California, Berkeley, and a bachelor's degree (magna cum laude, Phi Beta Kappa) from the University of California, Los Angeles.

Tom Doolittle, Ph.D., is the Corporate Communications Manager for Caterpillar, leading a team of communications professionals responsible for internal and external corporate communications. He completed his B.A. from Hamilton College in 1979 and his Ph.D. in clinical psychology from Fuller Theological Seminary in 1987, joining Caterpillar in 1996 to provide leadership for the Employee Assistance Program as part of the corporate Medical Department. In 2002 he took the position of Lead Human Resources manager for the newly formed Global Purchasing Division.

Nancy DeLay, Ph.D., is Kenexa's Director of Client Services, Europe. She has strong expertise in the areas of organizational development, international survey, change management, performance management, socialization and on-boarding, competency model development, and career pathing. She is also a thought leader in the area of telework. Her internal and external consulting and project management career has included employers such as Organizational Psychologists, Andersen Worldwide, and Eli Lilly. Nancy's client work and consulting experience has included organizations such as Sun Microsystems, the World Bank, PricewaterhouseCoopers, Eaton Corporation, A.P. Moeller-Maersk, Motorola, and Wachovia. Nancy is a regular presenter at the Society for Industrial/Organizational Psychology (SIOP) as well as the International Telework Association and Council. She received her bachelor's and master's degree in clinical psychology from University of Illinois and her Ph.D. in industrial/organizational psychology from Illinois Institute of Technology.

Tamara J. Erickson is President of the Concours Institute, a member of BSG Alliance, a firm supporting senior executives with an integrated platform of strategic research, leadership development, expert advisory services, on-demand software solutions, and technology professional services. Tammy has coauthored four *Harvard Business Review* articles, including the McKinsey Award–winning "It's Time to Retire Retirement" (March 2004), one *Sloan Management Review* article, and the book *Workforce Crisis: How to Beat the Coming Shortage of Skills and Talent*. Her blog "Across the Ages" appears weekly on HBSP Online (http://discussionleader.hbsp.com/erickson). The research initiatives she and colleagues have undertaken include *Demography Is De$tiny*, exploring the workplace implications of current demographic changes and generational trends, and *The New Employee/Employer Equation*, developing new and powerful approaches to increasing employee engagement through segmentation. She holds a B.A. in biological sciences from the University of Chicago and an MBA from the Harvard Graduate School of Business Administration, where she was the recipient of the James Thomas Chirurg Fellowship. She is a former member of the board of directors of PerkinElmer, a Fortune 500 company competing in advanced technology markets, where she served as a member of the Audit and Governance Committees, and a former member of the board of directors of Allergan.

Bruce Ferguson is the CEO, southern division, of i-Hire. He has over 25 years of operational management experience, emphasizing a collaborative and decisive style. He has extensive experience in planning and managing for growth. Prior to taking his current post at i-Hire, Bruce was at Exult, the first full-service HR business process outsourcing (HR BPO) company as its chief people officer. Exult provided across-the-board HR service delivery to global 500 companies. He held several positions of increasing responsibility for Ernst & Young's consulting services division. He has a proven record of sound fiscal management and is knowledgeable in budgeting and finance. Bruce earned a bachelor's degree from the University of Wisconsin. He has served as the co-chairman for the Human Resources Metrics Consortium and has authored a number of chapters and articles on the essentials of HR BPO and creating an effective BPO model. He is a past president of the board of directors for the U.S. Academic Decathlon Association, and he is a frequent speaker at colleges and universities on leadership development and career aspirations.

Brian Gareau is the manager of the Organizational Effectiveness + Engagement team in Caterpillar's Human Services Division. His global team focuses on organizational culture, employee engagement, employee opinion measurement, values-based support and behavior, and change management. He graduated from Hartwick College and then moved to the Midwest where he has been part of Caterpillar's management team for more than 20 years. Brian has worked in a wide variety of functions, including Manufacturing, Corporate Public Affairs, Customer Services, Logistics, and Human Services. He is the co-developer of a patent-pending Cultural Assessment Process and was actively involved in the redesign of Caterpillar's global employee opinion survey process and launch of the company's corporate values. He continues to work, both domestically and internationally, with his team on organizational effectiveness and measuring ROC (return on culture). Brian has been a featured speaker at the Conference Board, Dallas SHRM, Society of Industrial and Organizational Psychology, and CUE. He coauthored his first book, *A Slice of Life . . . A Story of Perspectives, Priorities, and PIZZA*, in 2004.

Kathleen M. Lingle is the Director of the Alliance for Work-Life Progress (AWLP) which is an affiliate of WorldatWork dedicated to creating healthy, productive, and profitable work environments based on a business strategy that integrates work, family, and community. An internationally recognized work-life expert, Kathie is a frequent keynote speaker, writer, and advisor to organizations across the United States and as far away as Singapore and Australia. She was a recipient of the Work-Life Legacy Award in 2007, which is presented to "outstanding leaders who have indelibly changed the American workplace." Before assuming her current position, Kathie served as National Work-Life Director at KPMG LLP, where she was chief architect of the Work Environment Initiative, a multiyear cultural transformation effort that continues to evolve. She earned a B.A. in diplomacy and world affairs at Occidental College in Los Angeles, and holds an M.S. in human ecology from the Ohio State University in Columbus.

Duncan Mathison is the Managing Director, Executive Coaching, for DBM, a global human resources firm serving the transition and executive development marketplace. He works with organizations and their executives around critical leadership issues during organizational transition as well as development of key C-suite executives and high-potential leaders. Duncan is a regular public speaker at key industry forums and is a noted source for media commentary. After receiving his undergraduate degree from University of Washington and master's in Psychology from Washington State University, Duncan began his career in the nonprofit and public sector as a family therapist, as well as an organizational development consultant. His interest in technology drew him to the business world, where he had a successful career in marketing and management in the telecommunications and computer industries.

Craig Mindrum, Ph.D., is a strategic and workforce performance consultant. Over a 26-year career as a businessman, researcher, writer, and a college professor at DePaul and Indiana Universities, he has focused on areas of human performance and organizational change, including communications, leadership, and the moral design of organizations. He is the coauthor of several books including, most recently, *Return on Learning* (Agate, 2006). Recent articles and book chapters include work in such areas as learning and culture change, risk management, and managing change to improve productivity. Following master's work at Yale University and Indiana University, he received his Ph.D. from the University of Chicago.

Kate Parker is a Marketing Consultant within Caterpillar's Organizational Effectiveness + Engagement team. A 2000 graduate of the University of Illinois, Kate has seven years' experience in marketing and communications at Caterpillar. She organizes an annual corporate engagement conference and develops communications to support engagement initiatives.

Dennis S. Reina, Ph.D., is co-founder and president of the Reina Trust Building Institute, focusing on research, product development, and operations. Dennis developed the original Reina Trust and Betrayal Model, the series of trust-measuring surveys, and many of the Trust Building tools and resources that the institute offers. He regularly consults, speaks, trains, and coaches leaders and their people in organizations across the United States. He has worked with organizations such as American Express, Boeing, Ben & Jerry's, Harvard University, Johnson & Johnson, Middlebury College, U.S. Army Chaplaincy Corps, Treasury Executive Institute, University of Tampa, Walt Disney World, and Wheaton Franciscan Healthcare of Wisconsin.

Michelle L. Reina, Ph.D., is co-founder and CEO of the Reina Trust Building Institute. An author, researcher, consultant, speaker, coach, and workshop leader, she oversees business development and partner engagement for the institute. Seasoned in areas such as strategic planning, change management, team development, and employee engagement, Michelle helps clients understand the needs of organizations, leaders, and individuals and apply trust-building principles to ensure those needs are met. Her clients include American Express, Kimberly-Clark, Children's Healthcare System of Milwaukee, Nokia, Johns Hopkins Medical Center, Microsoft, U.S. Army Corps of Engineers, U.S. Department of the Treasury, U.S. Army Chaplaincy Corps, West Point Academy, and Yale University. Michelle and Dennis Reina coauthored the book *Trust and Betrayal in the Workplace: Building Effective Relationships in Your Organization* (Berrett-Koehler, 2006).

Christopher Rice is President and CEO of BlessingWhite, a global consulting firm dedicated to creating sustainable high-performing organizations. Founded in 1973, BlessingWhite became employee-owned in 2001 under Chris's leadership. In addition to his responsibilities as CEO, Chris is the executive coach to several senior executives and provides consulting to clients like Johnson & Johnson, Toyota Motor Sales, and Euro RSCG on culture change, employee engagement, and authentic leadership. His expertise has been featured in *Fortune, Talent Management, CLO,* and *Harvard Management Update.* Chris's career includes leadership roles with Drake Beam Morin, the Gallup Organization, and Learning International (Xerox Learning Systems). He holds a B.A. and an M.A. from the University of Pennsylvania.

Sibson Consulting (www.sibson.com) is a division of the Segal Company, a leading independent firm of benefits, compensation, and human resources consultants. As a private, employee-owned consulting firm, Sibson Consulting has a long history specializing in strategic HR solutions that help organizations maximize the return on their human capital investments through the planning, implementation, and operation of total rewards, compensation, retirement, and health benefit programs. Sibson Consulting's services encompass talent management, benefits, organization design, sales effectiveness, and change management. Sibson has served more than half of the Fortune 500 companies.

Pat McHenry Sullivan has been writing and speaking about spirit and work for more than 20 years. She is the author of 26 *Vision and Values* columns on spirit and work for the *San Francisco Chronicle* and the books *Work with Meaning, Work with Joy: Bringing Your Spirit to Any Job* (Sheed and Ward, 2003) and *Purposeful Business Planning* (Visionary Resources, 2006). With her husband, John, she co-founded the Workday Wisdom Institute in Berkeley, California, which offers a large library and monthly spirit for all faiths, all types of jobs. They also host monthly spirit at work meetings. The Sullivans are in the process of creating an online spirit and work bibliography and resource collection at www.workdaywisdom.org.

Gordon Thomas is currently President of the retained search firm Trimarc Resources, where he conducts executive search assignments on a "deliverable-based" fee structure for *Fortune* 500 clients. Gordon has over 20 years of experience as an executive search and staffing professional. Prior to founding Trimarc Resources in July 2001, he served as the staffing director at AOL/Netscape, where he designed, built, and led the staffing function. Before joining AOL, he was the President and CEO of the retained search and project-based staffing firm, IPR/Staff-Net.

Leslie Yerkes is President of Catalyst Consulting Group, an organizational development and change management consulting firm based in Cleveland, Ohio. Leslie's business goal is to help people create sustainable organizations. Her life goal is to create a framework in which people can draw on their own resources to find creative solutions. Leslie is the coauthor of *301 Ways to Have Fun at Work; Beans: Four Principles for Running a Business in Good Times or Bad; They Just Don't Get It! Changing Resistance into Understanding; Fun Works: Creating Places Where People Love to Work;* and *Beyond Kicks and Carrots: Motivation in the 21st Century.* Her works have been translated into more than a dozen languages, selling hundreds of thousands of copies worldwide. She is on the faculty at the Weatherhead Dively Center of Executive Education and the Mandel School of Applied Social Sciences, Case Western Reserve University.

Sarah Zigler is a Communications Representative in the Corporate Public Affairs department at Caterpillar, developing materials for corporate initiatives, including employee engagement, career development, recruiting, and global diversity. She graduated from Bradley University in 2006 and joined Caterpillar the same year.